MW01294195

"The Devil in the Details III"©

The Art of Mastery
A Mentoring Trilogy

Volume III
Sustaining Structure & Training

LT Morrison
LT@LTMorrison.com

Copyright © 2012 by LT Morrison

Cover photo © LT Morrison

Second Edition

All rights reserved.

ISBN: 1466268808

ISBN-13: 978-1466268807

To All the Slaves I've Loved Before

All speech is vain and empty…
Unless it be accompanied by action.

Demosthenes

C ONTENTS

7

House Rules..**114**

8

Rituals & Protocols **154**

9

AUTHOR'S NOTE

Entertain, inform, educate, poke a little fun at ourselves, and mix in some lurid spice to stir your creative libidos. That is the style of this book with a pinch of pizzazz added for your literary enjoyment. It was just a way to convey an important message and make it as enjoyable to read as it was to write.

While the anecdotes and mindfucks enhance the storytelling and illustrate the message, the core purpose of this book and in fact the entire *Trilogy* is an examination of the principles and specifics of sustainable, consensual *master-slave* relationships. Making a *power exchange* relationship work in the real world, in real lives, on real blocks, in real houses, with real people, is the real goal.

As in *Volumes I & II*, the anecdotes, stories and characters contained within are true. They happened, delightfully so.

After writing this *Volume*, life will go on and more mindfucks, anecdotes, experiences and fun will follow. But, there will be no *Volume IV*, lest anyone wonder. This is a trilogy after all. There cannot be.

That said, ideas to grow the *master-slave* genre are constantly germinating. There are other avenues and tools under consideration, to augment, teach and expand *responsible master-slave* living to those wanting and willing. New literary and digital conveyances, as well as speaking engagements are all on the table. How the universe will bring those is unknown and not of concern. The ideas and drive to produce them is all that I control.

LT Morrison

ACKNOWLEDGEMENTS

There can only be one acknowledgement in this final *Volume* of the *DITD Trilogy*. Two very important slaves, both amazing women, with gifts far beyond my reality, taught me more than I can properly acknowledge or return.

Debbie and Kristi, you graced my life, more than you know. Your wisdom and dignity never wavered and I am grateful beyond words.

Thank you.

INTRODUCTION

This is the third and final *Volume* in a mentoring trilogy on *The Art of Mastery*. We have come a long way through the first two *Volumes* and learned of the theory and philosophies of responsible, sustainable *master-slave* relationships. The issues and required skills to manage a life in a power relationship were addressed and hopefully embraced. Now we come to the final and arguably most important *Volume* in the *Trilogy*.

When introduced to, then studying and learning the vast lifestyle we generically call BDSM, it is quickly evident there is much more to this lifestyle than apparent at first glance. From casual play, to top/bottom interaction, bedroom only submission, and *Erotic Power Exchange*, there is a slice of the pie for everyone, regardless of the level of commitment each wants to make. This series however, is specific in focus. The entire *Trilogy* explores the BDSM spectrum, but focuses on the *master-slave relationship dynamic, TPE relationship, 24/7, while living under the same roof*, and nothing more.

It looks at the theory and issues, trying to harmonize the diverse approaches taken, and if possible molding it into a sustainable power relationship model.

Volume I & II provided the necessary framework and understandings to ultimately produce a training regimen and sustainable structure style that is livable in the real world.

With that fundamental knowledge from *Volume I* and *II* in hand, we can now learn how to responsibly train a slave, thereby producing a *master-slave* structure you can enjoy for a lifetime. The goal is to train purposefully, with maturity, respect, knowledge and diligence, thereby creating the loyalty, obedience and devotion all masters want and slaves yearn to give.

Volume III is where we generate the peace and energetic tranquility for a lifetime of shared happiness.

1

THE FUN BEGINS!

Kneel her down!

Find a raggedy old piece of leather for her neck!

We are going to collar the beautiful wench!

Pedal to the metal, baby, it is time to *Git Her Done*!

And now, we interrupt your enthusiasm for a heavy dose of reality!

So, you have digested *Volume's I & II*. You have devoured and read each more than once. You have discovered how much you missed the first time through. Wonderful, and thank you. I am delighted for you. Undoubtedly, you discovered all the great stuff in there. Diligent readers now have a greater understanding of the foundations on which *power relationship* are built and sustained. But, until now, all this learning of theory and skills is just stuff. You know what I mean, things from the junk drawer that we all have, just taking up space. Unless it is useful, it just clutters our lives. It is junk, minutiae, and trivia – just crap, in short!

So, we either get rid of it and go vanilla, or find a way to turn it into something useful, tangible and real. Throw in a healthy dose of sexy and fun because we want those too. Now is time to close the deal, put gas to the engine, and take *responsible mastery* from the academic world, to her ass and of course - reality.

To your reality!

That is what *Volume III* is all about – *your sustainable reality*. It is all about training your slave and enjoying a special relationship for years to come.

This *Volume* of the trilogy is the main reason for writing the series from the outset. This is the important ingredient being lost with the advent of the internet generation of BDSM enthusiasts. *"Training and Sustaining"* is where real confusion lies in the practice of the *master-slave lifestyle*. Day-to-day reality is where masters make the most mistakes, which are too often destructive and irrevocable. It is quite understandable though, because this is where we *walk-the-walk*, and errors become obvious. So, let us avoid them.

To the slaves reading, hey, get ready. It is crunch time slavegirls and we masters love it. Now it is time we mount your cute little ass in the sling. We have done our work, we know how to be great masters - and you are about to find that out. Now you learn our structure, and the *SODS Principle* becomes your reality. We studied and learned, and can master well. Now we find out if you have the ~~balls,~~ wherewithal, to live indentured in slavery, as you keep vociferously telling us you want. So, *'Suck it up princess'*, here we go!

Investigating the state of mastery as evolved and practiced currently, it was clear, the art of training a slave, and what goes into real time ownership is at best, a murky pond. This is particularly so for those new, or of limited experience in the lifestyle. How do you prepare to own, then train and sustain structure over time, in a healthy, happy way? Those are the questions addressed and in a way that is both tolerant and flexible.

We have to train the little darling, that is a given. How we do it is the trick, or as some might say *"The Art Of Mastery"*. To old-timers it seems a lost skill on the next generation. It need not be and explaining that is the purpose. There are techniques and tools to train a slave that work, regardless of the personality of the master, or the niche he may choose. They are timeless. There is no universal manual of course, that would be silly. That there is not is good, we do not want cookie cutter slaves. We are after all each very different, but some universal training truths are time tested and still relevant. That is where we are going. We are going to explore and teach how to train a slave in a way that makes sense to both master and slave, but done by each in their own way.

Training requires specifics. Each master will do a lot of work in preparation of ownership, so that when she kneels to accept your collar and embrace your structure, she does so confidently. That confidence is in you, your life, your values and your structure. We need to train her to convince her. Let us begin at the beginning.

TRANSITION

"Master, what comes first when you first meet a slave, building the relationship, or building the master-slave component? Is it better to develop the relationship first and then overlay the power structure, or do it simultaneously?"

She was a curious little soul, cute, inquisitive, smart and sexy. He loved her for all that of course, but that she had the heart of a slave was the piece d 'resistance.

"Well pet, the chicken and egg were lying in bed and the chicken was smoking a cigarette. So I guess that answers that age old question."

He grinned at her puzzled look.

"It was a joke pet. Sheesh. You reminded me of it when you asked, so suck it up princess, laugh, or I will skin your ass raw."

She gave him that cock-eyed cute grin of hers and obligatory laugh.

"Pffft, slavegirls," and he bit her nose.

"Anyway, well it is an interesting question pet, and one many in the lifestyle banter back and forth. Like all these kinds of issues, there is no black and white answer. If it works for them, who are we to say otherwise. However, for me, it is most definitely black and white, and not because I love making your ass black and blue, which I do, of course."

He cackled, reaching under the covers to pinch her bruised ass. A little yelp and she wiggled her nose with a smile.

"Pet, they must grow coincidently. One cannot separate the two without incurring some unnecessary risk and work to the budding relationship. It makes sense really when you think about it. Understand though please pet, I am not advocating imposition of structure without consent. Just because two people meet and like each other, does not imply consent for the BigDomlyStudMuffin. By the way, that is my new meaning for the BDSM acronym."

She shook her head, laughed and he carried on.

"On first meeting, there is almost certainly no consent, nor should it be assumed."

"So then how do you proceed", she asked

Amused, he squeezed her nipple.

"Well, here is the dilemma. Should I impose rules she must agree to before she even knows me, when we first meet, even before consent; or should we spend time together, getting to know one another using vanilla protocols? That is the quandary and there are potential perils in both. Yet the answer is pretty obvious."

"Since they are just meeting, they have come together as vanillas, with no expectations or presumptions, or at least that is what one would expect. Yet both are obviously involved in the lifestyle, perhaps going so far as to respect each other's proclamations of mastery and slavery, though not to each other."

"But it is important, whether she knows or not, even now, this early on in meeting that the master leads. Do not misunderstand, he is not imposing his will, he is just leading while making it clear there are no assumptions of power by just meeting. She will respect that about him and it must be so for the master to remain consistent to the tenets of his mastery. He believes in consent, yet he is a leader."

"But if those meetings carry on and they decide to continue seeing each other progressing down a road leading to a power relationship, then a wise master is best having this discussion with her early on. The reason is simple and not only will she appreciate the candor, but if her interest is genuine, she will enjoy what is to come."

Oh-little-bruised-bum lay quietly listening beside him.

"An experienced master knows in advance, that if you allow a relationship to develop in what in effect are vanilla terms, before the power dynamics and master-slave structure is agreed to, habits of interaction form quickly. That is quite normal since they have lots to talk about getting to know one another. It is part of the healthy relationship building process. But, for the master, the danger is in the word 'habits'."

"In the exploratory stages of a budding relationship, if interaction is vanilla, which it must surely be at the start, if left to embed itself into the relationship, then a master creates a daunting and perhaps destructive task down the road. Unless you love vanilla relationships and that is where you want to go, at some point in the future you are going to have to say 'Ok dear, now the rules change.'"

"Why? Simply because the vanilla interactions you allowed have been building a false foundation. It is not based on what you want. In effect, you are saying that what has gone on so far is no longer valid. The result is confusion at best. Now you must start all over and rebuild the relationship with new rules, the ones you wanted all along, except now you have to break previously formed habits."

"Take speech for example. If you let her talk all willy-nilly vanilla and never point out "nilla talk", it becomes the norm for her. What is "nilla talk" you ask? Well, a simple example is "confrontational" or "antagonistic" speech, but there are many other examples. The point is, she will have developed a speech pattern and established a precedent that you do not ultimately want. She may like that because it is familiar, but you do not. So, at some point you have to change that habit. You have to now teach how you want communication handled. The rules change all because you allowed those habits to develop in the first place. Now you have the doubly difficult task of overcoming vanilla behaviors that may already have existed before meeting, and the pattern allowed to happen but did not like in the first place."

"See the conundrum pet? This consent thing really is a nuisance at times."

She smiled and nodded.

"So then the question is how do I coincidently develop master-slave structure to avoid bad habits when consent is missing, yet we want to pursue a relationship?"

"Of course, like much of this lifestyle, the answer to this conundrum lies in forethought and effective communication. The solution is mature and adult."

"I explain the situation to her. She is after all bright, listening, and quite probably wet, and she wants to hear it."

Very early in your time together, talk through the dilemma; explaining you do not like arbitrarily imposing rules and structure without consent. Smile, laugh and go further reiterating that you are not asking for consent either. You are merely showing her the problem.

It is an honest approach, though perhaps she may be leery at first, afraid of some sophisticated domly trick being played to get power without consent. It is nothing of the sort as she will see. Then explain the rules you want her to 'voluntarily' follow, and the reason you are doing it. Wanting to be with you, she will agree and enjoy this little step. It clearly shows her the care you take with your structure and the *master-slave* niche you live. In the coming days as she tries to obey, smile and highlight the positive difference in her behavior already. If you are good, she will love it.

MIND FUCK #21 "TAKEN"

She fairly skipped into the bedroom, freshly showered, wrapped only in a towel, a peaceful smile on her face. She could smell the coffee from the kitchen, her master beating her to the punch. He would not be pleased with that, but had ordered her into the shower. He liked dabbling in the kitchen anyway. Smiling and happy, she vigorously toweled her hair.

The welts on her ass were tender. The reflection in the mirror seen earlier was a testament to her obedience the night before. They were surprisingly raw. But, they were her first ever and she beamed with slavish pride. Badges of honor, a new feeling, unexpected, exciting and remembering what caused them, a shiver coursed through her body. Idly she wondered what he used, realizing it did not matter. So, that was sub-space. She liked the soreness, memories, intensity and then shivered again. It made her giddy. The bruises on her pussy even felt wonderful. Submission was primal and earthy. It had been a long time since she felt this alive, this in love. It felt so right. Bending and scrubbing her hair harder, she wanted to race downstairs and jump into her master's arms.

In the bliss of her moment and the deafening hair toweling, she did not hear him enter. Suddenly everything went black. The opaque hood changed her world and was the disconnect he sought, separating her euphoria from the world. It paralyzed her for just a moment, the second needed to shackle her wrists together overhead.

The sudden darkness disoriented her. In a short few seconds, joyous thoughts of primal mating had turned to immobilized blindness and unexpected fear. Surely this was her master she thought, but the sudden blindness and silence scared her. What was happening? She hoped. She reasoned. She trembled. Time went by and nothing but the paranoid feeling of darkness grew from within.

Sitting on the bed edge, sipping morning coffee, he was content and pleased. There was a surreal feel knowing her world was silent darkness in the bright morning sunlight. She was a beautiful woman, so completely surrendered, yet now disoriented and confused. She was as he wanted. For the moment, the towel covered her charms, but that would end and intensify her vulnerability.

It was an amazing journey already. From the first coffee so many months ago, who knew then it would bring them to this time and place. The ensuing months exploring concepts, needs and ideas together, seeing her open slowly to feelings she had, but could not voice. The barrage of questions she asked, and the probing answers she pondered.

He looked at her from the bed and smiled. Maybe the magic was in the unexpected, he thought. Neither of them had little idea it would lead here. Yet relentlessly forces drew them together. Their chats became more personal, almost mystically. Neither sensed what was happening, but the bond grew as if some relentless force pushed onward ensuring their paths would cross as fated. Now here they were, master and slave, as it should be, was meant to be, and always would be.

Sipping his coffee silently, again his gaze fell to her. She was a beautiful woman, the most beautiful in his eyes. He watched her stillness, hooded in darkness and uncertainty, a protective cocoon protecting against fear. Perhaps it was already gone. She knew his scent. Watching pensively, he was grateful for all the universe had brought.

Rising silently, he let her smell the aftershave then removed her towel. This morning would be special, something unexpected, balancing the savagery of last night. She needed to understand, their world held no boundaries now. Together, they were free to enjoy the entire human spectrum, the emotions and pleasures they brought. Kneeling behind her, he licked her heel and began the long wet journey of exploration. Tasting every part of her, evidence still of the open surrender demanded, the intimacy unparalleled.

Hours later, exhausted and sated, she released into his arms collapsing on the bed, cuddled tight and secure.

"Good morning slavegirl", he whispered.

She kissed his chest, "Good morning Master".

Looking into his eyes, utterly ravaged, she glowed.

"I love you pet".

Smiling, she pulled herself up and kissed him.

"The coffee might be burnt, but let's go find out and I will tell you about a strange girl I found last night with funny marks on her bum", he growled softly.

She laughed and jumped up, climbed on him, smothering him with kisses and questions.

"What did you use, OMG I flew, it was amazing, holy shit, can we do that again? How did you do it? It hurt, it didn't hurt", and he laughed.

My gawd he thought, "What have I unleashed!"

2

PREPARING TO OWN

It was their first intimacy and her first time bound. She felt anxious, a little frightened and utterly helpless. Naked spread-eagled on the bed, she shivered. Never before had she felt quite so exposed and vulnerable. He insisted their first time be in this backwater motel. Her heart raced. The modesty felt surprised her and she felt prudish, no doubt at the unabashed display and her need so obvious. That she was blindfolded only intensified everything. Her cunt was soaked and blossomed open. She was approaching her thirty-eighth birthday and had experienced a very active sex life for many years. But it had always been vanilla, never like this. Never with the surrender he now demanded. Maybe it was being completely shaved for the first time, unable to hide her wet need behind what had been her beautiful, thick dark bush. Oh how she wanted to be his slut!

The room was very still and quiet. Then like an explosion, he was on her, straddling her chest, the weight crushing her tits. His massive hand pinned her head to the bed and she sensed the sharp knife even before feeling the razor sharp edge pushed against her throat. The growled words in her face froze her and life stood still.

"You only thought you knew me girl. Now you find out about the real me".

And she fainted.

"What will happen tomorrow night Sir?"

He smiled down at her kneeling before him. "We have discussed this already, pet."

"Yes Sir, I know. I just want to hear it again."

"You are nervous aren't you girl?"

"Very Sir."

He kissed her and explained again.

"Your life will change pet. The ceremony will mark your ownership. A brand will be burned into your flesh, and my collar locked around your neck."

She shivered.

"We will sign the 'Master & Slave Contract'. You will sign your life into slavery to me, and I will accept you and that responsibility."

She smiled, but it was a nervous smile.

"Then I will hang on to you for forty or fifty years before trading you in for some young sixty-five year old hot chick."

He grinned and continued. "The fun part though pet, is that the signatures will be made using a quill dipped in a mixture of our blood. Then you can call me 'Master' for the first time."

She shivered again. "Yes Sir, and it will be with pride to become yours. May I make a suggestion Sir?"

"Go ahead girl, fire away, not that it will do any good at this late date."

"If you like, may we sign the contract with not just our blood, but with your semen mixed in as well?"

He thought quietly for a few moments and she waited. Suddenly rising to tower over her, he pulled her face into his leather clad crotch and roared.

"No girl! No! No! No! Out of the question! Red blood mixed with white semen makes for a pink mess and I do not do no stinking pink!"

They laughed, and she knew it was all good.

The guests arrived in an hour. She was dressed and ready. She had laid out his clothes, washed his back in the shower and waited patiently as he finished his usual routine. First the shower, then the shave, then that infernal aftershave face slap that always made him wince and her giggle. Next came the deodorant and hair grooming and always finished by brushing his teeth.

"Where is the new toothpaste girl?"

Her heart missed a beat. He had instructed her to buy more this morning and she had completely forgotten.

"Master, I forgot to buy more."

"You forgot? You forgot to do as you were told? Is that some sort of excuse for disobedience?"

Her eyes dropped immediately, she knew he was disappointed in her, but no more so than she in herself.

"Sir, I completely forgot and it is not an excuse at all. There is no excuse except inattention Master."

"Well, I have no time to deal with your behavior and disappointment in you right now girl, we have guests arriving momentarily. Haul your ass over here and lick my teeth and gums clean."

She gagged.

Three brief occurrences in a slave's life. Do they represent healthy livability? Which is fantasy? Are they just good stories, or sustainable reality? Or, are the anecdotes perhaps all just mind fucks?

There are many naysayers dismissing the master-slave lifestyle as unrealistic, unlivable and unhealthy. They love to make the analogy that *master-slave* as a viable structure is to relationships, as socialism is to responsible government. They are both great in theory but corrosive in reality. Socialism does not account for the very real human behavior traits of personal fulfillment, ambition, recognition and individualism. Socialism denies the human need for individual excellence and empowerment of the free spirit inside us all. It sacrifices these basic human traits for the collective good, to suit the socialist governing model.

The parallel is drawn-down to a personal level involving two individuals, a master and his slave. The reality of subjugating the slave's will, denying her personal freedoms and reducing her to dehumanizing chattel, thus stripping her of individual identity, life skills and self-worth all for the greater good of the power lusting, selfish master, are all strongly held opinions supporting the argument that real time consensual *master-slavery* is unhealthy.

The analogy unfairly misleads by making assumptions about the role of *responsible* mastery in a slave's life. That the analogy is drawn at all, is because in some corrupt relationships, there is abuse and it is very unhealthy. But the same can be said of many vanilla relationships too. That not all masters are perfect, does not nullify developing a workable relationship model. One cannot dismiss *responsible* mastery because some apples are rotten. Keep the good apples, and smush the rest to applesauce.

Volumes I and *II* explored the motivations of a master and his slave. It examined why they make the choices they do to live such an existence. Those books examined the theoretical components of responsible mastery, the importance of a *Vision,* and not just understanding why a slave's mind works as it does, but the importance of believing in that *mindset.* They examined the issues masters and slaves encounter on the road of their choice, guiding them along a successful journey. They certainly examined the potential for beauty and peace, treachery and sabotage; and of course, looked at power.

The entire BDSM spectrum as a whole, cannot be lived without breaching the tenets of mastery, such are the diversity of niches that exist. There are too many inconsistencies leading to breaches of faith. The choices each master makes to define his niche are his of course and are chosen wisely. Accepting some areas and rejecting others to create his *Vision* and happiness is a process he will go through. That some of these choices may not be ones you or I make, is not important, as long as he accepts the attending responsibilities and makes it livable.

And that is where we have come to, the juicy part of this *Trilogy.*

Talk of theory and philosophy is naught but wonderful natter and great talking points around a coffee table, unless at some point they translate into a real, tangible and healthy day-to-day existence. Without that metamorphosis, from theory to reality, we have made the naysayer argument that the *master-slave* TPE lifestyle is unhealthy, and accomplished nothing.

So, it is time to put the rubber to the road. It is fun time!

How do we live a life of master-slave in the face of all the BDSM issues facing us? Combine that with the everyday relationship issues attendant in any union and there is a lot to absorb and manage. Vanilla careers, children, in-laws, extended family, neighbors, finances, the law and even when Mother Nature visits to throw *Pretty-Much-Shit* at the harmony we call *master-slave*.

Well, let us have a go at it. If we are to fail, then let us go down in an honest effort at glory. If we succeed, well then, she can cum tonight.

We have had a good look and examined extensively the theory, philosophy and tenets that comprise a good master-slave relationship. We recognized early the *Four Pillars* of all relationships regardless of style, *Intimacy; Affection, Honesty/Communication* and *Sex*. We outlined the *Three Tenets of Mastery… Never forget she does not want control; Handle your mistakes without defaulting power back to her and Love women*. We identified the core powers that clarify the issues of exactly what it is we do. Whatever the combination you chose, there always remains control of her *Body, Behavior* and *Attitude*. All these concepts now have to become livable, healthy and reality.

It is worth a moment to talk again about what structure is, since making and enforcing structure is the core component of *master-slave* relationships. Clarity here is critical. Accepting there are only three powers to control, structure is the unique compilation of *rules, protocols*, and *rituals* you make, that define use of those powers. With a goal to develop consistent structure, it is critical to prepare a very extensive outline of how you intend to proceed, once you have met that special slave. Playing hit and miss with her emotions because of poor preparation is going to really mess with her mind, and yours too. In many cases just simple poor preparation results in bad outcomes that cause men and women, who otherwise would be good masters or slaves, to give up and leave the lifestyle in frustration. Some of the naysayers of *master-slave* living are dominants that did not understand the benefits of preparation, thus could not make it work.

The first pre-ownership task is easy, but one that requires enough thought that you can verbalize it to your slave, fairly early on in your time together. It involves developing a *Vision*. It is a conversation between you that gives an overall purpose and framework to the life you plan. It is the big picture if you will. A Vision is nothing more than important goals, ambitions and values you have. Perhaps it is as simple as a log cabin in the woods, with simple tastes, traveling, entertaining when the mood hits, and a quiet life with your slave, family and dog. For others, utopia is the suburban plot, in-ground pool, nice car, two point one kids and your slave. For others again, it could be a polyamorous *"family"* relationship with multiple slaves. Your Vision is yours, intensely personal and not open to criticism. Whatever turns your crank is right. Just be able to verbalize it to your slave.[1]

Thus with *Vision* in hand, there are only two other small items and then you are off to the races. The first is to develop your structure by identifying your *rules, protocols* and *rituals*. Once done, then figure out a means to responsibly enforce them. Ok, so they are not little items. There are however, tools to turn those rather daunting tasks into a series of manageable small ones. It then becomes achievable and prepares the way to ownership.

Building your structure and remembering it all, then teaching her requires you prepare four things to do it well. First, a *Me List*, then your *Master-Slave Contract*, then a list of your *House Rules* and of course delineation of the *Rituals and Protocols* you enjoy. That may sound like a huge task, but it all starts with this thing called a *Me List*. The rest falls quickly into place from that.

MIND FUCK #22 – "SNORING LUMP"

"I'm nervous," she thought.

It was bedtime, her first night sleeping with the man she would call master. She had dreamed and worked for this night, she hoped the first of many that would lead to a life of enslavement. Her nerves were on edge.

"Please let him be pleased," she thought. Focused, as never before and despite the tension she felt, deep inside, her soul was calm.

He inwardly smiled while watching her. Her face expressed the nerves she felt. Gracefully turning down the bed and preparing the end table, she was elegant in her movement and service. He had wanted her nervous of course, had in fact, encouraged it all day. Tonight was important. The time had come to delve into her soul, to examine whether the words and needs she spoke of ran to her heart. She had deep yearnings of romantic enslavement, a need she had felt her whole life. He knew she had sought out, learned and listened. She found external knowledge and searched deep within her soul. Her face expressed fear and anxiety mixed with courage and strength. He was delighted with her. She exuded the core traits common among successful slaves he knew, all of whom who thrived in structure.

---

[1] See Devil In The Details I - Volume I, Chapter 5

Tonight he would test the depth of those needs. He would probe and seek answers. Part of the happiness that guided him was understanding this woman and what made her so uniquely precious. This was but one moment, one step, into understanding those needs and how well they matched his vision and happiness. There would be no decisive revelation tonight, but it would be an important step, a small look into her heart.

He could only be happy with a partner of character and strength, whose ability to embrace the paradox of consensual slavery complimented his. He knew his own strengths, weaknesses, limitations, dreams and needs. Like the slave, he had looked within and grown, embraced the courage to face his realities. His mind was clear. Working to develop the tools necessary, he was at peace with himself, confident the path was healthy, fun and realistic. His morals, ethical platform, role in the community, his career and what he could bring to a relationship had crystallized over time into a life vision. What he could offer and needed in return was attainable and real. Was this lady before him of similar complimentary needs? He was falling in love with her, without a doubt.

Mustering the courage to test the validity of that love he took her by the hair, tilted her face until eyes met and smiled into her soul.

"Tonight you will sleep bound, girl."

The words raced to her soul. A smile came to her lips and eyes glistening she murmured softly. "Yes Sir."

This first night would be different from the usual nightly bondage he would practice in the future. It needed to be more difficult than the nights to follow. She would be probed for a reaction to the dark loneliness, bound unnaturally, alone with her thoughts, at a time when submission was not fuelled by lust and passion. He wanted her to awaken; wrists bound together, alone in the dark with her thoughts, a snoring lump beside her.

Would she awaken and sit bolt upright, alone with her thoughts and ponder the craziness of her decision? Would she see that a life of consensual slavery was not for her? Sure, it was sexy and romantic with wonderful aspects, but not a relationship dynamic she could travel through life in?

Or, would she find comfort and peace, knowing she had found where she belonged. Could she balance the paradox of strength and skills against the serenity of the structure she would live? It was crucial to know her feelings and answer.

Neither reaction was wrong or bad of course. This lifestyle is not for everyone. To reject it, would take the same courage it had taken to explore it in the beginning.

Perhaps the match was wrong, his vision not for her. Such a choice would not make her a good or bad slave, only reflective of thoughtful growth. Nor would walking away be a condemnation of his mastery and vision. Yet again, perhaps just simply a mismatch of needs.

The reaction he sought from her this night was not a contest, or competition, a right or wrong question. It neither sought to blame, fault, or pass judgment. It was but another step to discover who she was and lead her into a special relationship of lasting happiness.

Leather bondage straps lay like coiled snakes on the floor attached to the bed frame. They represented her choices, were symbols of the life this master led. She turned down the bed and made sure the end table was prepared as instructed. Learning his needs, his small protocols and little quirks that pleased him were important. She craved the relentless and patient teaching and more importantly seeing his smile. Setting out his reading glasses, all was finally ready. She turned and presented herself for his use and bed.

He had known she would wake up, planned for it in fact. He smiled to her over morning coffee. Last night was the first night of many to come. She had trouble sleeping. He had not. Their eyes met across the table and he smiled again.

"Give me your hands please pet."

She looked tired.

"You didn't sleep well last night pet?"

"I did not Sir."

"I knew you wouldn't. I hadn't wanted you to, but you will take a nap later. First though, we talk."

She smiled, "Yes Sir".

"Last night was a special moment pet, one we cannot have again. It was our first night together. I suspect you are stiff. It isn't easy sleeping in wrist cuffs fastened together."

"It was very uncomfortable Sir."

He nodded.

"There was a reason for binding you like that pet, an important reason. It is not how you will be bound often. Tell me please girl, did you awake in the middle of the night?"

"Yes Sir. I sat upright, in fact."

He nodded again.

"And you saw the snoring bold lump beside you blissfully cruising on through another sadistic, erotic dream."

She laughed, "Something like that Sir."

"Tell me what you were thinking, bound and sitting in the dark pet."

This is why he had gone to the trouble, why she had endured a night of uncomfortable bondage. To seek answers, to discover her heart and know the reality of her need.

It is easy to be submissive when you are horny. Taken and used, played with, teased, flogged, to feel the adrenalin, endorphins, to be helpless and forced. Submission for many, perhaps most, is about that innate passivity. That is the extent of their submission, in effect, just a way of enjoying and enhancing their sexual lives. But for this man and woman, consensual living master-slavery was at another level; a manifestation of their core needs representing their unique desires. Some would say it is how they are wired.

Her passivity has its place of course, but be complimented by more. This master would not limit her submission to having things done to her, though surely there would be a lot of that. Submission existed in a more encompassing realm of TPE, where her skills, strengths and intelligence would be nurtured and used assertively to enhance their lives. Like mastery, submission is work, a good work, but not for the lazy.

3

"ME LIST"

How often have you heard masters say, *"Well, I have taught her all I can. We've done everything. What now?"*

It is heard often enough, spoken usually by masters in frustration who have focused much of their master-slave dynamic in the S&M area of the lifestyle. They are either unwilling or unsure how to take the dynamic further, into the area of control of her day-to-day behavior. It is redundant to continue justifying that if folks want that limitation in their relationship, then fine. But this is about the all-inclusive *Three Power* niche, so will presume masters reading want more.

The question posed can be re-worded to a more accurate representation of what brings one to ask such a question in the first place. Have you taught and done everything there is to do? As master, can you remember absolutely everything you have taught your slave and everything about your needs, expectations and the scope of indenture you require? My memory is too imperfect to remember everything taught at a given moment, and even if it is everything I want her to know. I need an elephant!

Remember earlier in the *Volume II, Chapter Six* about training and the *One Year Training Discipline.* You want to get her trained to enjoy a trained slave and that is what she wants. She wants to please you. But, you also need to know everything you want to train, and the easiest way to accomplish that is with a simple tool called the *Me List*.

Over the years, I have endeavored to come up with a better name for this list, until laughing over drinks one day, a slave said, *"Oh don't change it, it's perfect. That name describes exactly what it is."* So indeed, she got an opinion, just not a vote, but the name remains.

The *Me List* is a simple technique to help organize your training and expand the master-slave relationship beyond sex and S&M. Make and keep it on the computer, it is easier to manage there, but never show it to your slave! There is no need to.

The *Me List* is beautiful in its simplicity. It is dynamic, on-going and ever changing. In essence, it lists everything you like and dislike, from foods, to eating habits, what hobbies you have, to fantasies and dreams of the future. It includes how you like your shoes stored and which celebrity you think would make a great slave. Write down everything about you, from the mundane to the ridiculous. It is all you, and all fun.

Make two columns. The first column is a simple checkmark indicating the item is taught. The second is a line item for each entry. Start up your *Me List* with your favorite color, why not? Then throw in your panty preference, bikini, knickers, petticoats, bloomers, grannies, or… none! Lace, sheer, cotton, edible, fret not, you ain't wearing them. I hope. Include big stuff, little stuff, crazy things and the bizarre. For example, it is important my slave can recite College football team nicknames. Why? Well, mostly because it is fun to see her face saying Horned Frogs and I laugh, yup that's me!

Just know, the *Me List* never ends and therein is its beauty. It is dynamic, changing as you grow and mature when life experiences alter your perceptions. As likes and dislikes change, so simply change the list.

It is a big burden to make such a list, so take your time. Add to it each week as things come to mind, when you are sitting at the computer looking for dirty pictures of slaves in bondage. There is no test or judging you. It is just your private tool to help your slave understand and please you. No one but you gets to see it. Then teach her everything on the *Me List*. It takes time, months, perhaps a year and needs prioritization, but that is ok, we are coming to that.

A good slave however, will want it all immediately such is her desire and need to please. That is great, but drag it out and take your time. Make it fun. Kneel her down, cup her face, smile and whisper...

"You are my treasure pet. I am your master and I love you slave girl. It is important you please and I know this in you. You make me smile each evening when I get home and you greet me as taught. But now also have a glass of ice water ready".

In that little act, you have created structure. She has learned a little way of pleasing you. You have taught her something. She knows it must be done and that is important to her. You have taught her something and provided a little way each evening for her to feel her heartfelt submission. When she presents the water, acknowledge her and reward her, a smile, a hair pull and a *"good girl"* is all she needs. She will know she is valued. In that one little act emanating from your *Me List*, you have created happiness for you both. Did I mention mastery is a giving art form?

Now imagine how long your *Me List* is! Imagine how much there is to teach. The master who is bored after six months must have a very small list. There are huge benefits that accrue from the *Me List* for the relationship. But it takes work. Mastery is not for the lazy, but then you know that already if you have read this far.

The *Me List* is part of your relationship preparation certainly, but also a neat tool to have ongoing. As it changes over time, think of it as a curriculum revision in schooling terms. Do not revamp the whole, just tweak out the old and insert the new. The beauty and effectiveness of the *Me List* is its ability to change as you do. Growth for the master is as important as for the slave. This technique is a mechanism to facilitate that growth within a set structure. Remember, as your list changes simply teach her the change.

An interesting phenomenon discovered over time is that the longer you use the *Me List*, the less you need it. Eventually you will have taught everything and as changes then occur in your needs and wants, you teach those immediately. There is no need to record them on a *Me List*. But for masters just beginning, or starting a new relationship, there is too much to remember in your head. Then the *Me List* is indispensible. You, but more so, your slave will appreciate it.

The reason not to show your slave the list is a simple one. The list is you! Now certainly you can dump it on her lap and tell her, *"Learn this slave".*

But I will hazard a guess that those inclined to that approach do not have the patience, or dedication to the master-slave genre to make a list in the first place. It is always your option to throw it at her though, if that is your style. Where is the fun though? Besides information overload, your slave will question your creativity, imagination and romantic heart. If you do hand it to her with the expectation she learn it, then she will have to hermitize (I made that word up and like it) herself for several weeks to pore over and memorize who you are. Undoubtedly, at some point in those weeks she is going to think, *"Wow, how fucking boring is this!"* It is much like hated memory work from school days and not at all what she likely envisioned as romantic enslavement. Remember also, it takes time. She is not a super computer.

Teach the list slowly, artfully, make it fun. Enjoy the joy of the master-slave relationship. Teach slowly building those shared experiences and intimacy. Yes, intimacy, that key word again, one of the four pillars of successful relationships. Teach her not only that she trusts you, but that you trust her too, with your most private being.

One last thing about the *Me List*. Remember not all on the *Me List* must be about you. Odd statement on the face of it to be sure, but list things you want her accomplishing in life as well. Add characteristics, habits, skills, achievements and goals, beyond the scope of your personal relationship. These are all things to put on your list applying to her. She has her ideas too, so mesh them together responsibly. In fact, screw it, have her make a list too. Call it the *Me Too List*. That is not to be confused with the vanilla wife's *Honey-do List*.

MIND FUCK #23 – "DIABOLIC DESSERT"

Ten masters and their slaves enjoying dinner, celebrating... well nothing really. They simply gathered as good friends do, bound by the camaraderie of a shared lifestyle, over a fine meal and an evening's entertainment. Not that it was spontaneous, or without purpose. While there was no specific occasion to mark the gathering, it did not exclude much aforethought and creative mischief being planned, naturally. What would a dinner party be, without some entertainment?

Good cheer, smiling faces and laughter complimented the exquisitely set dining table. Dinner was excellent. Florentine chicken over a cilantro-mushroom sauce, roasted herbed potatoes, and a wildly delicious salad of fresh greens, raspberry vinaigrette, with Cambozolo cheese and hazelnuts, had everyone raving. Topping the feast was a decadent assortment of desserts, though the chocolate cheesecake seemed to capture the imagination.

The evening was splendid with great appreciation of the slave's efforts. Course after course of pure ambrosia graced the table. It had taken time to dine and savor the offerings. Fully sated, time had come to turn attention to the master's fare. Could they match the culinary skills of these fine slaves, and serve up a feast of debauched mind fucking fit for a king.

Was there any doubt? The slave's were about to enjoy a "Diabolic Dessert".

"Gentlemen, your attention please". He rose at the head of the table, drink in hand.

"A toast to our slaves, gentlemen. They've exceeded, but not surprised us once again with their skill and talent to serve in a tradition of excellence. A toast to an extraordinary meal and these magnificent slaves".

Ringing crystal, and a hearty round of Hear, Hear befitted the occasion. The host remained standing, looking around the u-shaped table. Nine masters and their slaves, and of course his own slave waited for him to go on.

"Slavegirls, your attention please. The time has come. Your efforts tonight deserve rewarding, in the way we masters do such things. We cannot, nor would we try to match your culinary skills, but that is not to say we cannot cook, in our own delicious way. Tonight we have done just that, and prepared a spicy evenings' entertainment."

Smirks appeared across the chuckling master's faces and all slave eyes were riveted to the man standing.

"Slaves, tonight we test you. Often in the past, as you have lurched, been yanked and came crawling on your journey into slavery, you were told that learning and obedience weren't necessarily tests. As questions were posed and probes made, your answers were neither right, nor wrong. Those were times of exploring your feelings and understandings of slavery. They were not times to judge, but rather to teach. You were then just beginning to grasp the subtle magnificence of the lifestyle we live. That was as it should be, then, but not now."

"You're over it. If not, you have ten seconds to get over yourself, because tonight it all changes. This evening, here and now, you will be judged. You can succeed or fail, but know that your judges sit here among you and will decide your fate."

Well, you could hear a pin drop. The slaves, each with creased foreheads of concern, listened, absorbing every word. Were this coming from any other master, they would not fret, as much. But, when this master called for judgment, their hearts thumped, pussies moistened, and angst wrung in their sweaty palms. To a slave, their minds screamed, *"Oh gawd, what is he up to?"*

"Slaves, what I am about to say, is the will of all masters here this evening. There is no purpose served, no pardon given, no place to hide, by appealing to your owner. Reprieve and consideration are for naught. We speak as one. Hesitation and reserve do you no good. You will obey unconditionally. You will survive by wits alone. Is that understood?"

Heads nodded and "Yes Sir's" muttered.

Pointing to the middle of the u-shaped table, he spoke.

"Slaves, all evening, I am sure you have wondered why that solitary chair sits alone in the middle of these tables. It looks rather lonely methinks, by itself, isolated, out of place, rather stark. But, it is there with good reason. From there, sitting alone, with just your guile for guidance, you will be judged. Your grade and thus fate, rests in your quick wit, ability to perform under pressure and your cunning believability. You can survive this test by making believers of us. Failure to do so is…"

He paused appearing to seriously consider the consequences, then looked directly into the eyes of each slave.

"Well, let us say, failure to convince us of your sincerity will be very regrettable."

Raising his arms in the ensuing silence, he beckoned them.

"Arise please slaves and gather at the end of the tables."

Chairs shuffled as the slaves rose and took their place. Masters too shuffled places gathering their chairs around the head of the U. A tribunal for war crimes could not look more imposing.

"Here is the contest, slaves. In a moment, you will go to the basement together to converse among yourselves. There you will conceive a plan, the outcome of

which will decide the pleasure you will receive tonight. A passing judgment and you will receive incredible pleasure, beyond your wildest dreams."

"We have consulted and planned for several weeks now, how to achieve this for each and every one of you. Your masters have confided your secrets. Together, we have devised ways to make your secret fantasy into your new reality. We know the hidden desire deep within you. We know what is in your soul. We have gone to great lengths preparing ten separate scenes, one for each of you, if you pass the test. Do you understand so far?"

A chorus of "Yes Sirs" made him smile.

"Goodgirls. Now understand, slaves, that if you fail your test, not only will the incredible scene meticulously planned for you be denied, and all that work gone for naught, but it will be terribly disappointing to your master, as indeed all of us."

He paused. "In addition to that disappointment, fail and you will be punished."

The room was very quiet.

"Your task is simple. In a moment, you will proceed downstairs whereupon, in consultation with one another, you will come up with either a truth or, a wildly concocted untruth about your own master. Think of something he loves, or hates, a peculiarity he has, some fetish heretofore unknown to us, use your imaginations. Pool your ideas to help each other. The only rule is that when called upon, you cannot all say something truthful or, false. There must be a mixture of answers among you and you will have to decide who will tell the truth, and who will lie their sorry little asses off."

Grins appeared on the masters faces, each eyeing his slave. Even a couple of slaves were smiling, their master's private peccadilloes obviously already known. The idea of relating them was delicious.

"Now, how this works, slaves, is again simple. After your consultations, each of you will be brought here, one at a time. Then you will divulge to us, the story about your master. He will abstain from voting when you are here. You must convince the rest of us that the story is the truth. Be as full and graphic as you need to make your case. But, you must convince us. When you are done, you speak no more. We will debate and discuss your story as you wait in the chair. You will only answer questions put to you in the course of our cross-examination of your story. Then we will decide your credibility."

"Yes, or no - pass, or fail - pleasure, or punishment, your fate is in your ability to convince us. Then it is in our hands."

A texture of drama permeated the air. He paused then continued.

"Upon rendering our decision, you will tell us if we were correct. Your master will verify the veracity of your statement, so you cannot manipulate us. Do not even think of going down that road to receive your pleasure. Just make yourself believable and you will not be denied the greatest of all pleasures."

"We will keep a tally of how many, and who told the truth and who concocted a story. We will know who passed and who failed miserably. Do you all understand or have questions".

Before giving them a chance to answer, he said,

"Fine, that's good. Follow me" and led them to the basement.

Returning to much laughter and merriment, he chuckled. They all knew the slaves would be howling their heads off in laughter trying to come up with ideas. The consultation was as much for their amusement, as any need for real planning. But, that was part of the fun. Meanwhile the masters dimmed the lights, rigged the interrogation spotlight and brought in the gavels.

"Ok, everyone knows the rules, are we ready for them?"

More laughter ensued, each savoring the deliciousness of the plan.

"Bring up the first."

And so, in a darkened room, it began. Each slave brought before the jury to plead her case and meet her fate. Each in turn, chair bound, spotlighted, nervous and alert. On display, she knew an interrogation when she saw one. Each related her story with the most incredible pile of bullshit one could ever imagine. And funny, oh my gawd they were outrageous.

From one about her master sleeping with a teddy-bear he owned since he was a child (true), to the slave that tried to convince us her master was bisexual (false). Then there was the story of one master who only discovered his mastery after a dominant girlfriend tied him up and his claustrophobia was so bad, be broke free and tied her up instead (false).

But, the Queen of Bullshit was the slave who with utter credibility, could have won an Academy Award for her portrayal of masters desire, indeed deep need, to see his slave gangbanged by a dozen men, (false) and we blew that decision.

Each in turn received their judgment. The cross-examination and deliberations were as much fun as the story themselves. The debates raged on about each story, with more and more laughter. After the verdict, the slave, sad or happy, was escorted to a separate room, to await her sisters. As their numbers grew, they commiserated or celebrated, but each wondering what was in store now. Finally, all ten slaves were rendered. Some had passed, some failed. Returning to the masters, they gathered again in the center, spotlighted and silenced. Some wore smiles and some with looks of forlorn. It was time to administer the coup d'gras.

Rising, the host struck the table with the gavel. All masters were grim faced. Any elation the slaves felt was suddenly gone. The mood had changed. They sensed something amiss.

"I have been asked to speak by all the masters. We are here, all of us terribly disappointed in you slaves."

He had their complete attention.

"We are, in fact, shocked at your behavior. By our tally, six of you sat in this chair and flat out lied to us. It was outrageous."

"Were you not told, and had it drilled into you from the first moment of ownership, that you were forbidden to lie? Did your training not include, that respect for other known dominants was necessary?"

"And you other four slaves, what gall you have to sit before us and tell secrets about your master. Have you no respect for his privacy and wishes to maintain that privacy?"

He paused. The look of confusion on the slaves face was perfect.

"You all failed miserably. You lied and betrayed trusts. Your behavior seriously hurt each of us. You all deserve and will be punished!"

Not a murmur stirred through the room. Nothing happened for several moments. Silently each master then rose, going to his slave.

"Now"

And a great roar was hurled at the slaves.

And they were tackled to the floor in a heap of bodies.

Laughter and mirth erupted as the slaves realized they were scammed.

Lambs to the wolves, but was it ever fun.

4

SIGNATURE SCENE

As your time in the lifestyle expands, inevitably, experimentation occurs and you explore many types of scenes and rightly so. It is pure bliss to mess inside a slave's head, so we do it relentlessly, creatively, but always responsibly. Well, almost always. Letting slaves think we are not quite the perfect responsible creatures they believe, can be a wonderful thing too. Exploring the full range of emotion and sensory experiences of the S&M world is much of what we do. From sensually binding and teasing, to the harsh realities of hardcore S&M, the paths we take are relentless and innumerable. Imagination is our only limit. Undoubtedly, you have, or will, explore many uses of your slave, creating a library of memories and joy. Whether recreating another's memorable scene, or emulating the skills read about with your own touch of creativity, it is all wonderful fun.

Many passionate longtime masters have limitless skills and creativity. They see a tool, device, or situation and in time, a simple idea germinates into a scene. They create many scenes this way. However, those same masters often take pride in creating their one *"Signature Scene"*. They relish the creativity of devising something uniquely theirs. It does indeed become their signature. I am a great believer in a master possessing a *Signature Scene*. Perhaps it is ego, or arrogance, but no, I have none of that. It is just because it is mine. Here then is a classic *Signature Scene*. Enjoy it as I have.

"DOMINANT'S DELIGHT"

My *Signature Scene* is one, that while not harsh, nor particularly difficult on the slave physically, it is a mindfuck, and a classic example of *"less is more"*.

Through sensory deprivation, comes sensory enhancement. By limiting reality, one can alter her perceptions and prove beyond a doubt, that with minimal resources, a slave can mind fuck herself. Welcome to *Dominant's Delight*, my signature.

A word of warning though – this scene can be done, but once to your slave. It does not work twice. Allowing her to witness it performed on others, or if she reads this passage, know that it will no longer work on her in the future. It is a one shot deal.

Dominant's Delight is a mindfuck to overload your slave's auditory senses with evil...

Tis the time for her imagination to run wild...

To make cold feel like fire...

Where chains become oppressive...

And howling screams torture…

We will…

Stalk her mind…

It is time to cast our spell, mix the brew and plan relentless devilry...

The party was in a private home and had been a quiet one thus far. Many present did not know each other well enough to expose themselves to the vulnerabilities of public play, so shyness permeated the ambiance. It was fun nonetheless and a good party. They were good folk, though mostly inexperienced and just beginning their exploration into the BDSM world. He sensed a harsh scene would be inappropriate with these folk, but a scene was needed. *Dominant's Delight* was tailor-made for this evening and this crowd.

Taking their host aside, he explained the plan and gained permission for use of the hostess-slave. Neither the host, nor his slave had heard of this *Dominant's Delight* scene before, but it would be a nice thank you for providing such a fine evening. With consent and a slave volunteered, the master set about preparing the room.

Couches filled as people gathered to watch. Before the slave's entrance, he explained what would occur.

"Friends, our host has kindly offered his slave for my use. What is about to occur takes an hour. You are welcome to stay and watch, but to achieve success will require complete silence from each of you. No shuffling, coughing, loud breathing, gasps, snorts, or farts please. If you are going to observe, there must be complete silence, or all will be lost. For those unable to comply, please leave now and for those brave enough to want this done in the future, I ask you leave too. What you are about to witness will ensure it never happens to you in the future. The magic will be lost."

None left and he smiled looking directly at Bob.

"Are you sure you want your slave to witness this Bob? You will never be able to do it to her if she watches."

"It's alright, she can watch," he responded.

All then was ready. The slave entered and he began.

Before him, stood a lovely creature, a slave, the hostess and a lady of great imagination. The latter trait he would nurture and depend on. She stood silent and still as ordered, her eyes locked on the ground. Slowly he circled, stalking her quietly. She was a bit terrified of him before this night and that her master had given her away caused great angst. Her belly was in turmoil. He was experienced and unpredictable. She somehow knew this would be an evening not soon forgotten, and so the mind fuck began.

Dominant's Delight is a scene that requires prudent use of *"timing"* and *"silence"* for a mind-fucking success. Getting her mind to wander freely is the critical element. Her world must shrink to within the confines of her blindfold, imagination her only reality. Achieving this early on, through use of silence and time, enables the drama that follows to overpower her mind and senses.

There is little actual S&M in the scene, but enough to create the illusion of impending danger through uncertainty and surprise. It highlights feelings of helplessness, with a good old-fashioned dollop of fear thrown in. In short, it is a riveting, unpredictable mind fuck.

Here is how it works.

The scene takes approximately an hour. More than one couple can participate, though each dominant attends only one slave.

Attire her as you see fit. Nudity is not required, though bare inner thighs is highly recommended. Bare breasts intensify the scene and an exposed pussy can produce some wonderful twists. The scene begins with the slave ordered to silence. Absolutely prohibit her from speaking at all. Growl at her and make her feel the severity of the command. Give her no mental outs. Ensure she knows this is anything but easy. It is going to be dangerous for her.

Blindfold and sit her in a chair. A butterfly bondage chair is ideal, but most any straight-back chair works. Immobilize her. Bind her quietly and securely. Have her sit upright, arms fastened behind her back, or securely to the chair arms. Spread and bind her legs as wide as possible. If she is nude, you want and need access to her pubic mound. Ideally, do all this silently though do throw in some minimal grunts and growls. All through this scene, as you will see, *"less is more"*. Understatement and timely use of silence are key ingredients. If more than one couple is involved in the scene concurrently, dominants must refrain from speaking to each other and their charges.

Once tethered with blindfold in place, silently bring in the props. She has not, of course, the faintest idea what those are. When in place and ready, approach her in silence, but with the intention that she can hear you pacing and circling. The anticipation, fear of the unknown and elapsing of time begins to work its mind magic. Continue the silent circling to intensify her unsettled anticipation.

Do not short change the effect of silence. Longer is better than shorter, so let time and silence do their thing. Then when you sense she is there, using surprise, evilly growl in her ear.

"You have no choice now... you're mine... you're helpless... you're defenseless... your worst nightmare is about to come true... god fucking help you!"

Now, you must SHUT UP! Ensure the one thing you do NOT say... is that she is safe. The scene will not work if she thinks nothing untoward will happen. Then retire silently from the room. Leave her alone for a full fifteen minutes letting her mind brew those final words. Let evil ferment in her imagination. Fifteen minutes will seem an eternity and prime her well for what comes next.

Then the fun starts...

Oh my goodness. Did you really think I was going to tell you the details of my *Signature Scene, "Dominant's Delight"*? Did you honestly think I was going to write it in this book for the whole world to know? And your slave, what if she read the book while you were at work, or sneak reads it in the bathroom, behind your back? Then what? Slavegirls are crafty and give her an inch and she will want eight. I am actually doing you a favor. Now, I know you are miffed at me. What a prick eh? Well, get in line, many think that. But I will do this for you. *Dominant's Delight* will be available on my website in the future for download.

In the meantime, the important thing is, develop a scene that is special to you. It is fun, uniquely yours and feels great. Your slave already knows you are special, now prove it to her, yet again.

As for Bob at the party, well as the scene ended, Bob was shaking his head in dismay while his slave beamed and clenched her thighs.

"Well damn" said Bob. "I shouldn't have let her watch that!"

MIND FUCK #24 "OLD FRIENDS"

Being her first BDSM convention, she was in awe. Witnessed all night were things she merely dreamed of, and sometimes did not know existed. She had been on master's leash all evening, following and obeying as taught. Beautifully behaved too, she was. Being collared and leashed, knowing others understood that, turned her on enormously. Beneath her leather mini skirt, she was naked and wet. The incessant throbbing between her legs had not ceased since they arrived. It only intensified when master ran into friends he knew from over the years. He was warmly greeted and she took pride in the respect he garnered. She knew too, he was very pleased with her. Already he complimented her behavior.

In leather outfit, bare legs and thigh-high dragoon style leather boots, she was stunning and astonished how the wrist cuffs and collar provided a sense of peace and security. She loved being owned. Even the hours of practice endured learning to curtsy properly paid off when he smiled after introductions to other dominants. That several commented on her grace left her beaming inside, knowing he was proud.

They walked through the large dungeon packed with kinksters from all corners of the world. The outfits were gorgeous and eclectic. The creativity existing in the community amazed her and she felt at home here. That many understood her slavery was oddly peaceful too. Master pointed out several folks and their wild attire. The pony girls were spectacular and so well behaved, even down to their braying and sideway gait horses sometimes do.

Amazed and awestruck, she could only imagine the time spent training them so well.

Continuing their tour, master suddenly stopped, turned and kissed her hard on the mouth. When he whispered she was his most precious possession and the prettiest slave here, she could have fucked him on the spot.

"Well, well, look who has arrived", boomed a voice from behind. Turning to see from where the words came, there stood a giant of a man. Well over six and a half feet tall, he looked the size of a football player. Decked out in full leathers, salt and pepper hair and immaculately groomed was a man smiling, obviously an old friend of masters. Standing slightly behind and to the side stood another man, much smaller but equally well outfitted and groomed.

They greeted each other warmly, shaking hands obviously delighted at running into one another. "Scott you old sod, still kicking and brightening events with your presence I see", said master.

"Well someone has to show these young whippersnappers how it is done," he laughed in return.

"Scott, may I present my slave Carrie (name change, nice try). She is my treasure and I am very proud of her. Carrie please meet Master Scott, a dear old friend of many years." She was intimidated by the sheer size of the man, and felt dwarfed in comparison, but remembered her training and quietly, graciously curtsied.

"Aw, well LT you still have immaculate taste in slaves. She is a joy to look at and I can see you have been working her." Carrie blushed at the compliment. This was all still so new and different.

"And LT, you remember Phillip, my slave?" He turned to the collared man, who like Carrie, had not said a word. "Boy, this is Master LT." The man bowed with grace and ease, extending respect to his master's friend.

"So, you have not been persuaded to come over to our side yet Scott," laughed master.

"No not yet", he laughed, "though if I ever do, it would be an honor to have such a beautiful slave as yours to serve me." Both masters were laughing now, obviously bantering and sharing old jokes.

"Well Scott, are you sure not even this could persuade you," and master turned to his slave. "Lift your skirt and show Master Scott your cunt, pet". She was shocked at the sudden command and blushed furiously. Three sets of eyes were on her waiting, and slowly she lifted the front of her leather skirt to her waist, bare for all to see. Without waiting master reached down and parted her labia, exposing her wetness. She was trembling in excitement now and shook when his finger touched her clit. Her master was so cavalier with her body and demanding of her. It excited her beyond rational thought, and a trickle started down her thigh.

Master took a finger and thrust it in her cunt then licked his finger. "She is quite the delicacy Scott, are you sure even this tasty morsel can't convert you?" The men laughed at Scott's response.

"Well you know I prefer my slave's cum more white, and besides it is the other spot I have a penchant for." Quickly spinning his slave around, she found herself bent over with her ass cheeks pried open.

In mock earnest, spreading her wide, knowing these men and passerby's were gazing at her asshole, he spoke, "Even this delightfully tight pink little rosebud can't turn you, you stubborn mule". They all laughed as he pulled Carrie upright and turned her back towards them. Her face was crimson.

Master Scott yanked his slave forward and commanded him to unbutton. Phillip, perhaps more accustomed to his master's antics did not hesitate and Scott grabbed his exposed and impressively rigid cock.

"LT now this is what you need. With all due respect to your slave, she cannot produce the thrills this fine weapon can," and while they all laughed Carrie's eyes glued onto the slave's enormous endowment, fearful of what might come next.

"Well old friend," her master said, "I think this calls for a wager. I don't think the event staff would appreciate our bending these slaves over right here for a thorough ass fucking, but if we slip behind this curtain, I wager my slave can make me cum with her mouth, before your slave can you, with his. The tab at dinner tonight goes to the master who's slave loses the Battle of the Blowjobs!"

The two slaves froze in spot, while the two masters laughed and bantered.

"You are on Sir", said Scott. Both laughed as the slaves stood in either awe or fright, probably both.

"I have utter faith in my slave," said master

Drawing back the curtain, "Shall we begin then?"

Moments later the two slaves were on knees before of their masters. Thousands of people were just beyond the curtain. Unbuttoning his leathers, he looked down into Carrie's eyes, and saw her fiery competitive passion. He knew of her skill to make this quick and pleasurable. She would make him proud.

Whispering he said, "Don't spill a drop pet, or it will be your only dinner tonight." She winked and smirked knowing she would be eating lobster for dinner!

5

MASTER-SLAVE CONTRACT ANALYSIS

MASTER-SLAVE CONTRACT

So, with your *Me List* in progress, the next practical step in preparing to own that special slave is developing a *Master-Slave Contract*. Accepting it is a wonderful tool to spell out your *Core Value Expectations* and provide tangible evidence of your structure, as well as re-enforcing her belief in slavery, application of thought is required to itemize what it needs to say. Some might say the *Contract* is a document developed together, once you know who the slave will be. But is that true? Is not the master leading? Read on and analyze what a *Master-Slave Contract* actually says and why, before including her in the mix. You might well appreciate that she likes when you lead.

A *Master-Slave Contract* is fun. It is a symbol of who we are. While many take the contents seriously, it is understood *Master-Slave Contracts* are invalid as instruments of law. That enables us to have fun with it. Take lawyers out of the equation and many things become fun (editorial bias notwithstanding). The *Contract* is a symbol of ownership, much like a collar. It is another of the tools at our disposal helping ground her and provide a real sense of trust and security. That is ultimately what enables her service and affects the desired result. The *Contract* provides something she can feel, touch, read and see in detail, the level of commitments made to her. Indeed that works both ways as her commitments are also in black and white. The precious slave needs tools to understand the goodness of the choice she makes. It is not easy to sign onto a life of slavery, especially consensual slavery. The *contract* provides a piece of that assurance. It also serves as reference down the road to measure the existence of structure by comparing a master's actions against his words. With nothing to hide and notwithstanding human error, that works for slaves and masters. Masters can stand the scrutiny.

The actual clauses and format you ultimately use are, of course, personal and yours to decide. They represent, not transitory *House Rules* subject to change, but the values and standards of behavior that are inviolate. These represent the core delineation of your structure, the basis for the relationship. They make it very clear to your slave the standards you live by, enforce and expect. She enters into your life with her eyes wide open. You can and will glaze them later.

Like any contract, there is need for sections defining the parties, intent, terms for alteration, termination and agreements between the parties. That is all pretty standard contract stuff. The words are certainly different that vanilla contracts though. That is the fun part. A *Master-Slave Contract* should also itemize the rules and boundaries to frame the structure of your life in clear, specific language.

The *Contract* outlined here is mine, merely serving as one model to understand what goes into one. It is not the perfect contract for all, or necessarily anyone else. But it serves the purpose to illustrate why certain clauses work and others do not. It is important for you to understand that, in order to develop your version, and then teach it to your slave. You want a practical contract that makes sense.

Appendix A has the complete unabridged *Contract* for your perusal. Below each clause is detailed and analyzed.

CONTRACT ANALYSIS

1. PREAMBLE

1.1   THE essence, spirit and intent of this contract is based on the simple notion of a structured personal relationship between the parties identified hereinafter, wherein the responsibilities of both parties are clearly defined. Hereinafter, the party known as the "Master" will exercise responsible control for the day to day living of both parties. The other party hereinafter referred to as the "Slave" being fully informed of the responsibilities and expectations placed upon her, consensually, without coercion, or undue influence agrees to obey the Master in all asked of her within the Laws of Canada. Master will not command the Slave to act, plan, or conspire to act outside the law of the land.

1.2   THIS private contract is provided as a binding agreement, which defines in specific terms, the relationship and interaction between the participants, hereinafter termed the Master and the Slave. The contract defines the personal relationship structure of the parties. This agreement is binding only between the two parties listed and is binding only by the integrity of the parties. This contract in no way supersedes the Laws of Canada. This agreement is entered into voluntarily, both parties being fully informed, with both parties agreeing to the conditions and stipulations set out herein.

The *Contract Preamble* is an important portion of the contract. While essentially self-explanatory, it is included to establish context for the slave and perspective as to the legality of the document. It immediately bases the relationship in reality, rebutting the extreme fantasy arguments so often used by some, to validate arguments against the need for a contract. Arguments that cite irrational commands a master could potentially demand that skew the valid existence of responsible power exchange, while maintaining control with the master. That misguided logic often leads to the new age fashionable belief the "*slave ultimately controls*", a belief of utter nonsense.[2] If true, then the whole lifestyle becomes nothing but intellectual debate, not sustainable reality. One cannot be a master by definition when the slave ultimately controls. Acceptance of this sort of thinking changes the lifestyle to a game, or role-

---

[2]   See Devil In The Details I – Volume I, Chapter 4

play rather than a valid choice of personal structure designed to suit the identity and personality of the participants.

The *Preamble* clearly cites the contract is not a legally binding document. Its strength derives from the personal integrity of both parties, much like in any relationship. Regardless of the existence of a contract, without integrity all relationships are doomed. And let us bear in mind, we only come into this world with integrity and it is the one thing we can take with us, so why leave empty handed.

2. PARTIES

Hereinafter, the term "Master" refers to:

Xxxx X. Xxxxx,

And furthermore, the term "Slave" refers to:

Xxxxxxxxx X. Xxxxxxxxx

Some folks prefer to use their "scene" names in a contract, others their real names. That is a personal choice and really no big deal. As the saying goes, *"if it turns your crank, go for it"*. My preference is for real names, which re-enforces the legitimacy and seriousness of the commitments set out. Anything that creates positive feelings of submission in the girl and encourages her to understand the significance of her decision to submit is good, and using real names makes her feel that pending submission in her heart.

3. MASTER'S RESPONSIBILITY

3.1   MASTER accepts the responsibility of Slave's body; to do with as he sees fit, under the provisions determined in this contract. Master undertakes responsibility to define Slave's behavior and attitudes and teach, then enforce these elements to please him. Master agrees to care for the well-being of Slave and to arrange for her physical and emotional safety. Master accepts responsibility to fulfill Slave's needs to the best of his abilities, for as long as he owns her. Master also accepts the responsibility to treat Slave properly; to train, punish and use Slave for pleasure and useful service. Master recognizes Slave's desire for this relationship structure and works to build a life of peace and tranquility together, through intimacy, affection, honest communication, trust, love and romance, all embodied within structure. Master undertakes to make the decisions entrusted to him, for the betterment of both.

Well there it is! This simple relatively short clause speaks volumes! It embodies so much responsibility. Fulfilling the obligations of slave ownership contained in this small paragraph is the reason a slave wants to serve her master. Many ask what a master gets in return for the enormous work he obliges himself to in owning a slave. Why would a man bother and want to nurture, make decisions, punish when necessary and manage a girl's life in part, or in whole? Read the clause again. There is the answer. He enjoys the responsibility! He enjoys helping, leading, making those around him and close to him happier and better people. He wants his slave to be who she is, all she can be, free, happy and true to her heart. He enjoys having control, leading and the decision-making process.

For many men happiness is letting his partner make decisions, for others it is the joy of a partnership and sharing decisions together. For the dominant male, he is attracted to control, decision-making and to submissive women. Accepting responsibilities of leadership, providing the foundation, structure and guidance that allow her be who she is in her heart, a slave and contributing member of society is what makes him alive and vibrant. It is the crucial element.

4. SLAVE'S RESPONSIBILITY

4.1 *SLAVE agrees to submit completely to Master in all ways. There are no boundaries of place, time, or situation in which Slave may willfully refuse to obey the directive of Master without risking corrective measurements and punishment by Master, except in the activities relating to boundaries covered in this contract under Section 9 - Boundaries. Slave also agrees that, once entered into this Contract, her body belongs to Master, to be used as seen fit, within the guidelines defined herein. She agrees to be useful, utilizing her skills, talent, knowledge and experience in service, taking direction and using initiative within the structure of rituals, protocols and rules taught by Master. Slave agrees to please the Master to the best of her ability, with her primary focus now Master's pleasure, needs and wants. Slave is expected to seek the Master's comfort, pleasure and well-being, above all other considerations Slave may have. Slave will carry out these*

expectations, conveying her pleasure to undertake her responsibilities.
Slave will be loyal to her integrity and Master.

Not much there, eh? Obey girl. You get an opinion. What? You want a vote too? Is not this what you signed up for? Is not this the reason you are with him? So it is spelled out now, in black and white, signed in blood. Deal with it!

There can be no misunderstanding about who this girl is and what position you have in her life. You are her master. It says so, right there. You have a superior place in her life. So be a great master and take your responsibilities and her equally difficult undertakings of service and pleasure and run with it. Honor her commitment to you by recognizing this clause and using her. She wants it and you want it. In *Volume I*, we talked extensively about the *SODS Principle* and what makes this woman special. Her heartfelt need for *Service, Obedience, Direction* and *Structure* is real. That is just nice talk and nice theory, but you both want to live this in real life. Well, this clause is the *SODS Principle* in the flesh, real, tangible and very livable, if you make it so.

5. ALTERATION OF CONTRACT

5.1   *THIS contract may not be altered, except when both Master and Slave agree. If the contract is to be altered, the new contract shall be prepared, executed and the old contract destroyed.*

It is significant to point out the *Master-Slave Contract* is not an arbitrary unilateral bully document. This whole book deals with *"consensual master-slavery"*. The *Contract* is entered into by both parties and cannot be altered by either alone. To stipulate otherwise either creates feelings of insecurity in the slave, or shifts power to her that she does not want. Remember, the contract marks out your *"Core Value Expectations"* and unless something fundamentally changes in the moral code of either person, there should be no need to alter it.

6. TERMINATION OF CONTRACT

6.1   *MASTER may terminate this agreement as and when he sees fit. Master will not release Slave without adequately providing for Slave's welfare, as best able and sees fit.*

6.2   SLAVE has the right to terminate this contract, only after exhausting all avenues available to her to overcome differences between Master and herself and after discussion, or discussions with Master as to her reasoning. Master will determine whether all reasonable efforts have been exhausted. Master will accept Slave's request for release, only upon return of Master's collar.

6.3   SLAVE understands Master will not ever collar and own Slave again once she has been un-collared and released from this contract.

6.4   Master accepts that should this contract ever be voided and Slave released from service, it is his solemn oath to part ways having enriched Slave's life, both parties having grown, enjoyed and savored their time together.

There are many variations of *Contracts* in the BDSM world. Some are service-slave oriented, others read like employment contracts. Certainly many are familiar with the plethora of fanciful *Training Contracts* that fill the internet and cyber world. Each is interesting and has its place in the grand scheme of things. None serve the purpose of a master though, one who is embarking on a relationship of master-slave, twenty-four/seven. Those types of contracts fall far short of achieving the goals we have for this relationship.

Most BDSM contracts have one common characteristic. They are for a finite period of time. The contract starts effective this date and expires at some time in the future. They are tools for transient relationships, serving those with a multitude of motivations to explore this culture. Again, if that works for folks, great, go for it. Transience though, for the depth of commitment by the master and the balancing emotional vulnerabilities required from the slave, is relationship quicksand. We need a *Contract* that is timeless, that has permanence, yet is dynamic enough to accommodate separation when breakdowns occur. The wording in this model is stark. It plainly states a master can leave the relationship anytime he wants, and with little restriction, so can the slave. Do not get hung up on that stark wording though. The reality is, it is no different than any relationship. A husband, or wife can do exactly the same thing. A slave cannot be kept against her will, that is unlawful confinement, and anyone practicing it will be squeezing his ass, hoping not to drop the soap in Cell Block D.

What the *Termination* clauses do say though, is that the master is honorable and makes a commitment to ensure his slave, soon to be ex-slave, will be able to survive and thrive in her release. There is another old leather culture axiom that survives the test of time and is worth aspiring to.

"If a slave must be released, ensure you leave her better than you found her."

When structuring a TPE relationship, the master is asking for an enormous commitment. The slave is offering herself with all her incumbent strengths and vulnerabilities to a depth few will ever appreciate. A stable foundation for her to rely on, in good times and bad, will draw out her needed commitment and trust, and that foundation must be bedrock. Of course, the contract is but one of the foundation stones outlining structure, but it is an important one. Meticulous thought must go into it and to its termination. A *master-slave* relationship, in my context, is a commitment for life. The *Contract* reflects this and thus there is no time limit included.

Clause 6.3 is an interesting one and one many ponder quizzically as to why it is included. There is a very important reason why it is there and after explaining, hopefully masters do not delete it from their versions. It is a critically important part of the foundation you are building.

This whole relationship style being embarked on, is intense. Yes, it is peaceful and fun, but it is also full of risk. As stated before, that is one of the reasons we love it. One of the purposes of going to all this trouble to have a *Contract*, learn her mind, your needs, develop skills and learn the issues and be able to cope with them, is to change her approach to what this kind of relationship is. In effect, it is to make sure she always believes she is a slave. This is another tool to that end. She has not entered into a vanilla partnership. It is a relationship where you have a superior position in her life. You want it that way and she does too. You are alpha and she is beta. We do all these things to ensure structure is livable and satisfying, so that when the crunch comes and a difficulty arises, there are ways to cope with them while ensuring she does not question who she is. She does not hesitate; she does not have to consciously think about it; she just knows that she is a slave. This clause serves that purpose.

The one thing we do not want and will not tolerate is reverting to vanilla behavior under any circumstances. We will not be *topped from the bottom*. This clause addresses one of the most critical types of *topping from below* that exists: *The Collar Flit*.

If a slave attempts to, or is allowed to flit in and out of your collar whenever she decides it is time for a hissy fit, you have been *topped from below* in the worst way. She has made a mockery of your structure and all the serious work you put into building it, teaching her and providing a healthy structured environment. She is not accepting herself as a slave. She does not believe it. In her mind, she can always resort back to the comfortable vanilla world and decide submission must be a convenience for her, not a need. When that happens, release her. It is over. If she removes that collar, she is done. She will never wear it again. Now that may seem harsh, but it is something the slave wants too. She wants to know, you are as committed to this as she is and the collar means something. If she thinks she can rip it off knowing she can get it back when she has her own way, then you are topped. Control has gone to her and the master-slave power dynamic has fundamentally changed.

I am not advocating that slaves are a dime a dozen, are not precious and not worth every effort to own, control and live with, they are. But, there is a limit to the shenanigans you will put up with from her and she needs to know that, before ever accepting the collar. This is the way to show her. If the collar comes off, as painful and as in love with her as you may be, she must go. Time will heal the wounds and you will find a slave more serious in her commitments to herself and you. Rationalize the hurt you may feel in having to lose the slave you have invested so much into by understanding an old adage. It is said the perfect woman is one in a million. Well, there are three billion women on this planet, so I am thinking there are about a million perfect women for you. Forget her topping antics and pick one of the one million perfects.

Hmmmmm?

I think that is an argument for owning a vast harem. Get me a Pirate ship. This is going to be fun! Arrrrrrgh Matey!

7. Agreements between Master and Slave

The *Agreement* portion of the *Contract* is a very cool part. It is a lot of positive stuff for the relationship. It sets out the dynamics of the master-slave relationship predominantly dealing with positive, specific, lifestyle issues. It also serves as realization for the slave that this is not a bully document, that their relationship is an agreement between loving partners. Unlike the

Preamble, Master's Responsibilities and *Slave Responsibilities,* this section of the *Contract* lays out specific issues and addresses them. Addressed later are *Boundaries,* which define specific acts, *absolute no's* and thus negative in connotation. *Agreements* are the positive parts of the journey together. Often controversial lifestyle issues such as polyamory, sharing and humiliation are, or should be spelt out and are done so here. *Agreements* oblige the master every bit as much as the slave, ergo why they are *"agreements"*. Each master is going to have to give this section of his contract a great deal of thought, defining the restrictions, or openness he needs for happiness.

These *agreements* form a large part of the structure the slave will live within and emphasis on the importance of these issues is critical. The *Agreements* outlined below are mine, and certainly need tailoring to each couple, but will illustrate their importance.

> *7.1 WE agree that our relationship will always come first in our lives. We will not put work, or other outside interests before the relationship.*

The daily grind of earning a living, grocery shopping, family and all the vanilla activities we partake in, will at times try to overwhelm our *master-slave* structure. It happens to virtually all of us from time to time and if left unattended, could well result in the deterioration and even ending of the relationship, or in the least, the *master-slave* component. A master must be steadfast in prioritizing his slave as the most important part of his life. She needs this every bit as much as you. And who doesn't want to be the most important aspect of another's life. It is an awesome experience. Your partner and your relationship is what it is about, this person with whom you will share life's adventures.

Experience teaches us that career, hobbies and accumulation of material goods, while nice and all add to the life experience, are hollow and shallow, without sharing them with someone who gets you. Your slave is that person. It is a peculiar relationship style, no doubt, but while she is property, chattel and your slave, she is still your partner. You are dedicated to each other. So why not say it? Tell her, in fact, put it in your *Contract* that she means the world to you, is your priority and you are proud to make that declaration. The inclusion of this clause is important. It is a forthright statement of clarity, commitment and understanding.

7.2 WE agree to be fully truthful to each other at all times regardless of situation. Untruths, omissions and lies are forbidden in the relationship. Full honesty is committed to, in all things including feelings, thoughts and actions. There is no need for dishonesty and it is prohibited.

Honesty, one of the four pillars of successful relationships, here it is again! There is no way to over emphasize the importance of this element in the relationship. The way to explain it to your slave is simply that no lies, omissions, or half-truths are ever permitted, regardless of the size, or importance. Developing habits of being able to get away with even little fibs, has an unfortunate way, over time, of being a precursor and pathway to big lies down the road. They are ambushes, set to sabotage any relationship eventually. Think of past relationships, or couples you know and remember the arguments that occurred. Too often, the element of distrust was verbalized stemming from some recent, or unforgotten lie. Whether large, or small, inevitably lies break at the least, some of the trust fibers between you. You are the master. You do not need this in your life. Do not practice untruths and do not allow them from your slave.

Those living the *master-slave* lifestyle are barraged with constant awareness of how critical trust is in this style of relationship. That I would argue it is no more or less critical, as a uniquely defining characteristic for us, as opposed to loving vanilla relationships, is irrelevant. The fact is trust is essential. The *master-slave* lifestyle is often identified with and includes elements of sado-masochism and thus characterized as *"high risk, high reward".* Taking a slave responsibly on a journey into the S&M world requires trust, which is often a direct product of honesty. Conversely, for a master to lead a slave and enjoy the responsibility of ownership, he needs to trust she is being honest in her feelings and commitments.

So, honesty must flow in both directions. Her honesty is both your signpost to chart a course, as well as her protection against mistakes. Yes, masters are wonderful mind readers, magical illusionists, and skilled, brutal sadists at times. But, even with all these supreme gifts and skills, we do sometimes err. A truthful slave is your *"redundancy system"* for those times you misread her. Your honesty is a pillar supporting her ability to submit. Now, sure it is easy to pay lip service to this, but more difficult to live. It is said brutal honesty sometimes hurts and that may be true, but it also never leaves you sleepless at night.

So when she surprises you with a birthday party, just smile, grab her by the hair and promise her that just because she has been sweet and thoughtful, no precedent is going to be set on your watch. Then brighten her bottom with your birthday spanks.

> *7.3 WE agree that emotional monogamy is required in this relationship. There will be no additional partners brought permanently into the relationship.*

This clause is to poly masters, as a smack in the head with a frying pan is to cooks. It is painful and irrelevant. For exclusive relationships though, where the dynamic is one master and one slave, this is an important clause dealing with monogamy. It addresses the issue directly, in a way that reflects the permanent commitments to each other. It is another critical component supporting a peaceful *master-slave* structure. While the clause is straightforward and reflects arguably the most common viewpoint in the *master-slave* genre, each master needs to experiment and think through the issue to his own satisfaction.

Polyamory is defined for purposes here, as the master being owner of more than one slave involving long-term *emotional commitments* for all his slaves. Understanding others will quibble with this narrow definition is fair enough. There are valid BDSM niches involving service slaves and beta slaves, unrelated to this book. A definitive analysis of all nuances of the term is not the point here. Rather, understanding a realistic cause and effect involving long-term, multi-person, emotional commitments; and its effects on a *master-slave* relationship, is vitally important. This clause explicitly states the master will not entertain ownership of more than one slave concurrently. That is his choice. But, as this is an agreement between both master and slave, it must be her choice as well.

The master's collar around a slave's neck, symbolizes a *master-slave* partnership. For many, the collar is akin to a wedding band in vanilla terms. To be consistent then, collars to multiple slaves concurrently, can be argued as a form of bigamy, illegal in our culture. Making a case whether bigamy is right, or wrong, is again, not the point. Rather it being the fact that we do live in a culture where it is an unacceptable practice and that is reality, so we have to deal with it. Now yes, it is argued the collar does not symbolize a wedding band in the legal sense and therefore its value sets and legality are irrelevant in the *master-slave* context. This classic misdirection argument just confuses and minimizes the issue. Are you in control of her life or not? Are you effectively married calling it a new name, with all the attendant responsibilities of that traditional union? Do not beat around her bush. Well, ok, let us do that later, but do not play word games with your reality. You own her; she is yours; and assuming you want her unfettered and unconditional submission, give her the security to offer it. Demonstrate courage and include this loyalty clause. You then have the right to expect that unwavering loyalty in return.

The best masters make the best slaves. It is a recurring theme. As an outstanding master, you want to give her the tools and platform to be yours, in all ways, at all times, without reservation. This clause, this commitment and agreement between you, when honored, does just that.

Now, nowhere in this clause is physical monogamy addressed. Did you notice that? This only deals with emotional commitment, or if you are so inclined *"intimate emotional love"*. The reasoning is simply that *emotional monogamy* for most *master-slave* couplings is a key foundation for all that comes in the future journey. Master and slave oblige themselves to this ideal and reality.

Several arguments are made for adopting *emotional monogamy* as an integral part of the relationship. But, like all issues, it is a matter of personal choice. *Emotional monogamy* while not exclusive to building intimacy, greatly encourages its development. For me and I suspect many others, that is simply a requirement of my psyche and happiness. The depth to which a master must commit himself to his slave, for most, leaves no room, or capacity at the end of the day to nurture more than one slave. Often, there is simply not enough energy to do so. To those who can commit emotionally to a level deep enough to sustain *master-slave* structure for years with more than one slave, well then, go for it. But, that commitment and other factors influencing polyamory make it at most, an unrealistic option for many.

Now there are other structures wherein polyamory may be more successful than the committed one-on-one style explored here. A multiple slave relationship, where one slave is the alpha slave and one (or more), are beta slaves, wherein the beta(s) answer to the master and alpha slave, and where the beta slave(s) are not as deeply committed by choice, to the emotional intimacy of the primary coupling. This is often seen in relationships where the beta slave's needs are more service oriented. A *"service slave"* position can work, especially prominent among male submissives, sometimes with a cross-dressing element. In this case, *"to be in service"*, is more important than emotional commitment. Most of these tend to be transient in nature, but it is certainly a sustainable style for slaves with those particular needs.

One last point regarding this agreement item is necessary. The clause states that no others will *"permanently"* be brought into the relationship. That does not exclude temporary *"play"* partners, or bringing in another slave on a temporary basis, often done to re-enforce a skill, attitude, or behavior the master is teaching his primary slave. Overcoming jealousy immediately comes to mind as a purpose.

> 7.4   *We agree the slave may not seek any other Master, or lover, or relate to others in any sexual, or submissive way without Master's permission.*

A simple clause with clear wording that addresses the deeper issue of commitment and potentially conflicting loyalties, structure and vision. The slave cannot submit to anyone other than her master. I will not argue the semantics of whether sharing your slave with another master is having her submit to another, or in fact obeying her master's wishes. The fact is that while she may temporarily obey others, she does so at her master's command and remains committed to the relationship. Likewise giving temporary control of the slave does not abrogate master's responsibilities and oaths to her. The critical issue validating the need for this clause, is simply you cannot act to put your slave in an untenable position that undermines her trust foundation in you. She cannot have divided loyalties that act to undermine her ability to serve and obey. Conflicting commands from two sources can do that, resulting in confusion, perhaps a loss of confidence and trust. She needs *"her master"*. That is what enables her to serve without hesitation. Remember, you enjoy a superior place in her life. You may not want to express it so directly and politically incorrectly, but that is the case. As much as you need loyalty and focus, so too must she be emotionally committed and monogamous to the master.

> *7.5   We agree Master may engage sexually with others, but will consider
> slave's emotional response to such action and involve slave emotionally,
> or physically.*

This is the *sharing clause* dealing with the issues addressed in *Volume II*. In that chapter, it was theory and issues. Here it is reality, like a cold slap on the ass. No more theory, it is time to get livable. We know already, this is a contentious clause that many will oppose. That is good. Sharing is not for everyone and in fact, quite the minority within the lifestyle. But, if as master, you are to use other slaves in any way, this needs to be clearly spelled out in the contract. By doing so, you show her of the confidence in your commitments, being unafraid to address issues, nor intimidated by opposing views. Rather, you are telling your slave exactly what will happen, what her life in slavery will include. If you are smart, you do so by explaining the journey to get to the point of sharing, if it needs teaching. This clause demonstrates to her that you are honest and as importantly, the slave is fully informed.

While the clause reads rather starkly, in practice it is an advanced step in the journey and one that is incredibly intimate between master and slave. For me, using another slave is an incredibly powerful act. It is a way of demonstrating to my own slave, not that she is inadequate, but the opposite, that we share a commitment so powerful, that pleasuring others is a manifestation and instrument of that connection. We are not threatened by it.

The best, but by no means only way to use other slaves, in my experience, is to at times include your slave in the activities, or in the least, command her attendance. Creating shared experiences that later encourage intimacy as you lie in bed cuddling, whispering to her, stroking her hair and praising her, is powerful stuff for a *master-slave* relationship. Very powerful!

For many masters, another task incumbent with the responsibilities of slave ownership is to eliminate jealousy from their slave's life. That negative emotion often muddies the path he chooses, making their journey more difficult. This clause (and the particular attention to its wording) serves that purpose. Building a stable foundation, by ensuring she understands the framework in which you use other slaves and your motivations for doing so, largely minimizes, if not eliminates jealousy. She needs the freedom to savor and enjoy feelings of pride in her master, as he uses another for pleasure or teaching, both during and afterwards. Her freedom and pride can create rich feelings, becoming deep commitment drugs for the relationship. Dare I say, they are manifestations of love? To me they are, so reward her in some way. After all, it is her obedience you want, while providing her the opportunity to feel the goodness of her submission.

> *7.6 We agree Master may give slave to other Masters, Mistresses, or others on a temporary basis, provided the terms of this contract are upheld. In such a circumstance, Master will inform the new parties(s) of the provisions stated herein and any breach by them is a breach by Master.*

Well, here is the other half of the *"share"* equation. If sharing is to be part of the relationship, structure must be set forth to identify not just motivation, but establish dynamics to keep everyone healthy and safe. The piece of structure defined in this clause is critically important for the slave's comfort, safety, and positive self-image. Despite what some will sermonize and preach, over the long haul, a slave cannot be treated as a commodity. Sharing of her is often seen in that light. While objectification has a place from time to time, sustained mindless objectification is not healthy for a slave's self-esteem. Part of that is for her to see, directly and subtly, that *agreements* and *rules* are enforced, not rejected cavalierly, or applied inconsistently. The casual, recklessness of giving a slave away, wherein she is unsure of her status within the relationship is a form of objectification.

This agreement is designed to provide stability and structure for her, in an act that is often difficult and on the surface seems to objectify and harm her self-worth. For some slaves that is exactly what will happen, particularly if the master has not established a commitment and trust she believes in. A slave needs to know the rules. She needs to know the core values of the relationship are intact, especially when potentially sharing her, something many find difficult. When the time comes to share her with others, particularly the first few times, she is going to be nervous. Being nervous because she may not know what the temporary master will do is not a bad thing. In fact, it can be very meaningful for helping her feel her enslavement. Done well, sharing can be very powerful and if desired, very erotic. But nervous because she fears for her safety, or is unsure of the integrity of this master is not positive for her, or the relationship. Her nervous anticipation of new styles, different acts and approaches, perhaps sexual, sensual and pain exploration are all paths you can travel with the help of others. It is a beautiful area to guide and watch growth, sometimes for both of you. But, like many aspects of this lifestyle, there is risk and reward. This clause eases her angst by assuring her, that while her master may, or may not be present, he has provided for her safety, as he always does.

> *7.7 ALL sado-masochistic equipment required by Master, is paid for by Master and remains his property.*

Some slaves think that once an S&M implement is used on them, regardless that they did not purchase it, it then becomes theirs. Perhaps it is a favorite, or maybe it is just spite when relationships break up, but make clear who owns what.

> *7.8 WE agree that household tasks will be distributed between Master and Slave at Master's direction.*

Shall we laugh now? Every slave will highlight this clause if they find it before their masters amend, or delete it. Of course, do as you wish, but do not be lazy, gentlemen. Do your share of the work around the house, or hire a cleaning service. Few slaves will not feel misused if she becomes your surrogate Momma, her day spent cleaning up after you. She need not be lazy either. Insist she pull her weight. Ensure she remembers this is her home, but a master's home too. When that little fact seems to elude her, a simple appropriate reminder is to tape a sponge to her face and then, on her knees, clean the bathroom floor. That ensures she will not ever leave drying nylons on the shower rod again. The point is, you have a slave so use her and be considerate.

> *7.9 We agree that no command is given causing extreme damage to slave's life.*

When the concept of TPE is discussed in BDSM circles, those opposed to its health or existence, often point to the potential abuse by a master with control of a slave's life. They also often confuse TPE with micro-management, but that is for another section of this book.

"Would you walk off a cliff if your master ordered you to?"

That is an argumentative question often posed in derision by nay-sayers, to slaves when discussing the viability of living a TPE life. The questions obvious implication is, either you are a total idiot if you did, or there is no such thing as TPE. This extreme argument contributes nothing and fans acrimony. The argument embraces unfounded leaps of logic, cavalierly dismissing the oaths and reasons for entering the relationship in the first place. In a TPE relationship a master could order the slave to fling herself off a cliff. In theory it works. But why would he? The master has undertaken a healthy, loving relationship with a woman to guide and lead on life's journey. He has pledged to keep her emotionally and physically safe, albeit they both are risk takers by virtue of bucking the traditional societal norms of relationship dynamics.

The consequence of ordering a *"cliff walk"* whether obeyed or not, is staggering and not at all good. The cops might want a word or two with you and perhaps several years of your life; and she is going to be some kind of pissed off you broke your oath, commanding her to knowingly do herself harm. It is not a realistic command despite its theoretical possibility. No sane master would issue such an order. But because it is theoretically possible, those critical of TPE will attempt to make the argument that TPE is unrealistic.

There are times a master will ask a slave something she may think is harmful to her. But, she calls on that foundation of trust built diligently and obeys her choice to be led. If she knows no good can come from a command, her choice to disobey, not only rocks her own commitment to you and herself, but undermines the very essence of knowing her master will never act with malfeasance of the heart. The trust is gone! Poof... the relationship is up in smoke.

So why do it? This argument by nay-sayers of TPE has never held water for me for it presumes stupidity and a motivation of malfeasance on the master's part. The relationship dynamic of *master-slave*, TPE or vanilla, become irrelevant if the master/hubby deliberately wants to harm her.

This agreement simply spells out specifically for the slave, her master's intention. He will enjoy the slave and not act to deliberately damage her. What a wonderful cornerstone for her foundation. She submits in the knowledge she is safe. Never exclude this clause, nor ever forget its value.

7.10 We agree that Master will never strike slave in anger.

Just do not do it! Leave the bullying and abuse to the less mature. Good masters are above all this nonsense and have healthier, legal ways of dealing with conflict resolution. The slave must know she is safe. But then again, do not all partners need to know their home is their sanctuary, their safe haven, and they are bound to a rational partner with a semblance of common sense? The slave, even when bound and vulnerable must know deep in her soul that her master is not taking his anger or frustration out on her. It just cannot happen. It is a trust fiber guillotine. I doubt a master can be forgiven even once for this transgression. Nor should he expect it. At best, a power shift will end the *master-slave* dynamic. You can imagine the worst.

Hopefully, new dominants will know this instinctually, but may have to learn there is no fun, or constructive outcome to strike in anger. Nor does it accomplish anything positive to engage in S&M activities when your emotions are uncontrolled. That is what striking your slave in anger is. Out of control! Odd is not it, that as a master you are accepting responsibility to control a slave's life, yet demonstrate to her you cannot even control yourself. Any striking of a slave in anger stemming from a loss of self-control is not something any master wants to aspire to, or accused of doing. Yes, a master gets frustrated and angry at times, we are humans too. But a master has learned skills and taught conflict resolution techniques to control these situations and emotions. If he is smart, he has taught them to himself and the slave, before proceeding too far into the relationship. Enough said. Striking a slave in anger is relationship suicide.

8. RULES

"Core Value Expectations". Remember this is what comprises the *Contract Rules.* These simple and individual rules form the core structure for the slave's life. A great emphasis on teaching and re-teaching these expectations relentlessly, right from the beginning of the relationship is wise. Yes, even prior to collaring. While it is understood that during pre-collaring, structure and enforcement is less strict than later, primarily because commitments are still evolving and of the inability to punish, in my experience the expectations embodied in the *Contract Rules* cannot be withheld from the slave for any

length of time. Habits develop quickly, as much for the master being too lenient, as the slave's behavior taking on an unacceptable vanilla flavor. Tightening structure and enforcing stricter obedience after early patterns are established is very difficult to accomplish. What is that old saying? *"It's tough to teach an old dog new tricks."* Well it is something like that.

As you read through these rules and in time develop your own, it becomes obvious not all need enforcement, right away. But some do and a wise master identifies those, teaches them and enforces them right from the beginning. Most will find that if the slave is indeed serious in her desire for a relationship with you and wants to live power exchange, she will love your teaching and obey immediately and... smile doing it.

> 8.1 *THERE are to be discussion times regarding the relationship or any other issue, concern, need or interest anytime Master, or Slave feels it is necessary, except when Master is using the Slave, or while being given an instruction. A request for discussion will assure one, within twenty-four hours at Master's convenience.*

Effective techniques applying order to inevitable conflict occurring in all relationships are arguably, the most important components of any master's structure. This *Twenty-four Hour Rule* is such a technique, and the most important of all. Of the many rules I have come across, used or discarded, this is the one I treasure the most. It simplifies so much of the busy daily lives we all live, giving order to what is often a chaotic day. This simple rule, so vital to a healthy *master-slave* life is indispensable. Your benefit by imposing this rule, results in control of the communication methodology with your slave, thus ensuring she addresses her concerns and issues of the day in a manner acceptable to you. She does not get to control even how she speaks to you. You control it. The rule eliminates the nagging-wifey crap too often heard in many vanilla and some poorly constructed *master-slave* relationships. The way a slave communicates with you is couched in *protocol*, *ritual* and this *rule*. These three elements contribute enormously to the civil peace and tranquility in your home. That is your benefit.

For the slave, it is a powerful piece of structure she obeys without hesitation. She wants to. Doing so carves an avenue of unfettered communication with the man in whom she trusts her life. By having and using this rule, she immediately knows her value, trust and indeed her concerns, opinions and issues, matter. She is heard. She is listened to. She is important and relevant. She is also owned, chattel and without a vote. This all makes her happy. But she also knows, master is sincere in making her useful, recognizing she is a vibrant, energized human being, with needs, concerns and with much to offer. She needs a way to express all that in a way acceptable to her master. This one simple rule, more than all others makes twenty-four/seven, *master-slave*, TPE, under the same roof; work, endure and livable.

> 8.2 *SLAVE is required to fully obey Master's directions. When given instruction, Slave will neither negotiate with Master, nor hesitate to complete the instruction. Slave's only choice is to ask for clarification, if necessary and obey Master. Discussion is allowed later, if needed. Hesitation will be met with corrective measures and punishment. Slave will obey the literal and spirit of the direction.*

This rather important rule sums it all up succinctly, don't you think? Obey darling. Perhaps that is not clear to some, but slavery is essentially just that. Let us not get confused, or off on tangents. She obeys, serves, pleases and works to make her master's life comfortable, pleasant and as happy as possible. She has made the choice for a life of slavery, not for a lack of alternatives, or forced to that decision. She does so because it makes her happy. It is something she wants. If her needs for submission are genuine, then the combination of an alpha male and responsible mastery she respects mesh. There is no room for anything but obedience.

A slave cannot decide what she will obey and what to ignore. If her master's wishes are inconvenient, difficult, or tedious, it is irrelevant to whether she can choose to obey. If she thinks so, then this niche of the power exchange spectrum is not for her. A slave does not have the right to say '*no*' within the parameters of the powers she offered and for which her master accepted responsibility. That is important to understand. She is not asked to obey anything other than what she agreed to in accepting her master's collar. She knows he will not deliberately act to harm her, or their life together and if she thinks a command will do so, she has the mechanism right there to ask for clarification. This *Contract* clause makes it plain and clear. She obeys, without hesitation, with the right to ask for clarification if confused.

Her behavior has a consequence. If she does well, praise and reward may be offered. If she does not meet the standard her master expects, then she is punished. How much clearer can it be? She does not want punishment, nor does her master enjoy doing it. Negatives are not sought in their relationship. Joy for him comes from leading. For her the pleasure is in following and obeying.

Just remember, obedience comes in many flavors. Decide what flavor tickles your palate. Just try to avoid vanilla.

8.3 SLAVE will conduct herself with integrity and self-respect while exhibiting complete loyalty and honor for Master.

This is such a simple rule, yet very powerful. It sets the tone of dignity he expects from his slave. While she may be a tramp, slut, and fuck-toy, she is those things only to him. To the rest of the world she may never show that side of herself and she is much more than that. Integrity and self-respect are key words and critical assets in a slave for an enduring relationship.

Let us face some facts. Most *master-slave* relationships involve sado-masochism. Both partners are at risk when engaging in this practice. Whether the community wants to admit it or not, all a slave has to do is pick up the telephone after being bruised, call 911 and the master is going to jail for the evening, if not longer. He can plead consent until he is blue in the face, but the evidence is that she is bruised and you did it. Is any man willing to risk an arrest, possible conviction, loss of job, security, possibly permanently marked a sex offender and loss of family for the benefits of a few bum smacks? I dare say not a chance. Yet we do, and we do because our slave has a high moral fiber, self-respect and character. She has demonstrated she is loyal, trustworthy and is not going to send our sorry asses to visit Bubba in Cell Block D.

8.4 SLAVE must display an ability to be totally submissive to Master and furthermore display a positive attitude about her relationship choice and having entered this agreement. Discernable pleasure to be in service to Master is Slave's predominant outward image and emotion.

Body, Behavior and Attitude is the *Three Power Triumvirate*. An earmark of successful mastery is thorough attention to detail, without encumbering oneself in administration. This clause addresses the *Attitude* power and your expectations. She is not your nagging wife. She is a slave and assumedly happy in her choice. So she must display that. A lot of effort goes into owning a slave and it is not too much to ask that she show her appreciation for the commitment and responsibilities you assumed. This is not all about her. It is not a one-way street. A positive happy attitude makes for a fun life and a person pleasant to be around.

> *8.5 SLAVE must express her feelings, wants, state of health, likes and dislikes, at all times. Slave is free to express those needs consistent with her position as Slave, expressing not demanding.*

The slave expression rule is another critically important rule, but not just for the slave. While it is obvious a slave must be able to express herself, it is not as clear why this is important for the master. Yet it is.

Over the course of a day, week or month, a master charts a course with an overall goal in mind. That seems simple enough. In fact though, it is anything but simple. Blending all the various elements of a *master-slave* relationship, S&M activities, possible objectification, endurance, sharing, emotional jealousies, and the myriad of other areas traversed and conquered, means many choices for the master. Where to begin? What order? Are some pre-requisites for others? Where are the pitfalls? Have I properly assessed the risk/reward ratio? Is this worth it? Am I going overboard? What rewards should I employ?

All these questions go through a master's decision-making process every day. Alone and perhaps lacking confidence; and without communication with his slave, inevitably lethargy and inertia sets in over time. There is a lot of responsibility in leadership.

This rule simply provides the master with a critical component in the decision-making process; and adds enormous fun. Often, when contemplating a slave's journey, I have thought, *"Ok where to next?"* Now, I am not about to ask my slave that question, for inevitably it will introduce thoughts of a potential power shift in her mind, or even a doubt of confidence in me. Yet I want signs as to where her mind is. I can lead, but leading is best by knowing where you are at any particular moment.

Demanding her feelings, thoughts, likes and dislikes, on a regular basis, is one simple way of clarifying the choices available to you and avoiding the *'bull in the china shop'* approach to mastery. That is the effect of this rule. However, do not be fooled into thinking you are asking her to chart the course and do not let her think that. Clever masters can hear slave's words and see deeper issues than perhaps she understands. When she says *"Oh Sir, seeing that fire play tonight was scary"*, he might well know she is readying her mind to experience it. Then again, she may not, so be clever, but not overly clever. The fact is, she took note of it and it made an impression. Now go figure out how to use it.

Using her expressions of likes and dislikes is a helpful tool in decision-making. She is going where you want, make no mistake. This rule just helps order the progression in a way that is both fun and rewarding. The rule is a tool, so use it as such.

> *8.6 SLAVE'S speech to Master will always reflect a submissive, respectful tone and choice of words. Slave will never scream, yell, or argue with Master. Master provides opportunity and protocol to ensure Slave is able to voice all her thoughts and feelings. Use of submissive speech in tone and choice of words is not to restrict expression of thoughts and feelings, but rather to reflect on the unique structure and tenets of this relationship. Speech patterns are enforced to kindle harmony, peace and tranquility.*

In *Volume II Chapter 6* of this *Trilogy*, the difference between submissive-speech, baby-talk and vanilla-speak were analyzed. Notably, the rule about how she speaks with you is here in the *Contract*, not in *House Rules*, it is that important. Accepting you see the necessity for this rule, if a slave under consideration does not understand why it is necessary, then an examination of your slave choice is necessary. Experience has taught that a woman expressing slave needs, either understands and accepts these distinctions immediately, or never will. Perhaps that is unfair to some slaves who just need time to assimilate the rule, but she is the exception rather than the rule. This rule is a deal-breaker... for me.

> *8.7 A period of reflection and focus is required when Slave returns home after absence from Master for more than six hours. "Focus" is done on*

her knees in a spot designated by Master and lasts for a period not less than five minutes. Slave will focus during the reflection period to release her daily tensions and concerns outside the relationship dynamic and focus on Master, the happiness she feels in service and the consensual choice made to enter this Contract.

The *Twenty-Four Hour* rule, the *Laugh* rule and this *Focusing* rule, are three of the most important any master can make. Too many slaves are encumbered with a vision that slavery is all about things done to them. They want to live a passive indenture. There are niches and corresponding masters for those girls and if it works for them, then hey, have fun. Certainly, you will be doing lots *"to her"*, so she will experience that in spades anyway. But, the niche espoused here, requires a more active slave approach and this rule helps her focus each and every day to that end. Here is an *invisible rule* that is practiced every day. This is her chance for some personal quiet time to focus on your relationship. It redirects her away from the vanilla world, to the *protocols* of interacting with you. The rule enables her to address you with all the issues of the day, while respecting your structure. Enforced diligently, she will love this rule and come to rely on it.

There is another benefit derived from incorporating this rule. Countless times, I have heard conversations, or seen discussion topics on BDSM forums, asking how to mesh living as a slave, with the reality of a vanilla life outside the home. How can a woman go from career woman to slave, the moment she walks in the door, in an instant, each and every day. Well, the answer of course, is that she cannot. If you expect that transition to happen consistently, by itself, you are in trouble. It will not just magically occur. That is, unless you provide her the tools to do so. This *Focusing* rule is such a tool for her to make that transition. It works. The first few months it will seem awkward, or contrived, but in time, she will come to rely on it. It is a small piece of calm in what is often a hectic day. When the boy or girl spawn ask where Mommy is, tell them she is changing and will be out soon. She needs and deserves the few minutes each day, to refocus her priorities. Give them to her.

8.8 SLAVE will express her femininity in appearance, behavior and attitude.

I love this rule! It is quintessentially beautiful. But then to me, feminine women are beautiful. One of the pure joys and reasons this lifestyle means so much is the forum it provides for a woman to be herself. She is different from a man, so let her be so. Expressing her femininity is done in many ways, including clothes, demeanor, strength, care-giving, makeup, posture, grace, the list goes on and on. Encourage her, train her, point out what you like and dislike. But, if you do not like feminine women, well hell, then just change the rule, Boss.

8.9   SLAVE will conduct herself with dignity and grace in public.

These are two great words of value, worthy of a rule unto themselves. '*Dignity*' and '*grace*'. A slave is treasured for the rare and wonderful person she is. She is respected, treated with integrity and is entitled to the peace and tranquility her master enjoys. There will be times though, during her time in slavery, calling for behaviors the general public might find objectionable. In private, or semi-private settings, slaves are often deliberately objectified, called sluts, whores, cum depositories, treated worse than the family pet, whipped like beasts, humiliated and used. These behaviors are done mostly because both enjoy that aspect of the lifestyle. It is hot for them. These elements are not necessary to enjoy a successful *master-slave* relationship, but many do them anyway. Still, the intrinsic human worth of the slave must be re-enforced and respected. As complex individuals, we have a labyrinth of needs. While you may well treat her as property at times, to the world at large, she is your treasure, partner, strength and love. Ensure she projects that confidence to the world in a way society respects. This rule presents that opportunity. She is your slave, not the worlds and they need to see that demonstrated through her elegance, grace and dignity.

8.10 SLAVE will respect others responsibly practicing the master-slave lifestyle, mindful she only submits to Master.

If you prefer others must earn your respect before you, or your slave offer any, then go ahead and change the rule. Since a slave reflects her master, her behavior here is your behavior. Which perspective you choose, depends on whether your prism of life is reflected through a glass half-full, or half-empty.

> *8.11 ANY errors or breaches of this contract by Master do not abrogate Slave's obligations provided for herein. Slave may request a discussion, but should not expect an apology from Master for any perceived, or real error, or omissions. Acceptance of this contract is sufficient for the Slave to understand Master's intent is to provide a safe, healthy structure and life for the Slave and that errors are reflective of the human condition, not motivated by malfeasance, or desire to harm the Slave. Slave accepts any errors on an ad hoc basis.*

Well, to all intents and purposes this is the second tenet of the *Three Tenets of Mastery*. It is vitally important a slave live in reality, know errors will occur; accept them as part of the lifestyle she has chosen and that when they occur, they do not empower her. Whether you want to apologize when making a mistake is your style choice, nothing more. Many masters in this niche do not apologize, rather choosing to explain and accept responsibility. But, again pick your poison.

> *8.12 SLAVE will accept corrective measures in her heart. Slave must learn to understand that when Master deems Slave to be in error and corrective measures and punishment occur, she accepts that Master has the right and control to make these decisions whether she agrees an error occurred or not.*

Oh my goodness, if you are new to the lifestyle you probably have yet to realize the critical importance and subtlety of this rule. It may read innocuously, but the concept it embodies is the very essence of slavery.

I don't give a rat's ass whether you think you were disobedient, pet, I have said you were, so then you were.

The practice of mastery embodied in that statement is open to all kinds of abusive behavior in the wrong hands. Exercised responsibly though, with restraint and common sense, then it has the twofold effect of ensuring you are indeed in control and she can submit, knowing that while she may disagree and not like some decisions, she does not control and cannot *top from the bottom*. That is what she asked for when accepting your mastery and superior position in her life. So now in reality it is time for her to suck it up and accept the depth of the slavery you demand. If she does not and will not, then release her. You do not need her hijinks and she is not going to thrive in yours, or possibly any structure that demands actual surrendered power.

8.13 SLAVE has at her disposable the Laugh Rule. When Slave is due punishment and can make Master laugh in context of her disobedience, she may request invocation of this rule. The Laugh Rule when granted, relieves Slave of punishment and the Forgive & Forget mechanism of the punishment regimen is immediately in effect, ending the punishment and dismissing the disobedience to ancient history. Asking for the Rule does not automatically grant it, application of the Rule is solely at Master's discretion.

If you have a sense of humor and anticipate losing a ben wa ball or two in her puss, this rule is indispensable. Steal this rule, you need it, trust me on this one.

8.14 MASTER'S leather collar is to be worn by Slave at all times when in the home, unless guests who might be offended by it, or not understand, are present. Master will provide a more discreet marking of ownership available to Slave for use inside and outside the home where discretion is required. Slave is never to spend a moment un-collared except when bathing, or directed. Slave is the only person in the world permitted to wear Master's collar. The collar is never shared, or loaned by Slave.

Another self-explanatory rule that reiterates the important symbolism the collar represents. As vanilla women do not share wedding rings, a slave does not share her collar. For times when discretion is required, well, a brand burned into her hide is just marvelous.

8.15 SLAVE'S clothing will be selected and or approved by Master.

Knock yourself out and make this as detailed or casual as you like. The important aspect is there is a rule, whereby she knows that nothing about her life is exempt from control. But most masters are not fashion gurus, nor want to be encumbered with the daily hassle of dressing their slave. So, along with this rule, add a *House Rule*, that stipulates your current preferences. A quick nod in the morning when she asks to wear jeans is often enough, or being instructed in advance that for work, as long as she selects from her business wardrobe, no other permission is required. The *Chapter* on *House Rules* explains practical ways to make this rule seamless, effective and no maintenance.

> *8.16 MASTER will approve all modification of Slave's body including haircuts. Slave will be clean of hair on legs and underarms at all time unless directed otherwise. The genital area including vaginal and anal areas will also be hairless unless directed otherwise. Slave will ask Master's permission when shaving is required.*

This is a fun rule. The look on the hairdresser's face and the slave's blush are heartwarming. What? Of course you pick her hair style. Put her on speech restriction and just wink when explaining what you want to the stylist. It is just delicious when the hairdresser cannot get confirmation from the slave.

The rule is also sexy and ritualizes some daily, weekly and certainly monthly behaviors. Structure makes for a happy slave and this is another piece of the plan. Many masters in the lifestyle insist a slave shave her pubic hair. For most masters the reason is simply to use a control mechanism distinct from vanilla relationships. Removing the metaphorical *'bush'* is symbolically important. There is no hiding allowed. A bald mound represents open honesty. And... it is damned sexy.

Incorporating the razor routine into her life is easy. While each master has their way, what most prefer is she be shaved at all times. She has the responsibility (not a right) to decide when she needs a trim and must ask permission. A little trick to ensure she abides this rule is just put your hand down her pants, or up her skirt, preferably in a restaurant, to check for stubble. She will rue the day, if ever found lacking and disobedient. By having her ask permission, you have the choice to shave her and once again reinforces in her mind who controls her body.

> *8.17 SLAVE is not permitted use of chairs, sofas, ottomans, stools or other furniture to sit on when in Master's presence, unless specific permission is granted by Master.*

The floor is a slave's place, notwithstanding concerns over health issues. The rule is clear, its spirit equally so, and it is easily administered. It is another of the *invisible rules*, ideal for vanilla situations. Some folks have questioned why a master would impose a rule that is so inconvenient and often uncomfortable for the slave. What purpose does it serve?

Dismissing the common rationalization of immature raging testosterone, there is a simple purpose. This slave is not your vanilla wife, girlfriend, or significant other. She is your slave. Everyone is happy when structure re-enforces that understanding. Her indenture is tangibly evident by this rule. Her body is yours, not hers. You decide how to use it. This rule just ensures you are using it. Promises of convenience and comfort were never offered. She does not have a right to those things, and slaves are beautiful on the floor anyway. Most all will happily tell you, they would have it no other way.

Making this rule work consistently, takes some thought. For example, if you are invited to a vanilla friend's cottage for a summer weekend, likely your slave will be in and out of your presence many times. Remember now, the furniture rule applies only in your presence. So, for her to be jumping up and down from furniture as you come and go, will likely bring unwanted attention to yourselves and particularly her behavior. You will quickly become *"those strange people,"* to your friends. Unless you are trying to subliminally introduce the lifestyle to these folks, it is not going to work. On the other hand, vanilla folk can be myopically obtuse and miss the whole thing, so then do not give it a sneeze.

Instruct your slave before arriving of the likely situation facing you and that imposing on everyone's enjoyment is not your goal. So, for the weekend, lift the restriction. Prudence requires you amend the rule, but you want to keep consistent structure in place. Make sure she simply understands that by suspending the rule, you are not creating a vacuum for her, you are in fact, imposing a new behavioral *protocol* to replace it. How so you ask? Well, she is given a new furniture *protocol* for the weekend that permits use of the chairs. Granted it is different than before and appears vanilla, but she still must obey, thus serves and pleases as you wish.

It is important to develop non-verbal communication if behavioral rules such as this are going to be used. A simple nod, or wave of the hand tells her to use a chair. Signals are good to use and a simple way of incorporating structure into vanilla situations. Discreet *master-slave* practices that do not impose your relationship dynamics onto those unable, or unwilling to understand them, is also great fun. Be flexible and creative with your rules, enjoy them for what they are.

Perhaps in your situation, the dinnertime seating *protocol* is the extend of what is feasible around the kids. So then, change the rule such that she can use couches and chairs in other rooms of the house, as a more practical livable rule. If the key is discretion, then tweak the rule to your own advantage and situation, mindful that it must be a livable and consistently applied. Consistency is the key to successful mastery.

Remember too, that you are ultimately responsible for your slave's behavior. She obeys if you give her a way to do it. Make and apply rules that she readily understands. The best ones are those requiring little administration and come naturally. This is one of those. It is easy and takes virtually no maintenance. Do not burden yourself with rules that funnel you to micro-managing your slave. Doing that is the kiss of death. Micro-managing is a fad that passes quickly, so do not get roped in. Sure, it has its place and some days it is fun. But, for sustainable *master-slavery* to work, your structure must flow easily within your total reality. Careers, kids and the vanilla world are part of your life, whether you like it or not. Unless you have a 10,000 square mile ranch in Montana, with a few sand dunes thrown in and a bevy of beauties to serve you, our days of being a Sultan are gone. Today's reality is having some pillows on the floor and calling her your harem girl.

8.18 SLAVE will not use the words "No" or "Ok" to Master.

Masters have rules for any combination of four reasons. Rules enhance fun, they encourage positive behaviors, they create and sustain structure that enables belief in her slave identification, and they please. The *"No"* rule achieves all these goals perfectly.

Not all punishments need to be harsh, or prolonged. Inadvertently saying *"no"* is not a serious breach, or disobedience threatening anything more serious than your funny bone and her booty. It certainly does not affect the core relationship values. She made a booboo is all, so it is dealt with as such. Choose a light, fast and humorous punishment. In my kitchen is a waist high pedestal on which sits a large wooden salad bowl. Hanging from the side is a set of matching serving utensils. I happen to make a mean Caesar Salad, so it is natural to have a salad bowl out. But hanging alongside the utensils is a little *"fun"* that sits unobtrusively in plain view, its purpose unknown to all but slaves. It is my *"No Stick"*. Important people, like slaves and other masters, know exactly what it is and where it is kept. It is a sixteen inch wooden spoon that after a trip to the workshop; came back silky smooth, stained to match the salad set perfectly. I attached a little leather strap and presto, there it hangs, patiently awaiting the next slip of the tongue. It seems appropriate a kitchen utensil should serve as consequence for a tongue slip and tenderizing her rump is perfect punishment.[3]

Visiting a munch one Sunday afternoon, it seemed appropriate to have a bit of fun with the *"No"* rule. Folks attending were young and enthusiastic, though some quite inexperienced in the lifestyle, so it seemed like a good chance to help them out. For fun I explained the *"No"* rule and suggested we adopt it for the remainder of the munch. A hearty approval came from the dominant's and an eerie *"deer-in-the-headlights"* look came over the slaves. Amidst laughter, we tried it out. A wee young slavegirl, not yet twenty sat wide-eyed. We bantered and enjoyed some laughs, but as often happens, in a few minutes the conversation moved on to another topic. It was time to spring the trap.

Leaning over to the cute young girl, loud enough for all to hear, I asked to pinch her nipples. Well, she was young, I am old, she is naïve and I had a twinkle in my eye. No one had ever been so forward, or bold to ask her such a question and the word *"no"* was forming on her lips when she conscientiously remembered the rule. Hesitating, she seemed confused, then was lost, completely stumped and flustered. She did not want me to pinch her nipples (I think), yet in her panic, she cocooned the rule to mean she could not say "no" at all. After much laughter at the poor girl's expense, I explained expressing non-consent was perfectly fine. She just had to be a little more creative in how she did it. She learned *"Thank you, but I would prefer you didn't Sir"* is far more peaceful than *"No fucking way, you old pervert"*. It was a fun lesson however; it did not help the poor girl. She was flushed scarlet and at last check was still sitting there too shocked to answer… but with very hard nipples.

Slaves, particularly when discussing vanilla issues tend to slip into vanilla-speak. That is fine when she is talking to vanilla folk. But, the master-slave relationship is special and banning the word *'no'* is another technique and structure to feel the specialty of her submission every day. In a sense, the

---

[3] Since writing this book, the *No Stick* met an untimely demise. After splitting and falling apart over a slave's ass, it was duly committed to a ceremonious funeral pyre. The following day, the slave respectfully knelt and graciously offered to replace my long-time companion. With eyes lowered and a smirk on her face, she presented palms up like a goodgirl, the *No Stick's* replacement. It was lovely, matched perfectly, but was three inches long! Useless as tits on a bull! Slavegirls, you gotta love em!

rule is akin to the Gorean custom of a slave referring to herself in the third person. There is a distinct difference though. Many perceive the third person *protocol* as demeaning for the slave. Whether one believes it is, or is not, is not germane here and up to individual tastes. But, the *'no'* restriction has a positive effect by removing an easy path to confrontation and the word's negative symbolism.

The rule also includes banning the word *"ok"* to her master. While perhaps a strange word to ban on the face of it, there is a simple reason. The most commonly used word on the planet, regardless of language spoken, is the word *'ok'*. For that reason alone, it is banned. There is nothing common about a *master-slave* dynamic and choice of words is a good tool to reflect that.

Beware though. Enforcing the *'ok'* ban will inevitably result in the emergence of the word *'alright'* into the slave's lexicon. Slaves can drive you crazy sometimes. Whatever happened to the old proven, tried and true *"Yes Sir"*, or *"Yes Master"*?

> *8.19 THE sanctity of the bathroom is inviolate. When Master is in a washroom and the door is closed Slave will not enter unless commanded to.*

To hell with the habit of vanilla wives who routinely walk into the washroom while hubby is perched doing some of his best thinking. If the door is closed, there is a reason. She may not know the reason, but thank air fresheners for that. But if you like the tinkle of a slavegirl's pee then keep the bathroom door rule and get her a personal portable metal bowl.

> *8.20 SLAVE will be taught additional rules exclusive of this Contract and recorded in a Ledger entitled House Rules. Slave is expected to honor those rules as she would these. House Rules can be altered as Master sees fit to reflect change and growth. The Ledger is always available to Slave for review. No expectations are imposed on Slave, until a rule is taught and recorded.*

This clause of the *Contract* is self-explanatory and again reflects the existence of permanent *"Core Value Expectations"* and the transient *"House Rules"*. All are important in their prioritized position and she must obey both the literal and intended spirit of each rule. Of note and again stated at the end of the clause is the important reality of *master-slave* consistency. Taking responsibilities seriously, what is untaught is unpunished. Once taught though, lookout slavegirls, obedience is expected.

> *8.21 SLAVE will be taught Rituals and Protocols, which can be altered as Master sees fit and recorded in a Ledger entitled Rituals & Protocols. The Ledger is always available to slave for review. No expectations are imposed on slave, until a Ritual, or Protocol is taught and recorded.*

Similar to the rule above, the slave is responsible for learning *protocols* and adhering to them. Records are current, so if she needs to refresh her memory, the *Ledger* is there for her use.

It is important to point out the phases relationships go through and here is a good spot to do so. Not unlike any vanilla relationship, master-slave unions go through phases too. Certainly the *"dating"* phase is obvious and the *"teaching"* stage. The teaching theoretically never ends as the couple age and grow, but certainly, there is an emphasis on teaching towards the beginning of their time together. Then there is the *"living"* stage, wherein your slave has learned what is required of her; where you can then enjoy her service and obedience. Routinely a calm, yet vibrant ambiance is the tone within the home at this point. It is also a time ideally suited to explore some of the more edgier aspects of the lifestyle. The foundation has cured and can support the weight of risk that is often involved with edgeplay. You are at the point where the relationship will survive and flourish, even when mistakes occur.

9. BOUNDARIES

> *THE following is a list of boundaries both Master and slave agree upon. This section may be added to or subtracted from, only upon the agreement by both Master and slave.*

> *9.1 NO acts involving feces.*

> *9.2 NO acts involving children or animals.*

> *9.3 NO acts leaving permanent injury to slave.*

> *9.4 NO acts resulting in undue risk of contracting venereal disease.*

> *9.5*   *NO snakes, pictures of snakes, replications of snakes or any other representation of snakes are permitted in Master's home, car, office or any other area he may be present if the area can be controlled or influenced by slave.*

Need I say more? Ok fine, so snakes are my issue. Delete it if you want, but if you do, do not invite me over for dinner.

As defined in *Volume II*, *limits* and *boundaries* are not the same things. *Boundaries*, (often referred to as Hard-Limits) are areas both master and slave agree never to go, for the emotional, moral, ethical and physical sanity of all. *Boundaries* do not negate the power exchange dynamic, nor nullify its validity. They are areas many new couples do not take enough time to discuss. Some *boundaries* are straight forward, but others take a lot of thought. Do you really want to share her? Have you thoroughly thought through the work and financial responsibilities, and the fallout from everyone's family if you have more than one slave? These are important questions and while contracts can be changed, it is preferable to avoid amending them if at all possible. A change in *boundaries* oftentimes represents more than just personal growth, but may have been dishonest.

A slave acquaintance was involved with a self-proclaimed master not too many years ago. He wooed her with claims of total power exchange and all the goodies outlined in this book. She bought it hook line and sinker. It was exactly what she wanted. He spelled out right from day one, he was monogamous, there would be nothing more than casual play with other slaves. That too was something she insisted on. So, you can imagine her surprise a year later, upon returning home from work, to find another slave moving into their home. He had been developing this slave behind his own slave's back, arbitrarily collared her, then moved her into the home. Rationalizing his behavior, he went on to explain, *"I'm the master, I do what I want"*. He failed to respect his own proclamations made a year earlier. They are apart now of course, another tragedy born of a master's only convenient integrity and rampant ego. Fortunately, she has emotionally recovered, moved on and can laugh about his antics and false pontifications now. His whole structure was merely for show. It only existed at public fetish events. Behind closed doors he was; and still is vanilla to the core. Not surprisingly, the slave he moved in was twenty years younger than he, a neophyte with no understanding of what she was getting into. She lasted two years before he unilaterally and arbitrarily reset their boundaries again. At least his behavior is consistent.

If a master is going to make edicts, he is wise to live up to them.

10. SLAVE'S SIGNATURE

I have read and fully understand this contract in its entirety. I agree to give myself completely to my Master, and further accept his claim of ownership over my physical body. I understand that I will be commanded, trained and punished as a slave, and I promise to be true and to fulfill the pleasures and desires of my Master to the best of my abilities. I understand that I cannot withdraw from this contract except as stated in this contract.

Signature: _____

Date: _____

11. MASTER'S SIGNATURE

I have read and fully understand this contract in its entirety. I agree to accept this slave as my property, body and possessions, and to care for her to the best of my ability. I shall provide for her security and well being and command her, train her, and punish her as a slave. I understand the responsibility implicit in this arrangement, and agree that no harm shall come to the slave as long as she is mine. I further understand that I can withdraw from this contract at any time.

Signature: _____

Date: _____

Sign them in blood. She is yours for life!

MIND FUCK #25 "DINNERTIME"

It was a pleasant morning. Sunday's were their private time together and this one no exception. Showered but still in robes, they sat together on the deck, enjoying the birds and rising sun.

It was usual for them to be up so early. They both enjoyed the quiet mornings. Sipping coffee and being together. They silently enjoyed the peace and tranquility shared with the morning glory.

"Pet, I do not pretend to understand the Universe, its' beauty and reasons, but you know I believe we are together for a reason. Look around us, pet. Do you see the harmony of nature and good out there? The sun coming up, the flowers alive and fresh. Look at the squirrel, happily going about playing his role. It is beautiful. That is how you make me feel."

She was silent for a moment then squeezed his hand. "I love you Master". They sat and drank their coffee quietly.

"What time is brunch with your mother, pet?"

"I'm meeting her at 11:30 and we should have Dad's retirement party plans finished today", she replied.

"Goodgirl. I will meet you here at 2:30 then, and we'll head over to the golf club. I have a 3:10 starting time for us."

"Are you playing with your regulars this morning Master?"

"Yes and looking forward to it after missing last week in Detroit, though I think we had fun there."

She giggled. "My bum is still marked, though the bruises are yellow now". She was not complaining he knew.

"Well we can skip golf this afternoon if you like pet and have a refresher course."

"It's ok Sir, I like that golf pain too" and they laughed. Inwardly, he cackled a little more. Little did she suspect. So they went about their days, happy all was well.

"Pet, it is 2:30, are you ready?"

"Yes Sir, ready to rock that ball", she replied as she bound into the room looking very summery and pretty.

Goodgirl, before we go come here for a second, I want to show you something. She followed him into the small room reserved as their private dungeon. Against the wall was a new butterfly bondage chair, with all the leather fastenings and special leather seat that ensured she, or anyone tethered in place had no modesty.

"Oh my, what is that and where did you get it" she said excitedly, "How does it work, what do you do with it? Oh, it is so kewl Sir".

It seemed golf had slipped her slutty little mind for the moment. He just grinned and followed her over to it.

"Oh it is just a little something I picked up along the way pet", and her excited innocence evaporated when he grabbed her by the hair, spun her around and locked a kiss on her mouth. Releasing her, he growled "Strip slut!"

She started to say something about golf, but that look in his eyes and she thought better of it. In a moment she stood formally, naked, unsure, but with eyes down and wrists crossed. She knew her place.

He paced, letting her adjust to the change, knowing her imagination would begin the process he wanted for her.

"Bend over and put your palms on the floor slave". She did, now exposed and vulnerable. She winced and cried out at the sudden invasion in her rectum. The plug was large enough to cause some pain, but quickly subsided to just feeling very full. Grabbed by the hair, he stood her up and buckled the blindfold over her eyes, then led her by the ponytail to the new chair.

"Sit slave". She wanted to feel for the chair but he pushed her down and was comforted when the padded seat hit her ass. Quickly she was bound. The chair had a thick spine for a back, with leather straps that encircled her waist and neck, fastening her stiffly upright. Her arms extended sideways and they too were bound tightly to the beam with built in leather straps. She sat with her arms straight out to the sides, unable to move. First one, then her other thigh were spread wide to follow the seat "V" and leather straps bound them in place ensuring access to her sweet little cookie. The center of the seat was missing, and only a small bit of her ass sat on the leather, but enough to hold the plug securely wedged inside. Finally, he buckled cuffs to her ankles and the chair legs, and blindfolded she was now completely immobilized. She began to sink into space right then.

The silence seemed an eternity and had its effect. Instead of wondering what next, her mind automatically went in another direction. This happened when choices were removed. A peaceful acceptance transcended all else and she understood her happiness to be his slave. Nothing could be helped now. Whatever came next was not hers. He would own it. She would endure whatever pleasure or pain he might bring, because it was her duty, her peace, she wanted to please. Already she sensed an inner peace invading her soul.

He sat on the chair across the room and watched. Ten, fifteen then twenty minutes elapsed and her head was wobbling now. Without touching her, simple subjugation of her body and she could float away to sub-space. He was blessed to own her.

Silently he rose and approached. He wanted her to know he was there and the sudden cold steel of the knife against the palm of her hand did it. She shivered and her head bobbed more. For an hour he used her, in subtle ways, differently than she knew. The sharp blade ran over her body leaving red lines behind. The feel of the blade along the nape of her neck and the snip of a small lock of hair surely echoed like an anvil in her brain. She was utterly surrendered, accepting his control and path. She would follow as he wanted. He licked her cheek and growled softly as the knife pressed into her ear, then invaded her nostril. He pulled her lip out and scraped the sharp edge against her gums. A tiny nick ensured she tasted blood.

For an hour he played with her relentlessly, nothing spared. There was no protection from the invading knife. He could well imagine where she went, associating the blood in her mouth and the feeling of her nether lips parted as the knife eased into her cunt.

She was long gone, deep in that special world he created that joined them so intimately. Another hour passed and she was back. Incense candles and quiet music embraced the room. He pried her mouth open and forced water in. She drank thirstily. Again he opened her mouth and held it open. She knew what was coming and she wanted to suck softly with joy in her heart, giving pleasure. But she was denied. It was something else on her tongue.

"Chew" he whispered. The chicken surprised her, a small bite. Then another, and lettuce, a salad she thought, given slowly with his fingers. He fed her in silence.

When released much later, he lay with her on the bed holding her tightly. Kissing her forehead, he smiled.

"I thought I would make dinner tonight pet. I hope you enjoyed it." She moved up and smothered him with a kiss. Looking into his eyes the honest love flowing to his heart she smiled. "Master, it was the most romantic, most delicious dinner I have ever had. I love you."

6

TRAINING YOUR SLAVE

So now on to the good part - training this lovely vixen of yours, making her into part harem girl, part porn star, part executive assistant and one very cherished, devoted slave. It is time to develop a viable training regimen.

First, a cautionary word about the ineffectiveness of universal training programs. Even though below is the outline of a training plan, understand and accept that universal training blueprints do not work. Regardless of self-styled BDSM pundits, there is no universal blueprint for training a slave. Nor should there be and with luck, there never will be. Here again is an opinion for the *"Controversy Jar"*. But controversy notwithstanding, the simple fact is no two slaves are alike. By thinking what works for one will work for all, you are naively misinformed. Misogynists, cult leaders and the creatively challenged try universal blueprint training. Masters are none of those.

Scientific control studies prove that when presented with a constant, the very nature of people produces varying individual results. People react differently to the same things. Slaves are no different from vanilla folk in this regard. Knowing this, then it is worth exploring a methodology to train your slave resulting in the outcome you want, creating as much fun as possible, in an orderly and thorough fashion, but tailored to her.

Develop your training regimen personally knowing that how you train her conveys your attitude and style of mastery, as much as the specific structure itself. How you teach her is important to sustaining the long-term viability of your relationship.

DEVELOPING A TRAINING STYLE

By now, you have the essentials to set your structure. Your *"Vision"* is established; the *"Me List"* is in progress and your *"Master-Slave Contract"* awaits a pithy ceremony. You will need a set of *"House Rules"* to flesh out the details of your daily routine, rules that fit into the *"here and now"*. Many masters also develop their own *"Rituals"* and *"Protocols"* to go along with their *Contract* and *House Rules*. Those too have to be included and taught at some point.

The sums of all these elements form your structure. They represent the tangible evidence of the existence of a *master-slave* dynamic. That total creates the synergy for beautiful *master-slave* living, but only once training occurs.

In subsequent chapters, explored are examples of *House Rules*, *Rituals* and *Protocols*, their explanation and reasoning. For the most part, they are examples of general likes and dislikes that she must know to suit your particular wishes. The details in the samples are not germane to any particular personal structure, but do give a sense of the thoroughness one might want. Pick through them as you wish, understanding they are but examples to illustrate the scope of personal preferences, perversions, phobias and peccadilloes that make us unique. None is essential to a particular vision. Whatever *House Rules*, *Rituals* and *Protocols* you devise, just teach them well.

How one imparts knowledge of your structure however is as important as the content. A master's style of communicating, the tone he presents and the willingness to be patient, are important training elements. Develop the style that works for you.

Styles vary across the gamut of individual personalities, interests and character strengths. Some masters enjoy a cavalier and jovial approach in their training program, while others are ruthlessly strict. There are strengths and weaknesses in each style.

Failure to appreciate the iron will behind training, often results from the casual training approach. Trouble follows down the road in the form of *topping from the bottom* and a general ambivalence to the whole *master-slave* dynamic. Often slaves perceive weakness in the casual style.

Likewise, too strict an approach may create fear and stymie her identification as an individual. Too serious and strict may also force the master into a role his personality is uncomfortable with, resulting in an inability to sustain control. This undercuts credibility and will breakdown the *master-slave* dynamic quickly.

A blend of the two is probably the most effective style for most to bridge the paradox of rigid structure and personal growth. At least, it seems to work with most slaves.

With experience coaching at the international level in the sporting arenas of life, I have witnessed many styles of teaching and training. The result is my becoming a devout non-fan of the bully style of teaching. Too often, it just backfires, reducing achievement rather than enabling it. As individuals age and mature, it becomes even truer. If you want an *"in your face"* - *"you are a powerless slut"* type relationship; that is fine, but it is best developed in the reality of your *rules* and degrees of the *Three Powers*, rather than in how you teach structure. One-dimensional bully training is likely to be counter-productive for a relationship intended to endure.

Likely more effective, is a calm, reasoned, sincere, yet fun approach, rather than an intimidating *bull-in-a-china-shop* style. When she kneels, hearing your no-nonsense tone of voice, delivered firmly with clarity and calm, the message is clear - these are important words and pay attention, slavegirl. That dominant tone creates an aura that sends shivers to her core. Then she understands that she is getting exactly what she sought.

There are times for repartee and giggles; and times for somber attention. A slave loves that her life embraces all this. Suddenly her slavery is much more than bondage and a thorough fucking; and for the master, structure lasts beyond dramatic orgasms. Good training leads to consistent behavior and a peaceful home. It also removes the need for artificial personas and dominant posturing. You are training her to be reflective of the behaviors you desire. She is your slave, not a caricature of some stereotype embodied within the BDSM community, or a fantasy writer's imagination. If she is the slave you suspect, she will yearn for this more than most masters appreciate. Simply by training in a style reflecting your personality, you build an enduring relationship of honesty.

So now, finally, you are set to move forward and train her. All that is left is to create an orderly progression that makes sense and assign a timetable to "Git Her Done".

Bend'N'Brace: "The Training Model"

There is not a chance in hell I am going to preach a training program, going through every little step a good one requires. First off, it would be impossible. Without slave feedback, reaction and her understanding of what you are trying to accomplish, it is meaningless. Secondly, it would be tantamount to online fantasy, treachery to a master. Thirdly, it would bore us both to tears. A slave crying from nasty bum welts is far preferable than enduring detailed, hypothetical training gobbily-goop.

However, training systemically can be broken into manageable sections, and then tailored to your preferences. That accomplishes the task-at-hand, which is to train the little slut relevantly into a great slave.

With so much to train, so many details and nuances, and much of it very personal, the approach to teach aspiring masters how to train is best characterized by simplifying training to concepts that relate to time and priority. No other organizational chart style provides the flexibility that training a slave requires. It is a realistic and doable.

There is no point training a slave about the *Twenty-Four Hour Rule* and *Conflict Resolution* if, as part of it, the attending *protocol* requires her to kneel, dance and play with her clit left-handed while staring into a funhouse mirror and you have not taught those yet. Regardless of how well she knows how to address an issue with you, if how to initiate that is not enabled, you have not taught anything. So she is going to have to learn left-handed diddling and get a mirror, if she is going to resolve issues with you as you have decreed, or you have wasted everyone's time.

Teaching her *rules, rituals* or *protocols* without situational reality is just haphazard irrelevance. You are a master, so you must reflect that you have mastered how to train her in a way that is intelligent and relevant.

Rather than approach training by category, such as *Rituals, Protocols, Contract, House Rules* or any other order you conceive, let us develop it from a different perspective, blending bits from each on a prioritized *"importance"* and *"time"* basis. For example, it is rather important that on Day One she learn never to lie to you. There is no point having that way down in Section 47B, sub-section 2.11 taught in the third trimester, eight months from now. The relationship is not likely to last that long without this rule taught first. That is what prioritized time-sensitive training means.

Referred to as the *Training Triumvirate* it is the easy way to accomplish priority/time training. The *Triumvirate* is a simple way to determine what and when to train based on:

The Essentials

The Daily

The Rest

Try it. It makes sense.

The Essentials are absolute requirements from Day One, or very close to it. These are the rules she just has to know before going forward. *The Daily* is comprised of the parts of your structure needed on virtually a daily basis to function and achieve the goals you have for her. They represent the tangibles of everyday *master-slavery* that focuses her headspace and behaviors in line with your expectations. They are very important. *The Rest* are simply that… the massive volume of details that are not critical, are often situational, sometimes trivial, knowing them not a priority to initially build structure and a lifestyle together, and they take time to teach.

The *Training Triumvirate* charts a clear path for training her along a sensible road. That it leads to peace and tranquility is its unique purpose. Use of the *Triumvirate* model culminates with a trained slave, produced in a defined logical order, yet is flexible enough to follow and adapt to the curves life throws at us all.

Training this way ensures you can enjoy your slave as you want, knowing the expectations placed on her are completely understood. More importantly, she has the tools to meet those expectations. Her purpose is clear and enumerated within unequivocal structure. You have built the edifice to house belief that she can achieve happiness in slavery. In essence, she is informed and that is an integral part of consent. Do you see a symmetry building here? You are both happy – quirky, kinky and maybe a little squirrelly, but nonetheless, very happy. The *Triumvirate Training* model is another win/win situation. Now apply a timeline and you are done.

One last point before embarking on the *Training Model*: there is a wonderful characteristic of training, often overlooked and thus its benefit not realized. When a slave undergoes training, she focuses exclusively on you, your words and actions, but mostly on learning and getting it right. She will try very hard for you. She is going to study, learn, practice and repeat things, until they are exactly as you wish. Reward is a critical element in a good training regimen. When her effort and results are there, reward her. A simple *"goodgirl"*, a smile, or a hair pull - and then shoot elastics at her ass. Did I not mention about elastics? Every self-respecting master needs a bin full of those stretchy little miscreants. An enfilade volley at her bare thighs is just good fun, especially when she gets perched on the phone nattering to her coven for hours on end.

Reward, praise and reinforce honest effort and good behavior. Your effort are returned in spades. The joy of ownership is a happy slave.

So now, first up, the *Essentials*.

THE ESSENTIALS

Some things are too important to leave fallow and unattended. Far be it for anyone to dictate the process and order others train their slave, but experience is valuable and the wise often seek to use the wheel, rather than re-invent it. Here is but one path, a well-worn and tested one, but not the only one.

Theory is over, now you are training the cutie. Atmosphere and focus is important in the early days of training. You do not want interruptions or distractions so plan accordingly. A glass of wine, candles and her kneeling at your feet is a fine start. While it may seem gentle and un-domly, perhaps even vanilla-ish, better a slippery slope than an anvil to the head. She will experience a variety of settings in the weeks and months to come, some more acute and raw than this initial offering, but she identifies with this and so is more relaxed and in her comfort zone. It is just a start. The rockets up her ass come later!

Essential Step One

Spend ten bucks!

Training your slave is not going to be free. It will cost you. About ten bucks, all in. Bloody expensive these slavegirls. Pinch her bottom and tell her you hope she is worth it. That is the first *Essential*.

Head down to your local office supplies store and purchase a three-ring binder and a sheaf of printer paper. There is no need to go hog wild, just a cheap binder and some paper are all you need. If you are without a three-hole punch, well, invest in one of those too. Later, if you decide she is worth it (and have a sneaky romantic side), take that binder to your local leatherwork shop and have it covered in leather. Emboss, or gold leaf it with your symbol and she will appreciate the sentimental side of you. But, all you need to start is a simple vinyl binder. Black is a nice color.

Touched on earlier was the importance of knowing what you have taught as time moves forward. This might sound trite, but experience proves periodic confusion reigns, and memories are imperfect. Make no mistake, we forget what we teach, and so does she.

Now what is to come you will perceive initially as overkill. Trust me, it is not. It is immensely valuable.

Record everything pertinent to your *Structure* as you teach it. By doing so, while a lot of work initially, the practice pays huge dividends down the road. By recording rules once taught, you are giving your slave the playbook. Eventually, everything is there in one place, organized and neat. She can review your *Master-Slave Contract, House Rules* and *Rituals & Protocols* at her leisure to refresh her memory. Once recorded, it eliminates the *"Did I teach her that yet?"* phenomenon that happens and only cause's strife. Call your *House Rules, Rituals* and *Master-Slave Contract* binder the *Bible*, or maybe *"The Book"* for all I care, but have it.

Put each rule into *The Book* only after teaching and record the date taught. By titling each rule, a *Table of Contents* can be created with a word processor program and she can reference any rule quickly. Managing this on a computer is simple. You will appreciate it and so too will your slave.

Then you might think, *"What happened to No Master Maintenance?"* Good point. You do not think we are going to do this work do you? Oh no! While it seems the master should do it, no, the slave will. To those slaves reading, *"Suck it up princess"* you are the beneficiary.

Your slave is going to record every rule you teach! Know that I am laughing while writing this. I know many are thinking *"What the fuck!"* Be patient, realizing the benefits comes soon enough. Bear in mind, you are building a sustainable relationship designed to keep the *master-slave* dynamic consistent over time.

Master consistency has a premium in this lifestyle, so it behooves us to record our teachings. Doing so helps immeasurably to avoid unnecessary conflict. It also produces a tangible piece of *"you"*. She can touch and review it privately and will do just that, in her sincere desire to please. This little binder is yet another tool re-enforcing self-belief in her slavery, while ensuring your consistent mastery. So, with binder in hand ready to record what you teach as it occurs, it is time to move forward, but with one proviso.

Often asked is whether a slave should be collared during the training regimen. The answer is that it can occur anywhere, at anytime. If collaring is the symbol of permanent commitment, do it any time you are ready and she submits. It is not a necessary function, or dependency of training. That a collaring occurs during training is more coincidental than a product of good planning. Once making a mutual agreement to pursue exclusivity, there is a yearlong window to train her anyway.[4]

Many masters will not collar inside that first year for any number of reasons. Certainly the most important one is to ensure she can be happy in your structure, once trained. You cannot be sure until she has lived in it, and she cannot live it until she is trained. It is a vicious circle. But serious masters are focused on enjoying a trained slave, so take that year to train her thoroughly. Then when it comes time to collar, you do not have a loose cannon flitting about, lacking the tools to please, and unsure she will thrive anyway. There is merit in that approach.

Many do not like the transient crapshoot of collaring then training. Think of it as Picasso painting a picture. It might be fun watching him paint for an afternoon, but the real joy is in appreciating the finished art for years to come.

Rely on the old axiom, *"Train her immediately – Collar her when you wish – Make her cum daily!"*

Another word of caution before training begins. You have a lot to teach and she has a lot to learn. Training cannot be done overnight. She needs time to listen, assimilate, enjoy and appreciate the context in which you

---

[4] Devil In The Details II – Volume II, Chapter 7

present things. It will take time for the overall picture to clarify. That is time when trust evolves, growing based largely on your actions. Give her time to assess you. Masters are not afraid of that assessment. Many new-age and online domly-boys are terrified of it, but masters are not. You have six months to a year to *"Git Her Done"* so take your time. Savor each step, make it fun and do not teach too much in a single serving. Make each session more than just a lesson. Laugh and smile. Let her come to realize that, not only is trust growing, but so too are the opportunities to grow your intimacy together.

Take advantage of the time you have and you will both enjoy the results.

Now time to hit you with that classic sales trick, the old *bait and switch*. One binder is not enough. You need three, one for *House Rules*, another for *Rituals & Protocol* and a third for your *Master-Slave Contract*. Make it thirty bucks. I warned you, these slaves are expensive!

Essential Step Two

The beginning of any worthwhile training program starts with a review of goals and objectives. For slave training, the purpose is to enjoy your relationship on a day-to-day level, with the intention it endure for years to come. Happiness together, meeting each others' unique needs, consistent with the totality of our personalities and character, is where we are headed. This includes vanilla needs, while nurturing those embodied in the *master-slave* dynamic.

So, kneel her down and start by reviewing why you are together. Begin with the vision for your life, the goals, dreams and aspirations you have. Move to recognize, both those you see for her and the ones she has enunciated herself. Teach her your oath and the oath she undertakes for you. Explain your obligations and hers too. Highlight your path through life together, the explorations you want and the joy you hope to share.

Explain to her your version of the *"Master's Code of Conduct"*. Educate and train her about your understanding and practice of mastery. Teach how the *Code* applies to your personal relationship. Then, if you choose and become involved in the BDSM community, teach how it interfaces with your involvement there too.

Build the big picture for her. Build the foundation, the purpose, the raison d'être. Be her ethical and moral rock. It starts right here.

Essential Step Three

Many do not recognize this next step as a critical element of training. They prioritize it lower, or ignore it, thinking it is a *"given"* anyway. That is fine, to each their own, but it is included here and stressed by importance, prioritizing it so early in the training process. It is teaching her about the *"slave mindset"* and your belief in it. It is about *"who"* she is. Many women have simmering submissive thoughts and can identify with the slave lifestyle, but do not fully understand those feelings. It is important they do however. A slave, in my view, must be able to articulate the special needs that separate her from vanilla women. Teach her the *SODS Principle* so she understands those needs.[5] It is useful and practical knowledge. In quiet moments of reflection, when questioning herself, or seeking a better self-understanding, she has the tools necessary to do so. Finding comfort by identifying her needs is healthy. Take time to teach her the *SODS Principle* and stress not only her acceptance, but that you too, believe in it without reservation.

Essential Step Four

So, armed with your binders and knowledge, it is time to get to the nitty-gritty.

Start by stringing her hands up to the rafters, stretching her up onto toes. Using a big old Hibbons knife, machete, or urban-style switchblade, (if you can get your hands on one), start slashing away at her clothes until there nothing left but a heap of tattered rags around her feet. If you drool and mutter *"redrum"* at the same time, even better. Ignore her unexpected screams and mercy pleas. Make sure she thinks you have gone utterly insane, that you are lost in some demented reverie; that life as she knows it is over.

Squeal a little then clamp some clovers to her labia. They will not slip off. By now, she is drier than a cameltoe in the Sahara; and exactly how you want her. Pace about a few times and the twitch in your neck is good. Some loss of muscle control never hurt anyone's perception of insanity. Now grab a pair of five-pound barbells and hang one each from the clovers, stretching those labia until she has new knee curtains.

If you are doing well, she will have passed out from fright and pain and will not notice when you unfurl the twenty-foot bullwhip, almost taking your

---

5 Devil In The Details I - Volume I, Chapter 8

ear off during warm-up. These are all good things so far. Did I mention training is fun, at least for the master?

Ok, now get over yourself.

Did you really think this would be the next training session? Get real! No one would use a twenty-foot bullwhip first off. Everyone knows you start with an eight! Did I mention it is fun to mind fuck you readers too? Done in book form, you cannot retaliate.

It is time to teach some fundamentals, establish a baseline, and as important as all else, have some fun. Yes, we may as well throw in some fun right from the get go. She needs to know life with you is the whole nine yards. Damn the torpedoes, full speed ahead! Thank you Admiral Farragut.

It is imperative, for all that is coming, to create a solid foundation. There is no better foundation than understanding the *master-slave*, TPE niche, ergo, why this is an *Essential*. That is the next step. You may have gone over much of this in previous discussions with her, but those were discussions. They are now superfluous. This is training. Now she has to know it, recite it, explain it and understand it. Mostly though she has to believe it and that is what we do now. Explain it all again, making sure she understands, buys in and knows it. Proof of her knowledge is in the ability to explain it back, in her own words.

This is the *One, Two, Three, Four* lesson.

You own *One* slave. Teach her the *Theory of the Two Decisions*, the *Three Powers* and the *Four Pillars of Relationships*. One slave, two decisions, three powers, four pillars. You are not teaching your personal specifics, rather, she is beginning to learn the fundamentals of power exchange. You both need to know she *"gets it"*, knows what a slave is; and the theory behind it all. She does not need to memorize this book or any other (ok, my slave does, but bad luck for her), just understand the context, theory and philosophies of *master-slavery*. Ultimately, of course, her position is to please you on a personal level and this is the beginning. Also, if not now, in the future, she will have slave friends. She will enjoy talking intelligently with them and others about her choice, and why it works for her. That intelligent informed discourse is a source of pride for many masters and it comes from these lessons.

General knowledge, foundation building and intellectual conversation within the community aside, you need her to know this stuff. The specifics of *"Conflict Resolution"* and *"Punishment"* depend on this understandings - and that is the next *Essential*. But, before you move on, are you sure she knows this, can recite it and believes in it? If so, use the *"House Rules"* sample page in the Appendix, (or create your own) and have her type it up, then print it out. There is the first insert into your *House Rules* binder. She will refer to it for years to come.

Essential Step Five

The next logical tangible lesson is a simple communication *protocol* that is a bedrock for sustainable *master-slave* relationships. Since most of your interaction is going to be verbal for the next sixty years, start her off right and ban the words *"No"* and *"Ok"* from her vocabulary. The reasons are previously explained and, besides, it is fun. She will cringe, laugh and eventually just bend over for her swat when she realizes one of them popped out of her mouth. It is even funnier when she bends and you had not realized she said it. Have your *"No Stick"* ready to go. It will get a workout for the next few weeks.

Oh, missy slavegirl, I know you are reading… type it up and print it out and do not say *"No!"*

There are other certain inviolate precepts that permeate all the interactions with your slave. Knowing them and teaching them early is wise. Here are two more essentials to train now. They represent a nice blend of *"mature adulthood"* and *"master-slave specific knowledge"*.

Since, presumably, we are mature, intelligent adults, the training of complete honesty as a condition of ownership is straightforward. The rule is simply this" *"Lie to me and you are punished, pet. Lie to me habitually and you are gone"*. It is easily understood, and she will appreciate you both living to that inviolate standard. Pet, you can print that one, but it is coming again in the *Master-Slave Contract*.

Next up is *"Conflict Resolution"* and, as explained earlier, it is arguably the most critical training she will receive[6]. Along with teaching the *Twenty-Four-Hour Rule*, have her practice it early and often, even on mundane topics. She needs familiarization with the process until it is habit. Have you assigned an attending *Position Ritual*, or *Protocol* to go along with *"Conflict Resolution"*?

---

[6] Devil In The Details - Volume II, Chapter 2

Requesting a discussion is best with one, so teach that too. Standing or kneeling formally are ideal.[7]

Essential Step Six

Structure only works if there is accountability. To ensure that her breaches of your structure have consequence, it is critical to teach about *Punishment*. The entire dynamic including its use, role and purpose is the critical defining characteristic of *master-slave* living, so must come early in training. A slave's knowledge of the punishment dynamic might well be required sooner than you think. You are caught in limbo if she is disobedient and you have not yet taught her about punishment. The old axiom, *"You can't punish what you haven't taught"* applies, even when it is punishment that is untaught. Unless it is taught, you are faced with the setting of an ugly little precedent, a disobedience left hanging. So teach her the role of punishment, her responsibilities and its purpose now. Teach it thoroughly, it is a tougher concept to grasp than first blush may indicate. Understanding punishment is to understand slavery in many ways. The right to decide if she thinks she was disobedient is gone. She must come to realize, that in submitting, she offers an unqualified acceptance of her master's right to decide. That is a very profound difference from our vanilla culture and, undoubtedly, her upbringing.

Along with punishment, it is time to throw in some fun again and teach some *Rituals* that will nurture the critical belief in her slavery. So, if you use a *bedtime ritual*, teach it now. Again, it is fun but moreover, it provides her another tangible, active procedure to please you, specific to the *master-slave* dynamic. You are reinforcing belief in her slavery and at the same time creating a beautifully behaved slave.

How is that typing and printing coming along, pet?

Essential Step Seven

Living in a vanilla society as we do is tough on the *master-slave* dynamic. Transitioning from career-girl to slavegirl the instant she crosses the threshold after a long day's work is difficult. As with most people, she likely has a lot on her mind at the end of a day and yet, as her master, you expect slave

---

[7] Devil In The Details - Volume III, Chapters 9 & 10

attitude and behavior when she is with you. So, it is time to teach her the transitional tools to make that change. There are two to teach.

The first is easy; you have probably already done it but, if not, do it now. It is a *"Greeting Ritual"*.[8] The exact *ritual*, when and where to use it, are important. It sets the tone immediately on her arrival home. Greeting you each night is an excellent habit and when done with some creativity, is very intimate.

Now teach the *Focus Rule*.[9] Give her the five to fifteen minutes she needs each day to refocus her priorities where you want them. Those are always to reinforce belief in her slavery, and to focus on you and the behaviors expected.

Have you noticed a trend in the training regimen thus far? With the exception of some *rituals* and speech training, everything taught is from the *Master-Slave Contract*. This is as it should be. The *Contract* represents the core of your structure, so it makes sense to teach it first.

Essential Step Eight

The next series of *Essential Steps* include, in whatever order you want, the remainder of the *Master-Slave Contract*. All of it. It is really quite simple to teach and takes but one or two sessions. You are likely not ready to sign the *Contact*, but that does not preclude its teaching. Once taught, print out each item so she has a record to review and so can remember it. There is a lot to learn, but easy to teach if she is kneeling in front of you. With a smirk, have her adorned in leather cuffs only. It is a much easier way to learn. The butt plug is purely optional.

Teaching the *Contract* is actually one thing a slave looks forward to most in her training. After all, this is the primary structure for the rest of her slave life. She is keenly interested. She will love this part. It is very real to her. So reward her for the diligence shown. Afterwards, teach another *ritual* and this time, it is the infamous *"Pleasure"* position.[10] Once taught, she has in her *"repertoire to please"* a simple command to get naked, exposed and in a position

---

8 Devil In The Details - Volume III, Chapter 10

9 Devil In The Details - Volume III, Chapter 10

10 Devil In The Details - Volume III, Chapter 10

to receive your sexual attention. Practice, practice, practice! Teaching *"Pleasure"* is a dirty job, but must be done. Somebody has to fuck her blind!

In eight easy steps, you have taught your slave the essential theory and core rules of your *master-slavery*. She can now begin to put theory into day-to-day practice. You have provided the core structure she now lives within, and kept it fun by detailing a number of *Rituals* for your pleasure. All these are tangible structural details to feel and act upon her slavery. At this point, combined with an introduction into your S&M world, beginning exploration of the pain/pleasure paradox and some wild kinky sex, you undoubtedly have a very happy slave under your boot. See how easy all this is? Your *Binders* are beginning to fill up with lots of goodies. Your mastery is organized, consistent, manageable and tangibly real. Now take time to review and test her knowledge. She has to learn this. Then you have the basis of a trained slave.

THE DAILY

But Whoa Nellie, she ain't done yet!

Giddy-up little filly, we have miles to go!

Crack the whip…

Swish goes the ponytail!

The *Daily* routines, rules and protocols taught are as varied as the individuals involved. They are also intensely personal and often private. They represent the necessary structural components she uses to please, virtually every day.

There are many topics and issues requiring attention in the *Daily* portion of the *Training Model* and a great place to start if you plan to use her in any S&M context at all, is with *"BDSM Limits."* It is time to inflict on her vigorous discussions and your wicked sense of humor.

Your practices around *safewords* and *SSC*, as well as the various types of S&M use she will endure and enjoy - teach them now[11]. You must, because you are likely to use her, be it a pat on the ass, or a full-blown rough scene, each day. Here too, teach about *sub-space, aftercare, sub-drop, sharing, poly issues*

---

[11] Devil In The Details - Volume II, Chapter 11 "Sadism – This One's For Me"

and *snapping*. Teach it all. *Topping from below* is also a critical element. Understand though, teaching her to avoid *topping from below* requires ongoing development of a learned behavior and the first lesson is ensuring you recognizing when it occurs.

The BDSM issues are all identified in *Volumes I & II* for you to systematically go through and teach. They are all important. The purpose is to ensure the surprises you spring are motivated by creative mastery, not unscrupulous skullduggery. The result is the ensuing fun of inflicting the unknown on the knowing.

The second aspect of the *Daily Section* involves a great deal more fun. It is time to teach all the other *Rituals* and *Protocols* you have for her. These include all the *Position* and *Behavior Rituals* that make up your structure. Detailed in the following *Chapters* are a number from which you can pick, but certainly include others of your own making. Just because I wrote and use them does not make me the Boss – you are!

The third element in the *Daily Section* is training selective vanilla expectations based on the urgency they are required. These are non-specific to the BDSM culture being vanilla in nature, but they too are part of a slave's life. Many are acted upon, depending on whether you live together or not. They are very important, insofar as they broaden the scope of her indenture, moving it outside the bedroom and dungeon, to reflect the totality of service and the extent of her slavery.

Often asked is *"How do I make master-slavery work on a daily basis?"* Well, this is a large component of the answer, by responsibly controlling the vanilla aspects of your life together.   How important these are to your structure is, of course, personal. The more control assumed and training received though, the more encompassing her belief in slavery and the more useful she is to you. The opportunity to be useful is in large measure what drives many slaves. Even though they may not like every task and responsibility they are privileged to perform, they love the totality. The scope of duties encompassed in these vanilla areas really do, in the long term, feed her need for service as defined in the *SODS Principle* of the slave mindset.

The vanilla needs and services of our lives are so vast that addressing them takes time. Thus the first task is to decide what is important and relegating the lower priorities to *The Rest* section of the *Training Model*. Place the trivial there, where you can flesh out the body of your structure at a more leisurely pace.

Essentially our vanilla world breaks down into sixteen general categories that come to affect our lives and daily routines. Some are very simple, taught easily and quickly, while others are extensive, requiring time, patience and thoroughness. The *Chapter* coming on *"House Rules"* expands each category in detail. Remember though, nothing is etched in stone, though carving initials in her back is fun.

THE REST

The Rest, is your *master-slave "junk drawer"*. You know that spot we all have one in our homes. It is that special place where everything is tossed that does not have a place. *The Rest* is the junk drawer of *master-slavery*, where everything you have not taught her yet is stuffed. Frankly too, it is the place where the bulk of training is done. The contents are important, just less so, compared to the structure she has learned thus far. This is where flesh attaches to bone and your house rises from the newly cured foundation. It is the lion's share of the detail by volume, not importance. From behavioral, attitudinal and body rules, there is a mountain of information she needs here.

All of the minutiae of the various sections laid out in *The Daily* and omitted because it lacked urgency is now trained in detail. The next *Chapter* explains possible *House Rules* omitted in the *Essentials* and *Daily* sections of training. Now is the time to address them, filling in the blanks and thereby creating the *"trained slave"*.

Of particular importance is the section on *Self*, teaching her specific behaviors you want. Also, training of the *"You"* rules, where she learns how to manage your household and personal services, are detailed and vital for long-term peace and tranquility. This section is generally non-sexual at this point.

The first two sections of the *Training Triumvirate* did not take long, probably not more than a month or two. *The Rest*, however, is why training takes up to a year - such is the volume. The desire to *"Git Her Done"* challenges the best masters. If preparation to this point has been sloppy, or corners cut, this is where it all shows up.

This is also the section of training when she really wants that PDA you bought her. Remember that thing? No? Well read on, it is important. When you are driving for fifteen hours to get to your vacation spot and casually mention your favorite College Football team is the one playing Notre Dame, she is definitely going to want to remember and record that. Her ass will blister if she cheers for the wrong team in front of you. She can enter that little note in her PDA reminding her to print it in *House Rules* when home.

Undoubtedly, some readers laughed and ignored the suggestion that aspiring masters begin to develop a *"Me List"*. Well, surprise! It was relevant, in fact, it is an almost indispensable tool in a master's repertoire. Take the time to review that section and why it is important. It is going to save you enormous work.

The volume of detail is also, why your *Binders* are critical tools to sustaining the *master-slave* dynamic. The benefit of consistency they provide helps avoid slippage back to a vanilla union. That little ten bucks you spent at the beginning of training is now priceless. There is not a bumwelts-chance-in-hell that you or your slave can, or will, remember, first what you have taught, or if you even taught it. This is the only guarantee made in this book. Bank on it! Memories are not that good. Record everything. Print it and review it. It will avoid confusion, arguments and even verbal fisticuffs. It only takes a moment's upkeep. You have told her of your dedication to this relationship. Now prove it.

Outlined earlier was the concept of sustainable structure being of *"No Master Maintenance"*. That really refers to avoiding ongoing micro-management. It truly is a key element to sustainable *master-slave* living in today's busy society. But do not confuse that with *"mastery is not work"*. It is, and it is not for the lazy. There are things that just have to be done. Recording your own structure so your slave can learn and review it is one of those necessary things. It will not hurt if you review it at times too, for, if nothing else, it is a source for a good chuckle realizing how much you have changed over time. That is normal, so take the time to update them. Then everything stays good.

So as you consider and teach the minutiae of structure, do not forget that golden axiom of *master-slave* living. *Master-slave* relationships are fun. They always are. Throw some fun at her as she learns. If it sticks, great and if it does not, well, throw harder. Resort to unbridled tickling if necessary. She will scream, but screaming only makes you smile.

And Then Some More!

So you have got the wee wench trained, or are well along the way. You are smiling and she is banging her head against the wall. All is good. Now kick it up a notch. The mundane is for the vanilla world, but masters are nothing, if not creative. Here are some little tricks to keep vitality in your relationship and spike in some fun too.

The Slave Outfit

In your slave's eyes, you are a uniquely special person and without question, she is in yours too. She is worth the trouble of going to some expense over, especially when it leads to the fun this does. Give it some thought, indulge your fancy and purchase for her *"the slave outfit"*. This is exactly what it appears to be, your little fantasy and her manifest obedience. It is apparel of your choice, worn to nurture intimacy, privately, regularly, as a statement of identity. Choose well and she will surprise you with her love to wear it – unless it comes from Fredericks, where tackiness was invented.

It is not fetish wear for your romps at the local dungeon on Saturday evenings. That is a whole different trousseau. This is home wear, reflecting that she lives in her master's castle, her haven from the vanilla world.

In choosing the outfit, make it sexy, after all she is a sex-slave too. It might me a harem outfit, or a burlap peasant dress, maybe a loincloth, or French maid costume. It can be a pair of leather chaps and nothing else, or simply cuffs and your denim shirt. Whatever it is, it is her slave home wear, when circumstances permit. She is your slave and so adorned, she will be.

What you choose is not important to anyone but yourselves. It is your kink after all. At my home, it used to be a simple loose fitting sleeveless, translucent slave dress. It had a low neckline, slit from the waist and a rope belt keeping it all together. Sandals, a leather collar and matching cuffs completed the ensemble. That is all she needed and it titillated without being crass, yet is simple and functional. It is quintessentially a slave look and keeps her mind focused in her belief and identity. That my hands constantly groped her was the keenly anticipated side benefit. However, times have changed and now that little dress is in tatters, worn out. Today it is my oversized denim shirt, a collar, and her hair in a ponytail. Panties? Forget it! Drool! What more could a guy want?

Reserve the outfit for special times, or if your lifestyle permits, make it a requirement when home entertaining guests. The choice is yours. What wearing it does though is reinforce belief in her slavery. It is another little thing and in this case, a damned sexy one.

THURSDAY SUPPER CLUB

The slave robe is also ideal for another tradition worth investing in. It is the *Thursday Supper Club* and the robe is a lovely accent. Once a month, or every week schedules permitting and friends available, institute a *ritual* of entertaining another BDSM friendly couple for dinner. Not only is it fun, it is very beneficial when done as a wholly *master-slave* affair. It is simple to do, and starts with the rule *"Vanilla behavior is banned."* The slaves cook, serve, obey *rituals*, use the floor, get swatted for uttering inadvertent *"No's"* and generally have an opportunity to show who they are, absent from vanilla interference. You will be surprised how much they enjoy these evenings, especially knowing the pleasure you receive.

A regularly scheduled *master-slave* dinner with intimate friends creates many terrific opportunities to explore a whole range of options as master. For some slaves, it will be their first exposure with others in the lifestyle, and the first time anyone other than you knows of her needs. Admitting that outside your relationship can be very difficult, if not traumatizing for some slaves, so the tools you select to accomplish it are important. Intimate dinners are a good way.

Make the dinners useful beyond the company of good friends. Take little steps to grow your slave each week. Establish some goals and pursue them. If your aim is to overcome her modesty, then starting the first week by having her dress in a skirt and blouse, without panties. Her bare bottom may be unknown to your guests, but most assuredly she knows, focusing and aware of how she moves. She will grow and become comfortable, and in a few weeks time, will be tossing the Caesar Salad bare breasted with the flair of Emeril. Probably too, will her equally bare breasted slave friend. Use *security in numbers* to ease her along. Discuss your goals with the other master, for surely he too sees benefits for his slave in working together. In short order you may enjoy both slaves masturbating beside each other on the living room floor. Such is the power you wield. Harness that power and manage her slavery responsibly.

Where the dinners lead is your choice. The main purpose though is not to exhibit raging testosterone, or produce vicarious thrills, thought the latter is fun. Rather, it is to enjoy quiet, peaceful evenings in a safe environment, talking of the news of the day, as couples do, but in a setting of *master-slave*. After-dinner coffee often leads to lifestyle discussions that help slaves accept who they are, by recognizing others with similar profound needs. Ancillary benefits or not, in the least, you will enjoy a good meal.

MICRO-MANAGEMENT DAY

Total power exchange and sustainable *master-slavery* is not about micro management. It cannot be for it is too taxing. That was stated earlier. Likewise, the absence of *micro-management* does not disqualify the validity of *total power exchange*. So with these two parameters established, where, if anywhere, does *micro-management* fit into the *master-slave* dynamic? Surely, a slave just knowing he can manage her details with the snap of his fingers is enough. For most slaves, indeed, that knowledge is enough. However, there are pitfalls in a slave just knowing, but never realizing that level of control. Sometimes she just has to experience it to know of its continued existence.

Trying to *micro-manage* your slave on a day-to-day basis is most assuredly a path to failure. But practicing it in small doses is just quaint, purposeful fun.

Understanding the role of micro-management first requires a practical definition of the term. Those first entering the lifestyle are often bombarded with the importance of *micro-managing* a slave. It is a stereotype promulgated by fantasy novels and the inexperienced. The concept is that by definition, slavery is the constant management of a slaves' every moment, however minor, or trivial. The fantasy stereotype dictates this condition exists, or a master suffers loss of control, is accused of being pussy-whipped and/or is *topped from the bottom*. In other words, he is no master at all. That stereotype continues partly because of raging dominant ego, though more often because of inexperience and immaturity. An unwillingness to let go of even the tiniest control, motivates those with grandiose or low self-esteem issues, to *micro-manage*.

While deciding the slave's life minutiae, hour by hour, certainly services a dominant ego, doing so is not practical in this day and age. Unless one is so inclined and quite independently wealthy, it just is not going to happen. That it is tedious and mind numbing are also good reasons to avoid the practice. Unless of course…. you want to for a day… and therein lay the magic!

Negative stereotypes aside, *micro-managing* details of her day, even for just a few hours once in awhile is very beneficial. It is also fun. It does enormous good for the relationship and the *master-slave* dynamic. Having her feel submission is the goal. She knows that you control everything, even though she receives privileges to manage some details on her own. She enjoys that contributing responsibility and understands the impracticality of *micro-managing* her every movement. But, knowing it, and taking it for granted are distinctly different beasts, and there comes a time wise mastery dictates she be reminded of that fact.

Take a quirt, roust her from bed, kneel her sleepy little ass down and growl at her.

"Slave, until further notice, you don't pee, drink, walk, talk, or even breathe without explicit permission. You are a slave and no more needs to be said."

"Whatever plans you thought you had for the day are cancelled. You do nothing without express permission. If you need butter for the eggs, you ask, you need butter for your ass, you ask. The phone rings, you ignore it. If the house is on fire, don't even spit."

"You are a slave and you have no rights. You don't leave my side unless ordered to. You abide every ritual and protocol ever taught you. You stand formally when not in use, you walk as though leashed even when you aren't. You enter and leave room in protocol. You don't even fart without permission, or you will feel the wrath of this quirt. Do you understand slavegirl?"

There you have it. Smile now and know your slave just got wet reading over your shoulder. Then, for the next four or five hours, micro-manage every breath she takes. You have a wonderful opportunity to explore the depth of her indenture using this technique. Do so to reinforce those *SODS* needs within her.

Forget her morning coffee and reading the paper. Start her off at 7a.m. by having her scrub the toilet. Mentioning that you will wash her hair in there afterwards, is up to you. Keep her naked. Slaves do not need clothes, though a larger than normal buttplug is a delightful accessory for any slave.

If like most folks, you will find that a few hours of this serves the purpose. You might become bored after awhile because it is tedious and she will have felt her absolute commitment to you.

Occasional *micro-managing* does serve a purpose, so give it a go. Have the courage to press your will. Your motivations are sound.

That said, a word of caution is warranted. Lamented often by slaves, though rarely heard from masters, is that the only time a slave is really managed and *micro-managed*, is during public outings to fetish events and BDSM clubs. Slaves bemoan this practice, seeing it for what it is, that being nothing more than showing off by the dominant to his friends. Behind closed doors, in private, *rituals, protocols*, indeed any significant managing and control is imperceptible, or insignificant. Do not be a *showoff dom*. It serves little purpose when your slave's needs are genuine and she needs your consistent control. You may go to many BDSM outings and thus manage her many times in that venue. To balance and avoid her perception of showmanship, take a quiet Saturday or Sunday and spend some time alone in a strict *micro-management* setting. It is worth the effort for this reason alone.

TECHNO-SLAVE

One of the beautiful aspects of living in the age we do is having the benefit of history. And history tells us many wonderful stories about slavery in different times, on faraway lands, in a kaleidoscope of erotic adventure and service. We use those stories for amusement in a smorgasbord of erotic role play. Have we all not, at one time or another, pictured ourselves in the throes of ecstasy with a Medieval slavegirl at our beck and call, a Victorian chambermaid, or as Sultan, owner of a Persian harem. From controlling a Japanese geisha-girl and English ponygirl, to southern plantation slaves, there are a bevy of erotic fantasies bringing adventure into the boudoir. All that is good of course, each of us enjoying our personal fantasies. What none of those slaves of yesteryear had access to was a technology that promotes the modern day slave to another level of service and ability to please. Today's slave can kick it up a notch. Today's slave has access to the Personal Digital Assistant. The PDA. You guessed it, the personal electronic organizer that will have her humming as efficiently as a Sybian on full rotate.

Fine, laugh, it seems funny now, but when you see the benefits derived, you will be glad you were not born a Sultan two hundred years ago with a harem of nubile maidens to service – maybe!

Get your slave a PDA. You will never regret it. It is a fantastic tool, enhancing service and quite probably invented specifically with slaves in mind. It is the perfect device to turn her into your techno-slave.

The PDA revolutionizes her ability to serve. Not only does it do the mundane like schedule her appointments, but it has the capacity for note keeping and messages. It becomes a handy little sticky-note without the paper; a string around the finger without self-bondage. They are a place for handy reminders of onetime event, or regularly repeating items. Record new rules and set prompts to trigger her into performing duties, on time and without fail. She will not forget she needs permission to pee now; that master's new leathers are ready at 3:15, and what this week's menu is. She has a way to record and remember all those offhand commands made in the spur of the moment, as masters are want to do.

The PDA is a tool, like any other at her disposal, provided to improve service to her master. You have a vision, a structure, likes and dislikes and over time teach her all that. However, no one could possibly remember it all. Memories are too imperfect. The PDA is a tool to assist her serving beyond your wildest expectations. You deserve it - and she does too.

Training Summary

So now, you have a trained slave. What a marvelous treasure to enjoy! Priceless!

This *Training Model* and its content represent a radical approach to training by today's standards. It is radical insofar as it is very different from training as perceived by much of the current BDSM community. To be blunt, much of today's mainstream training is about dominant ego. Training is an excuse for the slave to pleasure/service/jack off the dominant. Too often, it is framed as training to confuse the naïve, while serving an entirely selfish agenda.

Bear in mind, these comments reflect the particular *master-slave* niche espoused in this work. Less committed relationships may well enjoy a more fanciful and playful training regimen. Many design their programs to suit that purpose. In keeping with role-play games, rather than misleading about relationships intended to endure, no quarrel is taken with that purpose so stated.

The *Training Model* requires work on your part – before and after you spill cum. It requires forethought, self-knowledge and transparency of your vision and goals. While not stated, it is there, subtly and crystal clear. The *Training Model* strips away illusions, delusions and bullshit. It requires, dare I say, commitment.

In large measure, helping masters understand training was a primary goal in writing this *Trilogy*. The rhetoric of today, by self-professed *"trainers"* was so diametrically opposed to traditional purposes of yesteryear, as to haul me out of the dungeon to write. Today's selfish banality and lies represent butchery of what is a noble purpose. Professing expertise is not enough, one must actually possess it, have trained for it, and understand the power it represents.

Today, when self-styled trainers are asked why and what is trained, the answer is too often couched in hackneyed platitudes, web-page sophomoric rhetoric, and how often she is beaten and punished. Self-serving intentions are clear. When *trainers* cannot explain purpose, nor have the ability to articulate specific training, beyond S&M role play and fantasy control, then a slave dedicated to her purpose, is in jeopardy and a miscarriage underway.

Train her honestly. Be forthright in purpose. If training is just erotic foreplay, the purpose solely sexual, then say so. If it is to enrich both your lives by building a sustainable *master-slave* relationship, then make that clear. Balance your teachings with intelligence and honesty, for therein lies peace and tranquility.

Training is an expression of a master's romance and consistent care for the most important person in his life. For the slave receiving it, it is a privilege and pathway to deep peace. Then, when you have trained her and all is said and done, ravage her ass like no one before, and no one ever will again. She will love and thank you for it.

MIND FUCK #26 "FISTING"

She was afraid and hated herself for it. All these years, while difficult and merciless at times, master had never subjected her to outright fear in a real way like this. Sure there were times she thought to be afraid, but settled her mind, knowing he would never harm her. This though, petrified her outright.

She awoke to a glorious morning, a weekend without kids, free to serve and spend time alone with master culminating in a party of lifestyle friends tonight. She looked forward to it and even more so after the thorough fucking received before breakfast. It was over pancakes he dropped the bombshell, so casually it seemed like he had not said it at all.

"Tonight will be fun pet", he said, pouring the maple syrup. "I'm going to have you fisted." Her mouth went dry.

Of course, she knew this day would come. He had told her many years before. Yet, it was the one thing she truly feared. Knowing the fear was irrational did not help. Just the thought of being stretched like that mystified and mortified. Why wouldn't master want her tight? What if she ripped? Worst of all, what if he did it too easily? Crazy questions went through her mind. The whole idea just squicked her in the extreme.

"Nothing to say pet?"

"I don't think so Sir." She replied quietly, then added, "Please be gentle."

He smiled and kissed her, "It won't be my hand pet. I have a special treat for you instead" and she shivered again.

The party was in full swing that included supper and use of the dungeon. In there, it was busy. All the masters were particularly creative tonight. She had been not used yet, but it was forefront on her mind, knowing what he planned.

"Pet, have you met Master Bryan?"

"I have not Sir, which one is he?"

"Come and I will introduce you."

They entered the kitchen where a group stood chatting. Among them was a giant of a man, surely over six and a half feet tall, built like a football player. Moving forward, he recognized master.

"Bryan, good to see you. I am glad you made it."

"And you too LT, a pleasure as always and thank you for having us. Now, who is this lovely small creature beside you?"

"Bryan, please meet my slave. I told you about her earlier on the phone. Pet, please meet an old friend, Master Bryan."

She curtseyed graciously as always.

"And please meet my slave Melissa" Bryan replied. A tiny sprite of a slave stepped forward. She could not have been five feet tall or a hundred pounds, but she smiled graciously and said hello. Master thought his slave was small, but this girl was diminutive.

Turning to his slave so all could hear he said, "Bryan is the man who will fist you tonight, pet."

Automatically her eyes dropped to his hands and she nearly fainted, then looked up, eyes pleading, but quietly responding "Yes Sir."

An hour later just the four of them entered the dungeon. By now she had overcome years of shyness among lifestyle friends, so when ordered, Melissa stripped her with quiet efficiency. Still, she blushed.

Lowering the sling, she was tipped in and tethered. The stirrups held her legs well back and apart, exposing her charms to whatever master planned. With wrists cuffed to the chains, she was immobile, exposed and without a shred of modesty left. Master fastened a blindfold and she was grateful for its black cocoon.

"Pet, it is time" he whispered. "Bryan is going to fist you now. Make me proud." Time stood still. "You can do this pet, you will endure it for me."

She nodded faintly. The dungeon was suddenly very warm, yet she had goose bumps. Reaching down, he touched her pussy.

"You are dry pet. I am going to have Melissa fix that." Expecting a tongue, the cold lubricant startled her as Melissa's fingers performed their duty. Yet none entered inside her.

When she felt the first finger begin probing, he kissed her hard and rough. Seeing her tense, he growled. "Be brave slut. I want to see you in pain. I love you, but need to do this for me." The fisting began in earnest then, her first ever.

Fearing the worst, she was grateful he went slowly. Despite that, the pain increased, the burning started, but it was not as bad as feared. Surprisingly it felt good and her hips began involuntarily moving in arousal.

Master stroked her face, whispering *goodgirl*, throughout. She knew the giant hand was in now and slowly began to fist fuck her. It was intense and the peak was near. She was going to cum and her master saw it.

"Fuck her hard now!"

Never had she felt the onslaught so suddenly. She screamed out in agony and ecstasy. On the verge, suddenly the blindfold was ripped away and he screamed into her face.

"Cum slut! Now!"

Clenching her face, he squeezed. Blood vessels in her neck and forehead bulged as the giant orgasm consumed her.

"Keep going, fuck her harder," he bellowed as the fist penetrated and stretched her as never before. Master forced her head up to watch and amidst tears of unending pleasure, her eyes registered the shock.

Collapsing back she was utterly exhausted, the fist still rudely inside. Sweat poured from her body. She was sore, tender and completely sated. Master looked down and smiled.

"A nice little mind fuck for you pet. You are my treasure." A lopsided smile came to her face, half surprise, mostly just exhaustion. He had done it again. Knowing her fear, he kept her safe and moved her forward. Lifting her head again she watched as Melissa slowly pulled her hand out.

"Goodgirl, I am very proud of you. Trust me pet, I would not let you come to harm." He smiled and she drifted off.

7

HOUSE RULES

I hate non-specific rules! You probably should too. I can guarantee your slave does.

Rules lacking specificity are usually a sign the master is struggling with his structure, possibly even his motivation and dedication to mastery. Likely he is confused about power management and the responsibilities incumbent with ownership. Certainly, he lacks an appreciation of the slave mind. His disorganized structure reflects this uncertainty. All of it results in vague and non-specific rules. Usually though he can *talk-the-talk* with flowery rhetoric. Without specific rules, tasks and performance expectations taught and enforced, he cannot *walk-the-walk* over time. Right there is a good lesson for slaves looking at a prospective master. Learning of a master's specific rules or lack thereof, is a strong indicator as to the quality of mastery represented. Control is in the details. You teach them and she performs them. We call it structure and direction, two key elements to a fulfilled slave.

Detailed rules do not have to mean a micro-management style, so do not make that confusion. It simply represents clarity for your slave with the happy by-product of minimal master maintenance. Developing this takes work, lots of it, and it takes time, but it is *"initial work"* and tapers off as time progresses.

Rules and *Tasks* are sometimes broken into separate entities and there is merit to that approach. The *'No Master Maintenance'* principle applies yet again. Anything that reduces relationship administration is welcome. Keeping *Rules* and *Tasks* together minimizes administration and maintenance and thus the approach used here. The number of rules and their detail clearly establishes your expectations. That in turn ensures she understands the life she is embarking on. Wise masters explain and even teach these rules prior to collaring, though that depends on your meaning of collaring. But, if the collar represents permanence, it serves no good purpose to spring a whole range of expectations on her if she is unaware that is what she was consenting to. Throwing *Rule Books* at her with a terse *'learn this'* does not do much good either. It is fun teaching your slave the rules so take your time, savor the journey and then drill them into her until she has them right, remembering the adage *'Do not punish what you have not taught'*.

Sort through then organize and teach your rules by thinking of various *conventional, traditional* and *historical "service"* roles, then impose on her the perspectives and pertinent responsibilities that turn your crank. Think of her vanilla service in terms of personal service to you and as career professional, but in context of being your slave. Her obedience and service are often comprised of these elements, depending of course, on the level of control chosen.

A major benefit accrues by doing this. All these rules, tasks and expectations are developed in advance of owning your slave. That is the benefit. There is no need to fly by the seat of your pants, and she will appreciate your thoughtful preparation, thus reinforcing trust. By preparing in advance, it is easier too, to modify rules later to suit her particular circumstances, skills, abilities, needs and wants.

An easy example regards kids in the house. If raising spawn properly is a priority and important, then demanding a rule that she be the best Mom in the world is irrelevant if you have no kids. Yet that is your desire, and before knowing who your slave is, it is a priority rule for when kids come along. So depending on your slave's circumstances, modify or eliminate it. Likewise, there is nothing gained from a rule demanding a bowl of soup served from her knees at lunch, when she is twenty-five miles across town at her job.

The rules laid out here as *House Rules* are livable and doable. The extent and scope reflect the all-inclusive *Three Power* niche commonly referred to as

TPE. Note their precision, specific and inclusive nature. There are two reasons for this and suspect you have guessed them already. Obviously, they are what the master wants, but secondly because she thrives in structure and direction. Here is a bit of reality. She cannot please you if she does not know what you want. Well thought out rules give her that. Be specific and avoid feel good clichés. A wonderful illustration of this point is a rule regarding *"respect."* Some masters make a rule reading something like:

> *"You will respect your Master at all times."*

Well Doh! No shit Sherlock! She knelt for you and surrendered control of her life. Is a rule like that necessary, or just a master ego boost?

Going out on a limb here, it is fair to say no one would submit to someone they disrespected. The rule is redundant, unnecessary and serving no purpose whatsoever other than perhaps to reinforce an insecure dominant. So do not make it a rule. Make rules she can respect, not rules demanding it.

Rules like this abound nowadays as inexperienced masters publish flowery nonsense on the internet, thinking it makes them wise and wonderful. Fifty rules of similar fluff and they are convinced they created responsible structure. In fact, they have accomplished nothing except maybe confuse some poor retch already pre-disposed to falling for romantic claptrap. Find romance in deeds and style, not rules. She needs tangible structure, not fluff. Your actions and style makes structure romantic. Structure by itself is not.

Successful masters often have many rules. Others do not, and rely on one.

> *"You know what I want, now do it."*

That may work for some folks. Most however, cannot relay their desires telepathically and I have yet to meet a slave who instinctually knows. So, she must be taught… dammit!

There are *Rituals* and *Protocols* masters can choose to incorporate into their structure in the next *Chapter*. They are essentially rules too, but unlike *House Rules* they are behaviors more explicit to slavery expectations than service oriented, so separated. There are far fewer *Rituals* than *House Rules*, but record them for her.

There are sixteen categories of rules for a slave and undoubtedly, you will come up with more or eliminate some to suit your needs. They are not etched in stone, so make them fit what works for you. If you prefer a different organization of your rules, hell, go for it. The easier it is for you, the better. Remember, *"No Master Maintenance"*, is a practical road to consistency and a keystone to making this all work.

Many *House Rules* pertain to duties performed classically in another age, by a combination of *Butler, Chambermaid, Housekeeper Groundskeeper* and *Personal Secretary*. Others are more contemporary designations, *Chef, Waitress, Hostess, Guest* and others are yet an eclectic mix, but of equal importance. Groups pertaining to *Sexual Conduct, Career, Family Relations, Cars, Pets,* the *Public BDSM Community* and of course herself and you.

When you have more than one slave, a common successful technique to manage slaves, is equally dividing tasks, particularly household duties, by floor, or rooms, making each slave interchangeable, rotating duties regularly.

When analyzing your rules the slave must know these duties and tasks are ad hoc behavioral expectations. She obeys them automatically unless overridden by a new command.

Here are some examples of the scope you can encompass. You might want to use all these or just some and that is fine. You know you, I do not… and neither does your slave yet.

SOCIAL ORGANIZER & PERSONAL ASSISTANT

Women, by and large are terrific social conveners. They seem better at it than men. That is certainly my experience, so take advantage of it. They seem more interested in it too. Of the numerous personal secretary privileges one can task to her, the one to establish early is responsibility for the *"Social Calendar"*. It is convenient and usually a task well suited to slaves in general. It keeps them in touch with friends and events in the BDSM community and relieves masters of the tedious task of researching BDSM functions. Task her also, with suggesting entertainment ideas. That is always fun. You of course, decide how to use her social acumen to your advantage.

Now before getting all puffy slavegirls, read that again and realize your master is not looking for a momma-slave. There is actually very little there, and quite frankly, the only important part is keeping him informed of plays, concerts, who's playing at the Comedy Club and what BDSM events are coming up, so he can decide what he wants to drag your sorry little ass to. So relax, he will pick what works for you both.

Also, take this time to establish the habit of accounting for her time. Often, a simple refrigerator calendar with her weekly *out of house* schedule does the trick. The detail of this will depend on the level of micro-management you want.

There are many other tasks you can delegate including all correspondence, opening mail, auditing bills, preparing payments, reconciling bank statements and filing. Those entertaining regularly might want to establish an *Entertainment Book* that records who and when guests visited, what was served, any allergies, or other special needs they may have, and their favorite drinks. Many slaves enjoy keeping track of that information making it an ideal responsibility to establish. Your friends will compliment your hosting, so enjoy the benefits accrued from your slave's diligence.

There are countless ways to enable your slave's usefulness. From making and recording appointments for you, to providing input to the monthly budget preparation, the sky is the limit. One of the most useful though, is being your extra hands, ears and complimentary brain. Schedule time to sit down and talk.

Enable her to enable you. A simple command heard in these parts is "Pet, please look after the filing or it will sit there for years!" I hate filing. Whatever rules you choose, write them down and enforce them.

ENTERTAINING

Teaching entertaining *protocols* is not critical if you are not planning to entertain in your home, particularly BDSM lifestyle specific guests. But, if you are, then move this up and train it now.

What are your expectations when entertaining? Perhaps you have general standards, but what specific ideas and conducts do you expect on a party-by-party basis?

While always a slave first, when entertaining guests, be they vanilla or lifestyle, she is also the hostess. As such, her conduct reflects the respect that all are invited guests. Guests are welcome and hospitality must be relentless. As hostess her actions reflect that attitude to the extent that her needs are subordinated to those of your guests. She must acquire the skill and grace to achieve that invisibly. Teach her that and make it a *House Rule*. Guests are to be made as comfortable as arrangements and facilities permit. At the same time, she cannot flit about, get upset, or seem to make a fuss on their behalf. Nothing makes a guest more uncomfortable than to feel their hosts are going to trouble for them, even though that is exactly what they are doing. That is what separates the distinguished hostess from the self-centered one.

With that general bearing, then develop other more specific rules of choice. Examples include that she cannot get angry no matter what happens. She must be interesting and entertaining without seeking attention. As hostess she already holds a prominent position, so there is no need to exaggerate it.

If you enjoy formality, have her offer to unpack overnight guest's bags and lay out their toiletries, putting folded clothes in drawers and hanging ones in the closet. Then really go overboard and at bedtime, determine when guests prefers to arise and if they would like breakfast in bed. If you want her to be the breakfast, well, make that rule too.

Continuing on a formal basis, task her with ascertaining guests breakfast likes, ensuring each order is to taste. Have her arise before your guests with sufficient time to have breakfast ready. If breakfast is in bed, establish rules to serve it, such as breakfast trays always having a cloth covering, a carafe of coffee or tea, milk and sugar bowls, napkins, utensils, salt and pepper with appropriate plating.

There are countless etiquettes and entertaining *protocols* to develop only limited by your wants. Consider enrolling her in cooking classes or taking advantage of the numerous resources that teach entertaining decorum. The ideas are endless.

Entertaining is important, and generally performed with good intentions though poor etiquette. Good hosting is a memorable experience for many guests and a slave's performance, guided by invisible rules, is largely responsible for dispensing that pleasure. Train her well, it reflects on you.

BEING THE GUEST

For many masters this is a particularly important element to train simply because her conduct reflects you. There is nothing worse than a slave flitting about being the center of attention while imposing on others. Also though, a low maintenance happy guest is a welcome one and keeping friends is a nice touch. It is not difficult to train, nor does it take long.

Make rules that when entertained in others homes or elsewhere, faultless grooming, neat appearance, dignified and graceful decorum is required. She will be unimposing, somewhat shy but not aggravatingly so, speak gently, walk and move elegantly and be unfailingly courteous and respectful to all, be they dominants, slave or vanilla people. She is to enjoy everything and not show disappointment or annoyance even if she hates the food, their kids and pets. To a formal slave, a rule requiring her to love any game a host suggests is ideal. Ensure she knows she is the quiet winner and gracious loser.

Hosts are thrilled when their guests project happiness with the hospitality and are honored to have been invited. Everyone loves her because she loves everyone, not a disingenuous talent, but rather a positive outlook on life.. She is tolerant and non-judgmental of others opinions, but strong of conviction, without a need to preach or convert others to her point of view. Her manners are impeccable but not arrogant, rather with a practical appreciative style.

There you go, presto she just became the perfect guest and a source of great pride. Later reward her in private ensuring she is a tawdry slut and groveling ditch-pig… but just for you.

CAREER HOBBIES INTERESTS

Her career, hobbies and community interests are important, not just to her but you as well. Like you, she aspires to be an all around contributor to this society, and that includes hobbies and outside interests she may well have or want. Encourage them and allow enough time and energy for fulfillment. The only limitation is in the event their focus becomes excessively burdensome on your relationship. Most masters are not interested in one-dimensional slaves, finding them boring over time. Seek to ensure she fulfills her other needs. That is vitally important. She needs outside interests. Some control of those needs and interests can be structure for her however.

A good practice having her feel submission yet without restricting her unduly is having her summarize her weekly commitments outside the house in advance and present for permission. It need not be terribly detailed, but if she plans to be out every night and you are ignored, you might want to know that. Have her require your permission before she involves herself with any activity or group outside the home. Perhaps a list is not needed, conversation simply sufficient. That is is decided by your style. However works, go for it, but she is to keep you abreast of the activities not shared. Then budget money for her activities. Also, make a rule that when she is away from the home unexpectedly, she notifies you, notwithstanding emergencies.

Then control her career.

Whoa dom-boy... I just heard that muttered a thousand times.

Control her career?

Yeah sure, why not!

Understand the statement's goal. It is not the intention to be anything but supportive of her career, or to be involved with her career on a day-to-day basis, except insofar as hearing how her day went. She does not need permission for the decisions and duties involved in her job. She is fully capable and her employer would not allow it. Likely, most masters are not qualified to make those decisions anyway. So reality check. She can ask for advice, but otherwise it is her career. So then why the statement *"Control her career?"*

My view is simple and may or may not apply to others. I will involve myself if her job is becoming detrimental to her health, long-term happiness, or raining on our relationship. In that event, taking a patient thoughtful approach, analysis of the conditions causing these problems occurs and if necessary, a search for a new career position begins. No job is worth ruining a committed loving relationship over. Those are my personal values and others might disagree. So be it, let us move on.

FINANCES

She must learn to manage money if not already able. It is an absolute life skill requirement. Addressing financial issues, particularly when a dual income situation exists, expectations must be taught in their entirety. Bear in mind, doing so requires you to expand on the earlier discussions located above in the *Personal Assistant* area. above.

Is this a priority training issue? To some it is not, though frankly it should be. Money issues are the number one cause of marital/relationship stress, so responsible mastery addresses, trains, and establishes good financial habits so the relationship runs smoothly.

The issue of money is often a thorny one, particularly with new master-slave couples and is one a master can take in one of two directions. Many slaves are most comfortable owning nothing. For them, to fully appreciate the wholeness with which they give control of their lives, it must include effectively signing over income to their masters. If that turns their crank, then by all means, go for it. Advocating one way or the other is not the purpose here. It is intensely personal to each couple and comfort levels needed to feel secure, vary so much, in many ways.

Certainly, a slave partaking of this practice is committing herself completely into the hands of her master emotionally, physically and now financially. That would be incredibly freeing for many slaves. To others, it produces insecurity issues they cannot overcome. That it also opens the possibility of fraudulent con men entering their lives is another reality she must consider. There is risk in every decision we make so she needs to understand her exposure.

Assuming a fanciful utopia for a moment, whereby all monies are master controlled with the slave having no access, if the couple could predict the relationship would last forever; that the master was responsible with money; and he would outlive the slave, then this works without reservation. If you know all that will happen, then go for it, spank the monkey. If you do not know all three things will happen though, then consider these factors.

Ensuring your slave has budget input, does the accounting, makes payment transactions and reconciles the bank statement, is to avoid stripping her of life survival skills, of which managing money is a key one. The reality of life is that the unexpected happens sometimes. Tragic circumstances sometimes do happen. A master can be hit by a bus and gone tomorrow. Good mastery requires we plan for that, as unpleasant a task as it is.

Should the unthinkable happen, the slave naturally is upset, perhaps devastated at losing the man to whom she dedicated her life. A grieving period notwithstanding, at some point in the future, she is going to have to pick up the pieces and move on. She has to cope and seek her happiness. Masterful life skills are required to do that.

As master, if you have passed on and are giving the Devil a run for his money down below, and paused to think of your loving slave, would you not be upset having left her unable to cope? If not, rather than enabling her as your slave, you provided a structure that stripped her of the ability to survive, let alone prosper. Then you deserve Satan for the broken pledges made to her. That would be poor mastery. So, she is not allowed to lose her life skills, in fact structure is in place to ensure she does not. So let us make financial rules that are consistent with responsible mastery, protective of the *master-slave* dynamic and enabling for your slave in the least, during an emergency.

Even if a slave signs over her paychecks, she must have access to all monies and working knowledge of its management. Make that happen with a joint bank account for her emergency protection, even if she does not routinely access it. There is no reason for you not to do that. If you have been upfront all along, without a secret agenda, then it is common sense and good mastery. Then the master sets his budget including her spending money and the slave deals with the details.

The alternative is to set a budget and divide expenses either through contributions to one account, or individually assigning budget items to each person. The joint account solution is easiest and if the master wants to restrict her practical, but not legal access to the money then it works well.

There is another way as well though, and one I like. Having the luxury to pay for my lifestyle without burdening her with a required financial contribution each month is indeed a luxury in this day and age. But even if some monies were required from her pay cheque to maintain the level of comfort they share, there is a way to manage it and maintain security for her in the event of tragedy or fraudulence. Simply have her maintain her own independent bank account for deposit of her earnings; and she transfers (by email nowadays, it is so simple), a set amount to the bill paying account where access is joint. She keeps the rest. It is her money to do whatever she wants.

Her master does not even need access to it. If she wants to spend it on her master, fine, it is her choice. But she need not. This solution goes a long way to maintaining her pride, self-worth and life management skills, not to mention some people need that security blanket, regardless of the dedication, commitment and love between them. If that works for her, just do it, it is no skin off an honest master's ass.

SEXUAL

Train it all. Was there any doubt? Perhaps needed are a few thoughts to inspire.

The most unequivocal of all rules is that she is used sexually where, when, how, by whom and with what, you chose, without protest, reservation or hesitation. Leave the whole *"Boundary"* issue out for the moment. Take the rules further so she knows her responsibilities include making herself sexually pleasing and alluring to the best of her abilities. Free her of any guilt or inhibition she feels to enjoy her sexuality to the fullest. Give her no choice but to enthusiastically comply. Essentially make her your slut. Everyone knows you both want it anyway.

To do it, explain and then establish a rule that sexual activities she is involved in are not of her choosing, thus alleviating any guilt she may feel. Require her to be both pro-active and passive in her sexual conduct when called upon. At all times, she must endeavor to maximize the pleasure of you and/or others even at the expense of her own.

Make a rule that she must express her sexual needs, wants and fantasies at any discrete time, but must do so in the basest terms. That is fun. Especially when you come home and find her at the door on her knees, face in the carpet and hands holding her ass cheeks apart begging you to fuck her in the ass. She is not a lady regarding sex. She is a Marseilles dockworker's wet dream.

Rule that she will constantly be vigilant in seeking new ways to give pleasure and will acquire those skills. Require by rule and then enforce it that she be adventurous, inquisitive and lack inhibition. She needs to understand, it is your cunt, not her vagina.

MEAL PREPARATION

If you want to eat, you might want to get this one to the top of the list!

The slave always does meal preparation and she better be a damned fine chef! Just kidding slavegirl. I love cooking and share that task. A custom personal recipe cookbook contains the recipes I enjoy and can cook. I like to add to it frequently. I enjoy exploring new cuisines as long as there are frozen pizzas in the freezer for emergencies. So task her by rule to be vigilant searching out new recipes to try. It is fun. Experiment with a new one each month. If they are successful add to the *Personal Recipe Book*. If cooking is a hobby, then time shared in the kitchen is *'our'* time.

If you like, have her prepare a weekly menu for approval. It is to reflect good taste and ingredients, be well balanced, healthy and nutritional. Dictate exactly your desires and do it by rule. Remember, you are the boss and can change a *House Rule*, so go ahead and make one that pleases you now. It might not tomorrow, no biggie. Just change it.

Maybe you are health conscious, so make sure she knows portions are small. As a society we serve too much food anyway, by in large. Ideally, five small meals each day are better than three larger ones and when time and circumstance allow, that is the choice of preference. If you have a food you detest, then make sure that rule is written quickly.

Breakfast is light and quick, toast or fruit, except Sunday mornings when you might enjoy a large breakfast together. Lunches are also light, a sandwich or soup or salad, but creativity is good. Ice water and coffee. Dinners are from the *Recipe Book* with exceptions noted above and creativity and surprises are good. A good rule is that unless specified otherwise she prepares the meals.

The booze rule is important too. Personal consumption of alcohol in moderation only and requires permission is a good one. You don't need her drunk to fuck her!

CHAMBERMAID

There is no need to lower the training priority here. This would be a Daily prioritized near the top. Doing so will only establish slovenly habits or, worse, if she is not a neatnik, create a mess in the bedroom. Messing with her ass is more fun than tiptoeing through her clothes.

Chambermaid duties on days you are not at your job are to ensure all beds are made, clothes put away or taken with any soiled linens to the laundry. Bed linens are changed weekly on laundry day. The bedrooms are tidied each morning, the drapes opened and lights turned off. Any BDSM gear used is cleaned and put away. On workdays, beds are made and clothes put away before leaving. Occasionally dress her in Victorian chambermaid garb for these duties. It is the responsibility of the Lord of the Manor to spoil her innocence!

WAITRESS

Fair enough, I confess. There are only fifteen vanilla categories. This simply reflects a personal peccadillo. Setting a proper dinner table, both for family affairs and formal entertaining is a fetish of mine. Knowing how to serve and remove courses properly is just very civil. It reflects good breeding and style. It is only prioritized here to appease my sense of decorum.

She best learn that all meals are served from the left and taken away from the right. She never leans across a table to serve or remove dishes. The table is set with appropriate utensils, plating, water glass, ice water pitcher, salt and pepper shakers, candles and paper napkins, or linen ones when entertaining guests. Seasonal floral centerpieces are encouraged but designed low enough not to obstruct vision and make dinner conversation difficult. Formal dishes are used only for special occasions or entertaining and require permission to use. Not all plating, utensils and glassware are used for every kind of meal so adjust accordingly.

Waitress duties vary depending on the event, particularly when lifestyle friends are visiting.

Got all that pet? There is a test Monday.

HOUSEKEEPING

To address this training issue responsibly, one must first establish a baseline of expectations. That is a very fancy way of saying who in the relationship is the neatnik, and who is the slob. Rarely do partners come to a relationship on an equal footing. Invariably, one of you is going to be messier. Who that is largely dictates how this issue is handled. If she is the slob, then this is easy – for you - and likely very miserable for her! However, if it is you, allocation of time and resources is necessary to maintain the house.

There are many aspects to the Housekeeping issue, but the most important at this stage of training is daily upkeep. Quarterly, semi-annual and periodic maintenance descends in priority to *The Rest*. By whom, when, and how thoroughly the daily maintenance is performed are issues requiring immediate decisions and training. Detail here is important and who does what is entirely your decision. You may have her barefoot, naked and cleaning all day, each day, and that is your right. She may not like it, may revolt and leave, but it is certainly your right. Use common sense and as importantly, keeps things fun. An apron is quite adequate apparel at times, especially when you are feeling frisky. Plan to lose some coins down the sofa sides. She then presents an inviting target.

Regardless of how you divide the daily housekeeping, teach it in the Daily Section, or suffer rampant dust bunnies and a sink full of dirty dishes.

We need to manage this potentially thorny issue. An important part of any happy household is its tidiness and cleanliness. There are annual and seasonal maintenance and preventative tasks needed in every home and the slave is responsible for bringing these to the attention of her master for decisions in a timely manner. If she does not know how, master will teach her. How she organizes her reminder system is her choice.[12] These tasks include annual eves trough cleaning; semi-annual window cleaning, inside and out; bi annual duct cleaning; furnace filter replacement; seasonal garden refurbishing; interior and exterior painting; and pool opening and closing.

---

[12] See Chapter 4 "Techno-slave"

A simple rule to handle all this is to give her responsibility to locate and maintain a list of High School studlys, her *"Stud List"* if you will, available for hire to complete those tasks.

Additionally, daily and weekly house maintenance duties are required. Masters must establish what is important. If he is wise, he takes advice from his slave. If for example he is a slob and she a neatnik there is strife if she is not given the time and resources needed to keep the house. A slob can live in a clean home, but a neatnik will go insane in a pigpen. Proclamations of omnipotent mastery where his word is law notwithstanding, cleanliness to some people is a need required for a healthy mind and life. Thus, the issue of household tasks takes on great importance.

If the slave is not working outside the house then all daily household maintenance tasks are her responsibility. There are no excuses accepted, the house must be immaculate, or to the standard demanded by her master. Housekeeping duties include the appearance of the house and contents. Everything is kept clean and tidy, walls, floors, furniture, pictures, ornaments, books, linens, laundry, bathroom fixtures and beds. Those are the slave's tasks if she is not working outside the house. How she accomplishes these tasks is only of masters concern from an overview perspective. However, if the slave is fully employed, rules must change and evolve.

I cannot recommend an outside cleaning service enough. Understanding finances can be tight at times, the relatively small monies required to bring someone in weekly for five hours is worth its weight in gold for your slave and ultimately you.

Hiring a cleaning service relieves so much of the menial work most do not enjoy. Having said that of course there are exceptions and some women take great pride in doing the housework. Using a cleaning service also tangibly conveys the message her master cares and values her time. She is free to serve making useful contributions utilizing her advanced skills and knowledge. She is not just a menial serf, but a useful slave. That creates peace of mind.

FAMILY / FRIENDS

Part of this issue, the exclusive nature and privacy of your relationship, was addressed while training your *Contract*. The issue is broader than that though. If extended family exists and assuming you have friends and children, then perform the required training to address this issue. Left unattended difficult problems may arise.

The vanilla world is a strange place. Folks profess tolerance of alternative lifestyles, yet when it enters their close circle, the *NIMBY* syndrome rears its ugly head. Tolerance is great, but *"Not In My Backyard"* is usually the prevailing attitude. Be cautious with who knows about your relationship style. Society still sees power exchange as *"hitting someone"* and thus abusive, if not pathological, or criminal. Deliberate, or even inadvertent disclosure, can cause an inordinate amount of angst. Early training on the issue avoids this. Review your position and teach it thoroughly, then handle any disobedience rigorously.

Rules that affect interaction with the families, in-laws and outlaws must be detailed and is easily done. Naturally, they will vary by situation and masters tailor them individually. If underage kids are home, the first rule is to be the best mother possible. She can spare no effort or energy for this task. I am imposing values here placing a premium on the children's welfare and others may not do the same. It is however fair to draw the conclusion that whatever values you place on child rearing; they must be the same for both the master and slave. If momma-slave gives top priority to the kid's welfare, one I would have no quibble with, but her master does not, their relationship will spiral down the drain in an eddying whirlpool of strife. Conversely, slaves entering a relationship are wise to express themselves honestly rather than seek a collar knowing they will seek to alienate Dad and his kids from a previous relationship for selfish reasons. Neither situation works. Now this addresses minor children.

There is no need for kids to be aware of Mom and Dad's power structure and that is the second rule. Keep your mouth shut and bum bruises covered. In-laws and outlaws have no need to know either, but nor do you need to hide it if they are understanding, mature, tolerant and discrete. The more that know of your lifestyle, the greater the risk of experiencing intolerance and persecution. Use caution if exposure can unnecessarily damage your life. Discretion is the better part of valor. Endeavour to insulate yourselves from outing. Do not be burned through naiveté. If your job is at risk were your master-slave status known, keep your own counsel. If you own a BDSM gear manufacturing company and your livelihood and all friends are lifestyle related, then do not fret being outted. You already are. Hell, promote it in that case.

When considering whether to bare your lifestyle to family or anyone, consider one thing carefully. Do not think just because you understand and see the beauty and peace of master-slave that others will. As eloquent as you may be and as tolerant as you think others are, some people do not get it and never will. Trying to explain this to most vanillas is absolutely a waste of time at best, and likely will cause loss of otherwise good friendships. Explain to those on a need to know basis only and move on. The rule for your slave is simple and specific.

"You will safeguard our unique relationship. You cannot inform others of our master-slave dynamic without explicit, specific permission." A *House Rule* in the least, perhaps best Contract included.

GROUNDSKEEPER

It is not necessary this be in the *Daily* section of your *Training Model*, or in *The Rest*, unless you own a landscaping business. That provision notwithstanding, either cut the grass, or she can chew it down, it is no skin off my ass either way.

Perhaps I have been lucky, or perhaps it is a heretofore unknown aspect of the slave mindset, but every slave I have known loved to garden. That is fortunate because I hate it though admittedly enjoy watching them. That is as it should be, seeing as so much of it is done on her knees. I am just saying!

Be that as it may, a slave is responsible for the gardens. Each master has different hobbies and interests so these duties are allocated differently for each couple. At my home while the gardens are her responsibility accountable to me, there are specific rules that guide her.

She is responsible for light duties and overseeing only. Major repair for fences or other heavy maintenance, for planting large trees or moving stone planters she has a list of High School studlys to hire as needed. Her primary responsibilities are encompassed in three rules. Keep and maintain the garden first. That includes seasonal planting, weeding, soil maintenance and watering. The second is to observe and make note of any repairs that need attention on the grounds. Perhaps the fence needs re-staining, the deck power washed, or the driveway a new sealant coat. She brings those chores to my attention that are then dealt with in a timely manner. The third rule is unambiguous and *Holy Master Law*. Do not touch my fucking lawns! That is my bailiwick. Keep your paws off them slavegirl. I feed them, water them make sure her rampant garden weeds do not encroach, cut it and edge it. If she is lucky I might let her walk on it occasionally but she has a better chance by begging. If she even thinks I am anal about my grass I will happily show her what anal really is. The message is clear, she has her gardens I have my lawns. Keep your distance and the universe will unfold, as it should. Naturally though, change the rules if you wish, just stay off my lawn. I can be snarky with a whip.

CARS

Again, this is not a time sensitive issue. If she runs out of gas on some distant road, well, then it becomes even less so.

Teach her and enforce these rules always. The hood is what she hops on, spreading her legs to be used in front. The trunk is for bending over, to be used in the rear, naturally. It serves the double purpose as storage locker for kidnapping scenes. The backseat is for necking and gropes when it is time to play schoolgirl. Passenger front seats are for diddling and flashing truckers and the driver's seat is where she rests her head. Yes, rests it, so to speak. Beyond that she is generally thankful I do not own a trailer or we would be doing the kinky traveling dungeon show.

Not being big on micro-management, cars are not an area I give a great deal of thought to for her beyond the basics. She does not touch my car, but must keep hers clean of clutter and trash. She must have a lube oil and filter change every three thousand miles, or I will lube oil and filter her fanny and it will not be pretty. Run it through the car wash when necessary and I will wax it when I do my own. Again, slaves I have known have all been considerate safe drivers, so have not had to deal with exorbitant insurance rates caused by carelessness. But if it happened we are past the lube oil and filter and into a private engine overhaul.

PETS

Feed them, water them, play with them. What else is there? Unless she is it! Woof!

She is the pet puppy. What more is there to know? As long as she is paper-trained and sniffs around your crotch, it is all good. She has her dog bowl, leash and a cage. If she could just lick herself, well then, you would not need those other bitches doing it for her.

You thought this was about rules for changing the cat litter? Bloody hell folks! You do not need me telling you how to look after the family pets. Just jam a ponytail up her ass and teach her to canter.

Hee haw!

SELF (THE SLAVE)

House Rules pertaining to her personal appearance, bearing and conduct is what *"Self"* rules are. They are important. For many masters, they are quite extensive and sometimes downright sexy. Teaching them all is too trivial and personal. However, some may well be important habits to instill early. They are tangible evidence of your structure. Again too, they are fun.

Some of the best are detailed below.

The best place to start is with a simple behavior, easily taught and remembered. It is a control issue, a bit of behavior reminding her that vanilla boyfriends are a distant memory. She lives subordinated to her master now, so give her something reminding her of that little fact.

The rule addresses neck hugging. Ban it. Just do not allow her to put her arms around your neck. Why is explained below.

The next simple rule is again tangible and invisible, making it ideal for vanilla circumstances. Prohibit her from standing directly in front of you. It is confrontational and there is no place for adversarial conduct from a slave. It subtly reinforces, once again, her position. Again, and like all these simple behaviors, the *why's* are detailed in later.

If you have not taken control of her orgasms yet, now is a good time. *"No more pet. Pussy blackmail is for the whipped vanilla fellows. I decide when and now is a good time… cum, slut!"*

The growth of her intellectually and socially is another rule affecting daily life. Those elements of her personality are important to many masters. Often, early in a relationship, a slave's intellectual and social growth takes a backseat to the new reality of slavery. As unknown worlds open to her, are explored and discovered, naturally, other long-term items get set to the back burner for awhile. They are still there though. All that is good, it is fun. Make rules to encourage intellectual and social growth. Charity work is a great way to do it.

Oh and then there is that little item called *"her purse!"* Yes, we all understand it is the shrine of feminine living, her holy of holies. Oftentimes it is not particularly small either. Since you are her kingdom and she has her temple, and this is not a democracy, it is time to mix a little church and state.

Trying to control a slave's purse is like trying to dam Niagara Falls. Inevitably, you will be electrocuted, so do not bother. Just let her know, that in that big old bag of hers, she had better have her *"slave necessities".* It might keep her ass from pickling.

Saved for last is the fun one. Her apparel. Clothes! You know the stuff you have been cutting off her. There should not be much left. That of course, makes it easy to establish rules. Who says there is not method to our madness? There are clothing details further on, but because you want me to see her adorned to your liking, keep her naked and send pictures. We are all voyeurs at heart.

Every master has their apparel preferences, panty twists and knickers fetishes. Far be it to delve through the countless permutations of slut-wear you might like. Just inform her the degree of control you want, from micro-managing her every outfit, to whether she wears panties, to teaching her how to put a geisha dress on without hanging herself with the obi. Review the numerous issues around dressing your slave before detailing your rules. It is a fun issue. Understandably, it can be a lot of unnecessary work; however, that is not a given and is your choice. It also produces tangible control with enormous benefits.

Designing rules for your slave is sometimes joyous and other times exasperating. Some things work marvelously, others, well, *"we'll scrap that one pet"*. As experience grows, you will find what works, what does not, what you thought was sexy that is not, what looked good on paper and is a pain in the ass in reality. All kinds of growth will occur. Embrace that, do not fear it. If something works, keep it, if not, have the courage to change it. Do not suffer your ego and fall prey to teaching a rule and when it does not work, ignoring it. She will wonder why and worse, wonder why you are leaving her in limbo.

That said, teaching behaviors and expectations is fun. Slaves do not want choice. They want to be heard, but enter the lifestyle looking for decisions and leadership. They are so incredible, they do not even demand perfection.

"Do something, anything, just don't give me a choice."

It is what tickles their fancy, moistens their knickers and pushes them to their knees. Teaching rules that apply to herself are important.

The critical initial decision is just how far to go in micro-managing her. Essentially that is what self-slave rules are – managing your slave. Many of course, associate TPE with micro-management, when in fact they are unrelated except by master choice. Micro-management though, is fun. It is a terrific technique to put a slave into a deep headspace of exactly who she is. It very effectively helps her feel submission. It is a small-dose tool though. Sustaining its practice over a length of time is both very impractical and very tedious. Good gawd, there is more to life than telling a slave when she can comb her hair. Use it as a tool, as an amusement, perhaps to teach, but beyond that, it becomes stifling.

To address rules for her though, consider the degree of micro-management you want and then establish rules to fit that goal. *"No master maintenance"* is again, a critical element of sustainable *master-slave* relationships, so design rules with that in mind too.

What rules you choose is wholly yours. No one can criticize. If it works for you and no one else, that is just fine. It works and that's all that matters. There are a myriad of rules to develop from and below is a small listing and explanation of some popular ones. Add and subtract at your leisure. Always consider the ramifications, workload, practicality, financial cost, maintenance and then teach them well. Enforce them even better. More than anything… have fun with them!

APPAREL

Start the fun right here.

By mere chance, luck of the draw, fate or happenstance, take what you will, I had the privilege many years ago, to play a round of golf with one of the legends of the game in Canada. He was an amateur with innumerable major victories to his credit, including an appearance at the Masters in Augusta, Georgia. He was by then in his 70's and from the back tees on a course hosting more than a dozen Canadian Opens, shot under his age. He was a remarkable man and a source of incredible knowledge.

Exploration of the lifestyle was only beginning back then. Having just met Wayne, I split time between the golf course and his home with his group. It was the *'learning years'*. Life lessons came relentlessly, from all directions and in unexpected ways. Playing golf that day, a casual remark, led to a lesson I could teach a slave in the years to come. It was new to me then, though now it is common.

Golf courses then, as many still today, had a dress code. Colorful polyesters were the rage of golf fashion in those days. But dressing up in lavender sansa-belt polyester slacks with white leather shoes and matching chartreuse golf bag was never my style. Watching Mike Weir win the Masters clad in all black works better for me. But, being me, stretching the staid autocratic rules of the golfing establishment seemed a noble purpose in life.

Waiting on the first tee, nervously paired with this legend, I needed small talk to break the ice and calm the nerves. Searching for anything to say, I blurted out some dumbass comment about his impeccable attire. He never turned toward me, just kept staring down the fairway in his own little world. Figuring he had not heard and about to try again, he pounced with a life lesson that stuck. Quietly, confidently he turned, smiled, looked me up and down and said, *"If you look good, you play good."*

He slaughtered me that day. I must have looked like hell.

And so it is for my slave.

"Look good, feel good, pet. Be who you are, an elegant lady, well dressed, well groomed, impeccable hygiene, and appropriate manners. You will serve better and be happier."

Rules for your slave's appearance and decorum definitely influence a slave's performance. She wants you proud of her. As master, of course, you are defining her path to meet your needs and standards. Insisting she look good makes it easier for everyone. Establishing an apparel rule is then a no-brainer. Do not misunderstand; she does not need to be June Cleaver vacuuming the living room in a cocktail dress, pearl necklace and high heels. Actually, writing that has given me an idea. I will be right back.

Well, it has been two hours, but I am back typing. I never did find any pearls; and the living room still needs a good vacuuming; but little old Juney-baby just got cleavered. She is laughing in the next room betting I will not write this into the book. Silly-assed slavegirl! How long before she learns never to bet a master, especially hers? Somehow, she does not think it fair that I can change the rules mid-bet. Well, look up *'fair'* in the Dom Manual darling, it says, *"fair – a word used by slaves to be silly."* But we have digressed, yet again.

A good rule regarding her apparel is simply this.

The slave's clothing will be selected and/or approved by Master.

There, all done. Clear and simple. Easily understood rules are a master's best friend. As simple as it seems though, it is a mouthful. Most will perceive it as a micro-management technique. Yet it best not be, if you want to maintain a consistent, livable lifestyle.

Popular opinion is that TPE relationships are about micro-management, yet they rarely are. Citing this rule is the argument often making the connection. On the surface, it appears to be an impractical example of TPE. But, like many rules, application of the rule is as important as the actual wording itself.

The rule clearly states master's intentions to control the slave's apparel. Ok, fair enough - on the surface. But does he want to tell her every morning what to wear? I dare say, some do, but not me. It is too boring and not being a fashion guru she would look silly in granny panties hoisted to her waist with a prominent cameltoe and baggy butt - but grant you that I may be in the minority. Application of the rule is really a question of wanting *"High Master Maintenance"*, or *"No Master Maintenance"*.

There are times I do want to select what she wears. Commonly those are evenings out of the house together, be they vanilla functions, or lifestyle events.

Now consider one reason this rule is important for the master, if not the slave. When social events call for more than jeans and a T-shirt, married vanilla men are subject to an inevitable and ugly situation at dressing time. Wifey is scurrying about, hair in curlers, clad in control top pantyhose, boobs flying about in a vicious attack on anything that gets in their way. They plaster on makeup while rushing to the closet holding dresses, then earnestly uttering the one thing hubby does not ever want to hear, in the honest, yet misguided expectation that he is some fashion god, which we know is patently untrue.

"Honey, should I wear this or this?" "Is this my color?" "Does this make my ass look fat?" (worse than I can ever tell you darling, he mumbles under his breath).

"Oh you are no help" and she scurries off, angry at everyone dangling a penis.

Now, while vanilla wife is turning hubby into Mr. Haute Couture, a task virtually guaranteed to fail, the master recognizes his utter lack of high fashion sense and tactical diplomacy. So, he controls his environment to avoid the no-win calamity in waiting. This characteristic is common among masters worldwide and easily identifies him in the lobbies of the world's most renowned fashion houses. It is evident to all. He simply does not put up with crap!

The earmark of good mastery, where there is the intent to clothing his slave, is a twinkle in his eye and some pre-scene preparation. Now, to the uncreative master, it is as simple as two sentences. *"Wear the blue dress,"* (never say black, she has forty-seven of those). That is followed by *"Yes Master".* There, the deed is done. Now that is almost as bad as putting up with vanilla wife's one act play.

But, for the more creative master, dressing your slave goes something like this.

Master: *"Tomorrow night we're going to the theatre with the Williams".*

slave: *"Yes Master, I recall and picked up the tickets this morning".*

Master: *"Goodgirl".*

slave: *"Have you a preference of what I should wear Sir?"*

Master: *"Yes, but I doubt lacing your labia rings together and running a chain through your nipple rings down to your clit and calling it a pantsuit will get us in."*

Sustained, nervous laughter from the slave, co-mingled with a thought of "oh shit, he's in the mood tonight."

slave: *"Oh Master, you are so clever"*

Slave is grabbed by the hair and forced over Master's knee.

Master: *"Aren't you the saucy little slavegirl tonight."*

A series of whacks heard followed by yelps, yips and moans. Two hours later the conversation resumes.

slave: *"Master, thank you. Do you have a preference for my attire tomorrow night?"*

Loud snoring is heard.

The following evening…

slave: *"Master do you have a preference for what I wear this evening?"*

Master: *"Wear the blue dress."*

slave: *"Yes Master".*

Ok… so that is one version of a typical apparel conversation, maybe not everyone's. However, there is sound reason to include the rule beside it being fun. Micro-management of a power is not necessary. Often, just as effective is the mere knowledge you have the power and can exercise it at your whim is enough to re-enforce belief in her slavery. This is a perfect example of that. The slave knows your wardrobe expectations. She is not stupid, nor do you think so. Have the confidence that she will present herself appropriately. Do so by expressing your tastes. Teach her, especially at the beginning. Select her clothing on a more regular basis, so she learns your tastes. As time progresses, she will know. Set the rule so she asks each day, then wave it off when you want. The act of asking is but another small piece of structure.

Controlling even the purchase of clothes can be managed and is a lot of fun. Surprise a few sales clerks and other shoppers. You are entitled into the change room with her, aren't you?

The ad hoc application of the rule is simple. Yes, control what she wears every day. Teach her to wear a skirt and blouse, or dress everyday – if she is with you. Do not ask, if she likes the rule, just do it. If she is away on business, who cares what she wears. You are not there to enjoy it anyway.

That is the ad hoc rule. The reality is such that when she arises and a dress is not appropriate, a quick *"Jeans today Master?"* is all it takes. A quick nod and she picks out the jeans she likes. No fuss, no muss, a quick nod and it is done. She learns what you like and wears it.

That said, there is no better look than a slave in leather cuffs and collar and one of my oversized dress shirts casually buttoned, hair in a ponytail and nothing else.

Emily Post wrote a wonderful article in the 1920's that both slaves and masters are wise to read and it is reprinted here.

The Old Gray Wrapper Habit

How many times has one heard someone say: "I won't dress for dinner, no one is coming in." Or, "That old dress will do!" Old clothes! No manners! And what is the result? One wife more wonders why her husband neglects her! Curious how the habit of careless manners and the habit of old clothes go together. If you doubt it, put the question to yourself: "Who could possibly have the manners of a queen in a gray flannel wrapper? And how many women really lovely and good, especially good, commit esthetic suicide by letting themselves slide down to where they "feel natural" in an old gray flannel wrapper, not only actually, but mentally.

The woman of charm in "company" is the woman of fastidiousness at home; she who dresses for her children and "prinks" for her husband's home-coming, is sure to greet them with greater charm than she who thinks whatever she happens to have on is "good enough." Any old thing good enough for those she loves most! Think of it! A certain very lovely lady whose husband is quite as much her lover as in the days of his courtship, has never in twenty years allowed him to watch the progress of her toilet, because of her determination never to let him see her except at her prettiest. Needless to say, he never meets anything but "prettiest" manners either. No matter how "out of sorts" she may be feeling, his key in the door is a signal for her to "put aside everything that is annoying or depressing," with the result that wild horses couldn't drag his attention from her, all because neither she nor he has ever slumped into the gray flannel wrapper habit.

So many people save up all their troubles to pour on the one they most love, the idea being, seemingly, that no reserves are necessary between lovers. Nor need there be really. But why, when their house looks out upon a garden that has charming vistas, must she insist on his looking into the clothes-yard and the ash-can? She who complains incessantly that this is wrong, or that hurts, or any other thing worries or vexes her, so that his inevitable answer to her greeting is, "I'm so sorry, dear," or "That's too bad," or "Poor darling, it's a shame," is getting mentally into a gray flannel wrapper! If something is seriously wrong, if she is really ill, that is different. But of the petty things that are only remembered in order to be told to gain sympathy, beware! There is a big deposit of sympathy in the bank of love, but don't draw out little sums every hour or so, so that by and by, when perhaps you need it badly, it is all drawn out and you yourself don't know how or on what it was spent.

All that has been said to warn a wife from slovenly habits of mind or dress may be adapted to apply with equal force in suggesting a rule for husbands. A man should always remember that a woman's regard for him is founded on her impressions when seeing him at his best. Even granting that she has no great illusions about men in general, he at his best is at least an approximation to her ideal; and it is his chief duty never to fall below the standard he set for himself in making his most cogent appeal. Consequently he should continue through the years to be scrupulous about his personal appearance and his clothes, remembering the adage that the most successful marriages are those in which both parties to the contract succeed in "keeping up the illusion." It is of importance also that he refrain from burdening his wife with the cares and worries of his business day. Many writers insist that the wife should be ready to receive a complete consignment of all his troubles when the husband comes home at the end of the day. It is a sounder practice for him to save her as much as possible from the trials of his business hours; and, incidentally, it is the best kind of mental training for him to put all business cares behind him as he closes the door of his office and goes home. When it is said that a husband should not fling all the day's trifling annoyances into the lap of his wife without reflecting that she may have some cares of her own, there is no intention to indicate that a wife should not have a thorough understanding of her husband's affairs. Complete acquaintance and sympathy with his work is one of the foundation stones of the domestic edifice.

Emily Post

A rule included in many *Master-Slave Contracts* involves the wearing of panties, more specifically, the non-wearing of them. It is popular among those in the lifestyle. Many consider it a *Core Value Expectation* and include it in their *Contract*. As a slave ages though, it becomes impractical, thus is better suited as a *House Rule*. The rule simply states:

NO panties, or thongs will be worn by slave unless in slacks, jeans or shorts, or if in the monthly menstrual period. Slave will only wear pantyhose when specifically approved by Master. Slave will not wear other than a skirt, or dress without permission.

What a wonderfully sexy and feminine rule that is so simply adapted to everyday living. No master maintenance here so let her wear dresses for awhile. Knowing your slave is naked and available will have her soaked.

THE PURSE

The rules for personal attention vary with health and needs, but some are relatively universal. Others are just flat out amusing. A great place to begin addressing these issues is right where it counts most, right at her core, that temple of womanhood: her purse!

You know coming into the relationship, a woman's purse has everything in it but the kitchen sink. Granted, there are things in there men have no knowledge of and, were they ever found in a time capsule, would puzzle generations for eons to come. The dark mysteries of a slave's purse notwithstanding, the right is yours to add to the collection, and by gawd, we will!

The first rule is more a beg than a rule, though dominants have trouble even begging to differ. Just, please, do not ever show us what is in there. That is *"Purse Rule One"*. We do not know what that crap is anyway. The second rule is that in addition to every woman's essential necessities of life, like lipstick, eye shadow and a panty-liner (yes, slaves, we know what they are), she will, at all times, carry with her a package of *Kleenex*. We know that is no big deal for most women, but hold your knickers, we have not got to the good part yet.

Then she needs at least one *latex glove* (and a clever slave will ensure it fits her master); one *latex condom*, (for the girl who has everything), and one small tube of a water-based *personal lubricant*. It does not matter whether its KY jelly, Astro-glide, Anal-eze or Oral-gel for that matter, because this rule is not about the master, it is for her! All these, she should be able to produce from her purse at any time you demand.

This is a nice rule not requiring punishment when found delinquent. Ask her for lube and she gets the *"deer-in-the-headlights look"*, you will know this one's for you. Yank her by the hair and bend her over.

"No problem, girl. No fuss. No muss. No maintenance and, oh - No lube."

"Oink for me little piggy, you're about to get ass-stuffed."

She will always remember this rule in future. Bummer eh!

STANDING

Another livable *House Rule* governing appropriate behavior is to prohibit her standing directly in front of you. It is certainly not hard to learn and in a day or two, it will be habit. It is also deliciously invisible to the vanilla eye. There is sound rational behind this rule. Standing in front, facing a person is considered a *"peer position"* traditionally adopted among equals. It is also interpreted as a confrontational and challenging position. That can certainly be the case for a slave. By explaining and banning such behaviors, your slave continually lives her reality, that it is not her position to challenge her master, either verbally or physically. That is not the nature nor within the scope of your relationship. Then expand the rule to include prohibition for her standing directly in front of any known dominant. Most dominants today will miss the subliminal respect accorded, but traditionalists will appreciate the training you provided.

NECK HUGS

Along the same vein as standing in front of dominants, teach your slave that putting her arms around your neck is verboten. Many demonstrative slaves love to greet dominant friends with a lovely warm hug and the sentiment while appreciated, is lost if she hugs your neck. I absolutely forbid it from any slave whether I own her or not. The practice stems from wrestling classes back in high school. Now, I was never much of a wrestler. It was a mandatory Phys-Ed class and I was out of there as fast as the parole came through. Rubbing my sweaty body against another sweaty man's body while wearing spandex was not the intimacy I sought in those days, or come to think of it since either. The first lesson of wrestling is that to control another's body, you must control his head. Where the head goes, the body follows. The body-part that controls the head is of course, the neck.

Well, how more appropriate rule could there be in the lifestyle? The slave does not control the master's neck. He controls hers. That is why slaves love their hair pulled, or taken by the back of the neck and why a collar is the symbol of ownership. A slave instinctually knows her body must follow and thus submits. Conversely, grabbing the master's neck is an action banned for slaves. She is not permitted control, even subliminally. The exception is if in the throes of lovemaking, in the heat of passion, if she flings her arms around your neck, well then, take it as a compliment. She is out of her mind in passion and you caused it, cut her some slack Big Boy. In other circumstances though, it is a no-go mission.

ORGASMS

"Go ahead, pet, arouse yourself. Tweak your nipples and rub your pussy. Use a vibrator, the running water from the bathtub, hop on the Sybian, oil yourself up, bring yourself right to the edge anyway you want. Go for it pet, diddle yourself silly, drive yourself nuts. Any time, anywhere, if that floats your boat. I so spoil you."

She beamed like a kid in a candy shop.

"But, under no circumstances will you orgasm without permission. Masturbation to climax is forbidden. In fact, just because you are so special and I love you dearly, all orgasms are forbidden without my specific permission. Clear enough pet? Was that a groan I heard?"

A very common rule many lifestyle masters use is prohibiting their slave from achieving orgasm without permission. He controls her pleasure. It is a common rule because it is easy and directly links to control of her body, one of the *Three Powers*.

A longtime friend, Charles, a master with a lovely slave living the master-slave niche, is the only master I know who does not enforce this rule. He cannot. He wants to, he just cannot. It is beyond him, and it is hilarious. He is like a smoker trying repeatedly to quit, he just cannot. It's just not within him to deprive her of that pleasure.

He has told his slave for years, countless times in fact, he will decide when she cums. Then he succumbs. Immediately the next time she is aroused he just cannot bring himself to deny her. He gets so frustrated with himself and vows next time for sure. But we know he is delusional. His slave just smiles quietly. She knows, and it is the funniest damn thing to watch. It does not help, of course, that we call him *"Nilla-boy"* but in fact, he is a terrific master with wonderful consistent structure, but with this one idiosyncrasy.

For several hours now, the party raged. Good food, good weather, great masters and lovely slaves on a wooded tract of land isolated from prying eyes. Some bottoms were already well welted, and for several slaves, sitting would be uncomfortable in the coming week. The dominant talent present was at its creative finest.

The Dungeon had been busy since noon and the host was pleased. It had just been fitted with new solid maple suspension beams triangulating one corner.

Walking in, the host chuckled to himself. It was no surprise to see the DevilDom Dennis was using a slave. He was at his dervish best again. Standing below the center beam, he had bound her hands overhead. There was certainly nothing was unusual there. She was naked and moaning. With Dennis in control, that was nothing unusual either. What was unusual, and not seen before was the stretchy latex tubing tied off to the ceiling beam in front and behind the slave. How devilish that she was being forced to straddle the elastic tube. It stretched tightly between her legs, parting her lips, a knot against her clit and another pressing into her bottom. It was fully stretched and taut, stimulating her at even the slightest movement. She was moaning hard as the host settled in to watch.

From her appearance, she looked to have been enduring intense stimulation for some time now. Marble hard nipples and a brow damp with perspiration exposed the intensity of her arousal.

She was an experienced slave, trained well and would not cum without permission. The host had seen her endure hours of intense arousal without relief many times before. She had wonderful self-discipline. Despite begging for release, she would not cum without her trigger. Dennis looked up and grinned.

"Let's see what she can endure", he smirked.

Grabbing the crop, he started, but didn't beat her. With flamboyant precision DevilDom began striking the tubing above her head. Erratic, pulsing vibrations rippled down into her pussy. It was a seriously nasty thing to do to a slave already heated and moaning to cum. She would be begging soon.

"Tell me how long she makes it: and the host headed out the door to his other guests and to find his own slave.

He found her in the sunroom giggling. A half naked slave was turning her tits into mice, drawing whiskers and faces around her pink nosed nipples.

He laughed, "My little tit-mouse."

It was on an hour later when he returned to the dungeon to see the results of the Rubber-Rope-Trick. DevilDom was still there and so was the poor slave. She was prone on the hardwood floor. He entered quietly. DevilDom was standing over her with his trusty riding crop. He smiled down at the slave, now splayed out naked with both hands digging in her crotch. Primal moans flowed from her throat. She was flying in an overwhelming need to cum. He had been edging her for ninety minutes.

"Well, it's our Host this evening", DevilDom said to her. He viscously cropped her nipples again to make sure she was paying attention..

"Keep your fingers moving girl! Stay there. Right there on the edge. Hold, hold, hold it!"

Turning to the host he said, "I told her the next person through the door would decide when she could cum. Do you mind?"

He was smirking.

Looking down at the writhing slave, the host smiled. "Well, she looks cooked, basted and ready to serve."

She moaned barely above a whisper, "Please, please let me cum."

Not to be overindulgent, the host winked at the DevilDom.

Well, I need a drink before deciding girl. I will be back in five minutes. Be ready or you won't cum at all this weekend."

The scream of frustration was torturous to the ears but he left her under the tender care of DevilDom's crop. Her swollen nipples were mercilessly beaten again.

It was fifteen minutes before he returned and she was still on the floor, fingers still burrowing, her arousal still maddeningly on the brink. DevilDom was still exercising his wonderful patience and relentless sadism. Her nipples were still inflamed under the crop.

The host moved like a pouncing cat and was suddenly imposing his weight on her chest, straddling her, resting his crotch on her chin.

"Now bitch", he screamed into her face.

"Now or you will be covered in piss in ten seconds" and he moved up and sat on her face.

She exploded violently, making a hideously painful screech and she came.

It was an hour later, at dinner that the host grabbed her by the hair. "You didn't even realize I was still fully clothed did you girl?"

She looked down unable to hold his gaze.

"No Sir, I just heard "piss" and then everything went black."

A concern heard frequently from slaves new to the lifestyle is concern for this rule. The thought of orgasm control excites them, yet fear their libido will not be sated terrifies them.

Providing sexual pleasure without having their own needs met, too easily reminds them of their vanilla past. Address this concern with her. Assure her that while indeed her pleasure is controlled, and she does not have the privilege to cum when she wants, nor needs to, you have a secret solution for her. Then, if you are like me, just walk away, but hey, I am a sadistic prick that way.

Ok, so do not walk away. Kneel her down and explain that she can arouse herself and in fact, masturbate as often as she likes, so long as she does not cum. Let that hang in the air awhile, let her stew over it, then throw her a smirk and let her in on a little dominant secret.

"Pet, all I can assure you is that while you cannot orgasm without permission and you will undergo training in that, you will cum more than vanilla women. You just don't know when."

She is getting exactly what she wants and needs. She is going to be the slut you want of her. Likely, she will want to prove it to you, right then and there.

A quick check of her panties will assure you she understood. Now, if this is your first meeting ever with her, then you can only assume she has panties on. Do not fall into the wannabe trap and tell her she cannot have any for a first meeting. That is presumptive nonsense, assuming powers not offered. If she asks why you do not insist she be bare, smile, lean in closely and whisper to her…

"Because pet, I want you to offer them. I want to see your eyes, your soul and your blushing cheeks when you present them from your knees, in all their glorious dampness."

Then casually mention about *"trigger"* training, cumming on command and eventually, without being touched. She will not believe you, of course. She will assume it is one of the *"myths of BDSM"*, but that is her issue. You will have a little surprise waiting for her down the road.

GROWING INTELLECTUALLY & SOCIALLY

The slave mindset represents her core needs as a slave and the *SODS Principle* examined that essential part of her personality. But it is not all she is. She is most healthy when enjoying a balanced life that explores all the world has to offer. She does so of course, from the foundation of your personal relationship. There is a rule that directs her to understanding the importance of balance.

You want a healthy slave and her outside interests are fun and interesting for you both. Encourage them, in fact, insist on them, particularly to develop friendships outside the lifestyle, as well as within. Spirituality is a large part of many people's lives and co-exists in the master-slave lifestyle without conflict. Again, ensure rules direct her to maintain and grow those interests and give her the time and economic resources to fulfill them. A rule, or series of rules guiding this aspect of her life works.

> *You are encouraged and given the opportunity and resources to maintain and expand yourself intellectually, spiritually and socially. Membership in Civic organizations, Charity work, hobby interest groups and friendships are important and your involvement pleases me. Becoming involved requires permission.*

There are countless *"Self"* Rules you can design for your slave. They cannot all be listed here. Realize their purpose though. Thoughtfully construct them understanding the basis evolves from the *Three Powers*. Their real beauty lies in knowing what they achieve. They create exactly the home and slave you want. They nurture her headspace in tangible ways. Most importantly, they are practical without reducing your relationship to a level of unsustainable micro-management. At the same time though, they do provide more than adequate structure and tangible, real aspects to her life that reflect your wishes through her behavior.

YOU (THE MASTER)

Master-slavery, to hear the critics, is not about you, so skip this part.

Oh wait - it is about you, the critics are merely irrelevant. So perhaps it is best to read on.

"You" rules. What an interesting concept.

Does that mean they are selfish? You bet.

Does it mean there are many? Oh, believe it!

It seems a little too personal, is it necessary? No. Of course, it is not necessary. Do not do it if you lack interest, or it seems invasive. Just demand perfect service, assuming your slave knows all about you. Demand openness and honesty from her, but you need not offer the same. She is just a slave you know - meat, chattel, sub-human. It is crazy to think she wants to know the details of how best to serve and make you happy. Keep her in the dark. Blindfold her with your insecurities.

Fellas, we are past talking about structure. It is time to put rubber to the road, to separate the talkers from the walkers. Ask yourself if you really are a master and will make the effort to be a damned good one, or are your needs grounded in sexual fantasy? Are you are prepared to give her the tools to really make your life together special, by recognizing her real need for all encompassing slavery and the work that entails for you? If so, then you need to get selfish, take the time, do not grumble about the workload, and teach her about yourself - in fine intimate detail!

Yes, it takes effort. So does fucking her and that never stopped us. The results are just too glorious. Besides, most everyone will tell you that masters are arrogant bastards who think the world revolves around them. Since we are labeled as narcissistic asshats anyway, we may as well get the benefits. We will make it about us, and what better display of arrogance, than to talk about ourselves and what we want.

Now, it is pointless to itemize the unlimited personal idiosyncrasies we all have. Each though, can manifest itself as a rule, so we are all going to have vastly different *House Rules*. Make as many as you want. It only affects your happiness.

Many people, including some dominants, live *a glass half-empty* outlook on life. To those folk this will be an exercise for naught, for they wish it that way. For those seeing the bigger picture, who are indeed masters of their domain, itemizing specifics of your personal happiness, is not just selfishly important, but enables contribution and service by your slave. Decide what you like, teach it, record it and then enjoy it. She will do her damnedest to ensure you smile, for that is her joy.

So we are at the gist of it. You want a slave to please and serve, and she wants nothing more than to do just that. So all the hullabaloo about master oaths, slave mindsets, power, rituals, kinky sex and S&M are nice, but it really comes down to teaching her about yourself. It is time to get down and dirty and teach her the fine details of daily routines, silly quirks and personal habits. Take control of your household, become *Lord of the Manor* and *King of the Castle*. It is your home, complete with a slave, now make it exactly how you want it.

No more chintz sofas and flowery wallpaper. No more over-priced interior decorators telling you the pink carpet is really coral. No more pantyhose hanging from the shower curtain rod. Wait, skip that one, pantyhose was banned. No more hunting for a lost sock or, finding shoes unpolished as you head to an important business meeting. All that is gone!

You need a litany of *House Rules* that are only about you and your castle. They are uniquely yours, never wrong and not subject to negotiation. The range and details are your choice. Having more, rather than less, is a good thing, bearing in mind, the more tools she has to please you, the happier the home.

From the obvious to the mundane, make rules for everything. Where do you want your golf clubs stored? Do you like a glass of ice water presented when you arrive from work? Should the bathroom tissue unroll from the back, or front, if that matters to you, it all gets recorded and taught. Spare no detail you think is relevant and important. Where do you want your shoes kept, what football team do you like, how hot to make the chicken wings, that you prefer Advil to Tylenol, and most importantly, that you do not want to feel teeth during a blow job. Oh my goodness, the detail!

Well, fear not, there is no need to do all that – you have already done it. It is the *"Me List"* and it is evolving and growing as you do.

"You" rules are simply a reflection of the *"Me List"*, which you created and likely are still creating. Moreover, you likely always will be. Use the entries and teach them at the appropriate time. Record them in the appropriate *Record Binder* and presto, all done, snap, crackle, pop! How easy was that?

In time, your *Me List* merges to become a major component of your *House Rules*. All the fine detail about you is contained right there and by compiling it as a living document, it has saved you enormous amounts of work. She wants to know everything about you and you have the tool to do just that. The result is a very happy slave and a very well serviced master.

Now, surely you are thinking, that appears terribly selfish, arrogant and one-sided. Perhaps it is. However, perhaps it is exactly why she is with you.

She will have suggestions too. Use them. Allow her to contribute. She can and will have useful suggestions, so incorporate those, understanding she is contributing, not deciding.

It is obvious in presenting the niche this book endorses, that the *master-slave* dynamic places great respect and consideration for the slave's needs, wants and happiness. While she is owned and chattel, if not legally, then by choice; quality mastery always recognize her humanity. We work hard to ensure she is strong, able and capable. We provide every opportunity for her to thrive and succeed in meeting life goals. We encourage her ambitions and pursuit of happiness.

Nevertheless, understand, *master-slave*ry is not all about her. It is about you. You are the alpha dominant partner in the relationship. She is with you because of this, so ensure things run as you want. She has a voice, rules and a *protocol* to express her needs, but you are the Boss. Be selfish, just do not be inconsiderate. Make your rules and enforce them.

MIND FUCK #27 –" THE AMBULANCE"

He had not been to a public fetish night for years because they had grown into something anathema to his practice of the lifestyle. The frivolity and casual adherence to protocols miffed him. He stood on hierarchy, respected others rules and expected no less. That politics, malicious gossip and judgmental analysis of what occurred was incessantly debated on mail lists subsequent to the party, offended his sense of privacy. Confidence born of experience and knowledge was confused with arrogance and the subtle, but profound difference was lost on many only acquainted with him. His friends and peers understood the difference, so for years he had not attended. Tonight that would change. Tonight it was time to squick the newbies!

If they wanted to gossip and condemn, to 'gentle' the lifestyle to be virtually indistinguishable from vanilla, he would give them some meat for the mill. The local scene needed a good headshake. He was happy to put the rabbit in the puppy's mouth and let them break its neck.

For weeks he planned the scene meticulously. It had taken some expense and effort, but surely would be worth the work. It was set, his friends lined up, instruction received and understood. Cell phones were fully charged and the props in place. Tonight would be special. It was said he specialized in mind fucks, well, tonight he would mind fuck the BDSM community. He smirked, this would be fun.

The master's pal, Dennis-The-DevilDom was already inside the club. He had reserved the hanging chains in the play area and all was ready. The fet nite had been in progress for ninety minutes and the turnout was big. The club was full. Play had begun and people mingled, watched and socialized. The time was right, the phone call made to the parking lot.

It was not often he dressed in full leathers, and rarer still when the slave entered hooded and leashed. That she was anonymous to anyone noticing them was planned. Her identity was secret. The hood had only a mouth opening and breathing holes, but otherwise encased her head in leather. Her part in the scene was not really part of the mind fuck he was pulling off, but her role was critical. He was going to use her without mercy, hard, the old fashioned way. She had endured intense S&M before, so knew what was coming. She gave not a rat's ass about the scene he was pulling off for the audience, she was totally focused on what she knew lay before her. She began to drop in the car when hooded and it continued when led inside. Submission was raging in her soul as she focused on this master and what was coming. She trusted him with her life and would obey, follow where he led, peaceful and fulfilled, but she knew this would be difficult.

Marching directly into the play area, DevilDom and his slave awaited. They took his coat and the Devil-Dom's slave unpacked the Insanity Bag (Toy Bag) as previously instructed. Without delay or ceremony, he grabbed the slave's arms and tethered her into suspension cuffs, attaching them to the overhead chains. He spread her legs and lashed them to floor bolts. Fully secured, she was in place, immobilized and defenseless. He worked quickly wanting a no-nonsense, professional tone to the scene. This was intended to show what master-slavery was and is, could be, maybe even should be again. Responsible S&M was not for the quivering, timid or faint of heart.

The others withdrew and from the corner of his eye he could see people gathering to watch. Already a sense this would be different was racing through the crowd. Interest was piqued. Grabbing the machete first, he started. Within moments she stood bound, now naked, her clothes a ruined mess at her feet. The effect was immediate. Her head bobbed. She was dropping fast.

"Good" he thought, she needs to endure this one. This would be a "Me" scene, with no ramping (warmup). The pain would be excruciating until she was gone. But, that was the point. It had to be this style to pull off the mind fuck.

He stalked her for some moments, growling, letting her feel the heat from his body. A hand smothered her face and she struggled to breathe. Continuing the stalk, whip in hand, he suddenly kicked her with the soul of his boot, then with staccato pace, began slapping at her, barehanded, constantly growling, letting her know where he was. Her arms, thighs, cunt and tits were turning pink from the hard spanks, but he kept up the torrid pace. Normally rhythm helped her float, anticipating what was coming and where, but this was entirely different. The rhythm was in the speed, but where he hit her was random. The effect was deadly and he knew she was gone before he even unfurled the whip. Unfurl it he did though and began a ruthless assault on her back and buttocks. There was nothing gentle or considerate about it. He had chosen an eight foot bullwhip, one without a cracker. This would not be a flicking singletail sting, it was a good old-fashioned horse whipping. The skill on display would be apparent to those knowledgeable of whips, to the newbies though, it would have a brutalizing, traumatizing effect. He could hear gasps from the crowd and other scenes stopped.

He swung with ferocity. Long welts rose immediately across her back. She cried out at the first few, then moans and finally nothing. He swung hard and relentlessly. In short order her back and buttocks were a bloody pulp and he could see the Dungeon Monitors moving in for the kill. But this too was anticipated and while he continued the whipping, his friends surrounded the DM's distracting them with placating words. They would not be stalled long, so he finished quickly. She hung limp, her head resting on her shoulder, her legs having given out much earlier. She shivered occasionally and if he did not hurry, the convulsions would start while she still hung like a slab of beef. The scene was brutal. It was tough, hardcore S&M and most would have never seen it before. He knew where the slave was, she was fine, flying so deep it would be an hour before she opened her eyes again. But there was still much to do before then.

Standing before her, he looked quizzically into her eyes. With a cocked head he sensed something was wrong - very wrong. Two pals came rushing over on his signal and began unfastening her ankles as he released the wrists. Grabbing her under the arms, they gently lowered her to a blanket and all three crouched around her. He took her pulse and in a flash had his cell phone out dialing. Concern was written all over their faces. Gently slapping her face, she did not move. It was not but a few moments when the EMS crew arrived. They took charge immediately, shooing everyone back while assessing the prone slave. The crowd formed a semi-circle now and many slaves were covering their mouths in concern and fear. A hush had grown over the venue. The EMS crew was efficient and fast. They knew a critical situation and without delay an IV was in the girl's arm and she was moved to a stretcher. In a matter of moments they were gone. She was wheeled out to the ambulance and loaded. Her master was permitted in as well and the last thing he *saw as the doors swung shut was the crowd spilling out into the parking lot, gasping, watching and somewhat terrified.*

Her eyes opened to the smiling face of her master. It took a moment for them to focus, but then she saw the others too. DevilDom and his slave were looking down at her, as were the ambulance attendants. Everyone was smiling.

"Welcome back pet. You were marvelous. It worked to a charm and you were spectacular." She smiled weakly and everyone laughed, exchanging hi-fives. Only the six of them and the two event organizers knew the scam that was pulled off. They were all in the ambulance, sitting in a dark parking lot several blocks from the club. For thirty minutes they had been sitting, waiting for her to come back. That she was fine was a given, she had never been in trouble. With a few bottles of beer passed around, everyone started to laugh as the stories flowed of what people saw in the crowd during the scene. The master had called on some friends who were EMS specialists and they rented an ambulance for the night to pull off the charade. No IV had actually gone into the slave, just the drip line taped to her arm.

It had been a mind fuck of monumental proportions and by morning the mail lists would be on fire with condemnations and judgmental arrogance. It would be beautiful to watch as the community fought and argued over what they had seen. They would let it ride for a few days, staying mum until the fury ran its course. Then the coup d'gras could be administered. The community would learn a lesson in maturity. In the meantime, it was time to head home and have a party.

Postscript:

In the introduction to this book, I promised only to use true stories throughout. This is the exception. It is entirely a fabrication. This scene has yet to be done, but it is coming. It is too delicious to neglect.

Who says you cannot mind fuck the BDSM community… and for that matter, you the reader!

8

RITUALS & PROTOCOLS

Repeated actions of slave behavior demanded by voice, signal or situation are *rituals*. Developing and using them is a great joy for many *master-slave* couples. They also provide some of the most tangible aspects of structure that allow a slave to feel your rules, your control, and her submission.

Many folks view *rituals* as part of the fantasy *master-slave* world and undoubtedly restrict the benefit of ritualized behavior as just that, good fun in a role-play setting. However, the purpose of including them here is that to understand structure, a core slave need, and recognize that structure is composed of *rules, protocols* and *rituals*. Structure is nothing more. *Rituals* are physically real for a slave and thus serve to re-enforce her submission. They work when used consistently. They are not a game and are not presented as such. Nor are they fantasy. Herein are some that I enjoy but they are not set in stone for every master. As always - keep what you like and leave the rest.

Rituals come in countless flavors, each tailored to your individual needs. They reflect the style of dominance you prefer and can be as elaborate, or simple as you choose. Some masters even prefer to exclude *rituals* from their slave's life. They want a more direct approach to obedience, preferring to command her differently each time. For example, *"Kneel and open your legs pet"* is a command often ritualized. Some masters they could care less about how the slave does it, as long as she obeys. If he wants her legs together, he just tells her rather than developing, teaching and remembering a *ritual* command.

Others use elaborately taught and memorized word or hand commands for each *ritual*, often with a number of related variations of each. Hours and hours of teaching, training, memorization and practice goes into them. Masters employing them enjoy the physical interaction, deriving great pleasure from the tangible control of his slave. Some of these *rituals* and their variations are very complicated becoming not unlike an intricate slave ballet. Even an outsider observing these complex *rituals* though, can appreciate the training involved. Executing her *rituals* to others is both graceful and elegant and a compliment to the efforts of her master.

However, whether you choose to incorporate *rituals* or not, neither style is better than the other. They are just different ways of expressing the *master-slave* dynamic and whichever style you choose, it will be right for you. Understanding she needs structure and that *rituals* are part of structure is all that matters. Excluding any physical impairment a slave may have (and bad knees are common), there are four factors to consider when developing your *protocols*.

Consistency & Maintenance
Practicality
Slave Headspace
Boredom

Whatever *protocols* you develop, teaching them is fun, be they simple or complex, so spice it up, teach, practice and create some intimacy as she learns. The strength of your *protocols* become evident once training is over and they are incorporated into your daily life. That is the true test if they are what you envisioned. If they are not of course, then change them. That is your prerogative and do not take any slave sass about *"wasted effort"*, or *"a dom not knowing what he wants"*. If she complains about the hours spent learning a complex *protocol* just to have it tossed out, well that is just too damned bad. *"Suck it up princess"* and a cold night in a cage might temper her displeasure, refocusing her mind on who she is. However, I digress.

A theme throughout this trilogy of books is that mastery is not for the lazy. While true, it also needs saying, that mastery cannot be onerous or oppressive on a master's time. If you are careful in designing your *rituals*, minimal maintenance is required. People generally prefer to create things rather than maintain them and this applies for *Rituals* as well. Creating is natural and fun while maintenance is not, at least for me. Creating is where it is at. Yet in the *master-slave* world, maintenance of structure is crucial to success. So to bridge the *"create vs. maintain"* paradox, use simplified *rituals*. Simple *rituals* not only avoid unnecessary maintenance for you, but also influence how often they are used. She needs some *rituals* to feel her submission and she needs them used regularly.

Here then is a critical factor for developing your *protocols*. Wise, successful, long-term masters have all developed *rituals* creating the minimum amount of work for themselves. Now at first blush, some slaves reading this might think, *'Well is not that just typical of dominants, making us do all the work, the lazy sods'*. Making that conclusion is so wrong as to be into the realm of the absurd. That thinking displays their naiveté.

Ask a slave what she prefers, detailed complicated *rituals* that are beautiful but take time and focus to accomplish and by their complexity diminish the frequency of use, or a simple elegant *ritual*, used frequently, that takes little work from the master, but is easily learned and becomes a seamless part of their everyday life. If she chooses the first, explain the meaning of *"Tough, too bad, you have no vote. I want your submission to last"* It is a no-brainer.

Too many fantasy books and the spillover from online *master-slave* role-playing games have resulted in a tendency to over-create *rituals*, making them dramatic statements of good intentions, but poor reality. The last thing a master wants to create is a *ritual* for his slave to get a cup of coffee that results in a symphony of contortionist dance moves with a slave clad in flowing silks. Add in a ponytail plug hanging out her ass, bells dangling from pierced nipples perfectly tolling Ravel's Bolero, served in a coffee cup soaked with rank pussy juice freshly swabbed between her legs after a long day at the office, served from her knees while impaled on a Sybian, and, well, you get the picture. It ain't reality.

Now lest you think there is no maintenance involved in that *protocol*, think again. Good mastery is consistent attention to detail, rules and structure. It is what a master does. In simply asking for a cup of coffee, that *ritual* has condemned him, by his own words and oath, to ensure she follows the *ritual* correctly.

Try to follow along here. First he asks for the coffee. Then he waits while she peels off her jeans; climb into her silks, slaps the bells on her tits, tunes them and run the buttplug up her ass. She will want to comb out the plug's horsehair, not daring to present herself with messy hair even if it is coming out her ass. Then it is onto diddling her puss to get some juice, fetch the Sybian from the closet, plug it in, add the attachment, dial it up, get herself impaled, then and only then, realize she forgot the freaking coffee and is out of cream.

Now she has to get into her jeans again, get the car out of the garage, run to the ATM machine to get some cash before grabbing cream from the store and racing home to begin the whole thing all over. Now, one little mistake, one innocent tiny variance from this painstakingly taught *ritual* and of course he needs to stop her, correct the behavior, re-teach and then punish her for disobedience. After that and assuming she finally has it right, conservatively some two to three hours later... presto, a lovely cup of stone cold coffee for her wonderful fucking master!

Did I mention above slaves would appreciate masters with simple no maintenance *protocols*? There is method to our madness slave girls. Gentlemen, just have her bring the coffee and serve it with two hands. Mission accomplished. Fresh hot coffee and a *ritual* he can quickly observe she obeyed in the blink of an eye.

Create simple, useful low maintenance *rituals*. You will thank me later, or your slaves will.

The next factor to consider is the practicality of your *protocol*.

We stood patiently waiting. Patrick, my slave and I stood quietly expecting his slave's overdue arrival.

From around the corner came a flurry of motion and finally, breathlessly she arrived immediately dropping to her knees to greet as trained. Extending her arms around his legs, she leaned forward and kissed his boots saying "I am here to serve you Master".

How beautiful I thought, kneeling before her Master in elegant supplication, her words spoken from the heart. Patrick's faced conveyed the pleasure that her greeting entailed and the glowing complexion of one mortally embarrassed human being.

He wished with all his heart, that as she knelt respectfully as so arduously taught, that he had been a little more thoughtful and applied some context to the

Ritual. He was quite sure that standing in the lobby of the theater waiting for the movie with a slave around his legs while being gaggled over by hundreds of men, women and children and one cute Goth girl, like some freaks from another planet, that the Ritual was out of place. Some re-thinking was needed, especially if all he would get from her was the blind, unhesitant, obedience that he demanded.

Well, at least suburbia would be talking about them now. And there was always the benefit of seeing the Goth chick's nipples harden the minute the slave's ass was stuck in the air.

The lesson illustrated so poignantly above is not Patrick's failure to develop a terrific *ritual*, but in not anticipating the environment it may be used. While appropriate in a private setting or among lifestyle friends, the *protocol* was just not suitable for public consumption. His slave obeyed, there is no criticism of her. Patrick simply had not thought through the practicality of his wishes. Some folks may think the greeting, even done before children, is not offensive. If that is your view, then so be it. Most people, myself included though, respect the general public and are hesitant, if not downright intolerant of imposing our lifestyle on others to whom it might be offensive. There is no need. On the other hand, a little threesome with that obviously aroused cute little *"Goth-chick-slave-to-be-if-I-get-my-paws-on-her"* could not hurt. But again I digress.

What *rituals* you decide for your slave is your business. Many new masters however, are unaware of what they are or can be. So, here are some choices, how to teach them, there effect and why they are used. Steal the ones you like, alter or expand them or do not use them at all. The choice is yours. It is no skin off my ass. But, the ones you do use, have fun teaching and more fun using them.

The easiest way to develop *rituals* is to separate the choices into two categories. Many *rituals* build on one another so *"Positioning Rituals"* need teaching first. Once complete, use them to develop *"Behavior Rituals"* afterwards. The goal is to keep it simple and use them frequently. Start with the basics and as the years go by, if you want to develop more sophistication then do it. Always remember, that simplicity creates beauty, a great headspace for the slave, and instills a behavior you enjoy. Remember too, the fundamental purpose of *rituals*. You are creating structure for her that is essential to the master-slave dynamic.

Position Rituals	Behavior Rituals	
Formal Kneel	Greeting Master	Entering a room
Relaxed Kneel	Focus	Leaving a room
Formal Stand	Requesting Discussion	Body Inspection
Begging	Begging	Punishment
Pleasure	Use	Presenting Items
Bend'N'Brace	Bedtime	
Inspection	Wakeup	
Humility	Coffee	
Bend	Shaving	
OTK	Scene Protocol	
Breeding	Leashed	
Boots	Greeting Dominants	
Her Place	Speech Restriction	

Before exploring *body positions* and *behavior rituals*, a word about specific word commands used to order *rituals*. The key to sustainable structure is *'no maintenance'*. There must be no bad or, unnecessary work for the master. That is the law. You have enough responsibility managing two lives without piling useless crap on top of it all. Rigid adherence to specific word commands to exact a specified behavior is useless crap. It might sound pretty, but it is a major pain in the ass. Do not self-impose this but if you must, keep it to a minimum. If you are the Sultan's Harem Keeper with nothing to do but train slaves, then fine, go for it. Unless you are the quintessential detail freak with an elephant memory, it actually ends up destructive to your relationship.

Using specific word and/or signal commands requires that you memorize the exact wording taught for each and every act you want. Bored yet? Failure to use the command you have trained her to listen for, does two things. Either, she becomes confused and unsure what you want, thus not achieving the result, or you give the perception of being unable to follow even your own rules. Neither is good, but that last perception is a disaster waiting to happen. Under no circumstances do you want her thinking you lack self-discipline. Questioning your commitment, focus or integrity is catastrophic and anything creating such an environment wreaks havoc with her trust and faith. A watershed shit storm will have begun. And why? All because you just said *'Kneel bitch'* instead of the command you taught of *'Kneel formally, pet'*. Rather than obey, likely you will get a cocked head, hands on hips and a snarling *'Sheesh Buster, what the hell do you want?'* No, this is not good for anyone.

MIND FUCK #28 NEW YEAR'S EVE

New Year's Eve arrived and this year celebrated by hosting a party with lifestyle friends. Typically, she was nervous. Was everything prepared as he wished? Despite her experience hosting, this was her first hosting of lifestyle folks and their peculiarities.

Master planned the itinerary, now it was up to her to execute it. Arrivals at four, cocktails, then dinner by six. Slave use in the dungeon to follow. She really wished the slaves were not being used at once. She loved watching others scene and that could not happen. But, that was the plan and it would be special nonetheless.

"You look beautiful pet, I'm very proud of your effort today, goodgirl." They hugged and he cupped her face.

"I have a special tradition tonight at midnight for us." He smiled as her eyes begged the question.

"You'll know soon enough pet." Now kiss me slave girl," and she did.

The evening went well. Everyone relaxed enjoying the camaraderie of difference shared by lifestylers. She beamed inwardly hearing the compliments master received. "Stunning Sir, she looks good enough to eat" and they laughed when master bit her nipple.

Master had splurged this Christmas, indulging her in new leathers. He had always insisted on black in the past, so she was surprised at the pure white leather corset. In the bedroom mirror, she blushed seeing how little the matching leather g-string covered. Only her very entrance and clit were concealed and she blushed modestly. The corset pushed her breasts high and the stiff nipples stood proudly exposed. It is not for the prudish and that familiar twinge started between her legs. What a slut I'm turning into she thought and knew she'd be wet the whole night. Blushing again, she secretly beamed with pride.

He had not really decided how he would use her after dinner. Pondering all evening, he watched her mingle with their friends. She laughed enjoying herself, carefree and happy. You could see it in her eyes. Dinner was marvelous and the slaves served well. They all looked stunning, but none more than his delightful pet. He was blessed to own her and grateful for her coming into his life. Still he wondered how to use her tonight. There was of course the special tradition at midnight, but that was hours off yet.

"Gentleman, the slaves shine again. What a marvelous feast. Well done slaves. Speaking for all, we are pleased. Moreover, your reward waits in the dungeon. Gentlemen, if you will seize your sluts and drag them along, we shall amuse ourselves with debauchery, pain and pleasure."

Grabbing his slave he smiled and spoke with menacing quiet, revealing his mood.

"Listen carefully slavegirl," he growled. "I have treated you well, brought you along slowly, with patience and compassion. Right now, that changes. Tonight you are my meat, a slave, to be used, beaten, whipped and fucked without regard. Do you understand slavegirl?"

A ripple went through her body. She merely nodded, and found herself suddenly hair dragged to the dungeon, bent over and supplicated.

By ten that evening, she had been taken to a new level of devotion. Stripped of clothes, she rode the intensity of pain until it was no more. She floated in a happy place, devoted to her master, unaware, uncaring, just being for him. In the mists of her mind, her head cocked, looking magically at him, she felt the love of which she had only dreamed. The pain hurt, she felt it, but it was ok, she wanted it and needed it for him.

Her eyes opened to his soft kisses. Cuddled in his lap, embraced and secure, she was wrapped in his blanket. Slowly she focused and smiled. His voice was very gentle, "Goodgirl. You were beautiful pet. Goodgirl".

The dungeon scenes over, the slaves came alive again. Blanket wrapped and well used, they kissed their masters. It was nearing the witching hour and the countdown to a new year. The hostess remained on her master's lap. She gobbled and smiled as he fed her pieces of melon and strawberries. He knew her so well.

"Well folks, ten minutes, shall we bend these slaves over and begin the countdown on their asses," someone announced. Hoots of approval arose and slaves found themselves bent over couches, chairs and tables around the room, bare fannies everywhere. Except one slave.

"Come with me pet, I have something special planned for you," the host whispered.

They rose and he took her to the living room corner. It was darker there. She stood in front, holding her blanket tight, ridiculously happy. She had never felt so at peace and happy at the same time. Cupping her face, he stared into her deep rich eyes.

"Obey pet, I want you to cum for me, when I say. Not before, but when I say, do you understand?"

Cumming when told was difficult for her and not something for which training was complete. "Trust me pet, now open the blanket."

She obeyed and gasped when he took her cunt in his hand. Two fingers invaded and her thighs bowed open to receive them. Suddenly, unexpectedly she was close. He drove in and vibrated his hand against her entire mound. She needed to cum and heard his words… "No girl. Not yet!" She clung onto him fiercely trying to fight back the waves that were coming.

"Now slut!"

The relief was instantaneous and the first wave crashed into her cunt and rolled up her body. Convulsing, he held her upright. Her face contorted, ears ringing in orgasm, she never heard the countdown, nor the cheers as the New Year arrived. The waves continued. He would not stop and she came again, even harder. The blanket dropped. Grabbing him, her nails raked his back while humping his hand. The rolls kept coming. Finally, he held her tight and smiled.

"That is the proper way to end and start the year. Happy New Year pet. I love you", and they kissed.

9

POSITION RITUALS

The *Position Rituals* here are but some of the *rituals* any master can develop. These do however, represent a realistic goal for daily living, master-slave style. *Position Rituals* beyond these begin a slippery slide into the world of fantasy. They will be gone in six months.

Teach elaborate *Position Rituals* if you like them by all means, but use them as a game rather than a piece of permanent structure. She will appreciate that context on realizing they are used only infrequently. The *Rituals* listed here are useful, realistic, achieve structure and most important, endure.

FORMAL KNEEL

This is the fundamental first position a slave learns and is a staple for her life in slavery. Ironic perhaps than many organized religions demand this position as part of their prayer services. As *Charter Member of the Church-of-the-Holier-Than-Thou* perhaps too it is appropriate I insist she learn it.

Kneeling properly is to slavery as a bat is to baseball. You can use a stick but it is not as much fun, does not feel like the Big Leagues and the results are not as good. Your slave learning the *Formal Kneel* is a skill she

164 / LT Morrison

needs in many places, at many times. It really is where theory meets the physical reality of slavery.

Now it is easy but there are some things that go into it making it special.

"LT you have a lovely slave, would you mind if I asked her to kneel?"

"Kneel for you Nick?" It was a strange request and I was unsure what he meant. Was there some protocol I was unaware of that might be granting powers over my slave to this man that I was not prepared to offer?

"Yes, just kneel is all. I have been watching her walk around tonight and she has a grace of movement that is quite beautiful. I just thought it would be nice to see her kneel too."

"Thank you Nick that is kind of you to say." Nodding to my slave, *"Go ahead pet"* and she knelt formally understanding what was asked.

"Your slave kneels with elegance. That was graceful."

I was pleased and my slave beaming. That was the first time I focused on how she assumed a *ritual* position. She did have style, something I had taken for granted. It was all her doing of course; I had only taught the actual position previously thinking that was what mattered. Nick's request opened a new dimension of control. Here was a physical way to re-enforce and teach *Attitude,* one of the *Three Powers.* Now I focused as much on movement to a position as much as the position itself. Both reflect so much on us both.

The *Formal Kneel* is simple. She does not need any special accessories, obeys wearing whatever she has on and can do it anywhere. She kneels upright, no slouching, straight backed with knees together. There is nothing sexual in the position nor is that the intent. The purpose is similar to a soldier coming to attention. He cannot fight from that position but it marks the discipline and respect he extends to the armed forces. So it is for the slave and the *Formal Kneel.* Her wrists are crossed and placed in the small of her back with the palms flat, fingers together and pointed straight.

Pay attention to detail and accept no variance for this position. Few other positions will exact the degree of detailed perfection called for in this supremely submissive representation of whom she is. Her behavior reflects on you too. A relaxed style can be practical in other parts of structure, but this is time for precision. She will appreciate it as much as you will enjoy her.

Her head is bowed and eyes are looking at the floor before her. She is acknowledging your superior position in her life. Do not allow her eyes to wander. She can look up when commanded, but must maintain the integrity of the rest of the position. She is also prohibited from speaking generally while in the *Formal Kneel*.

Not being much for rigid specific voice commands that I have to remember, I just tell her to kneel. She knows that means *Kneel Formally*. It matters not if we are at a formal lifestyle event or if I am telling her to come and watch TV with me, when she hears '*kneel*' in any command form it means *Kneel Formally*. The exact words are not important. She has only one response. If I want a long discussion or if I want her watching a movie with me then I just amend the kneeling order by throwing in a '*relax*' somewhere along the way. That instructs her to '*Relax Kneel*'.

Doing it this way makes use of the position easy. It is effortless, puts no maintenance on me, is as clear as a Lucite buttplug up her ass. It keeps structure livable. Making work for myself is not the goal and simple positions ordered by simple everyday words make it easy and sustainable. Simplicity does not detract from mastery. Enabling consistent behavior enhances it though. Aspiring masters are wise to keep that in mind.

The wonderful extra benefit of formal kneeling is grabbing her by the hair and throat fucking her. With hands behind, there is nothing to wipe away her choking tears.

"Cry if you must, it only makes me smile."

RELAXED KNEEL

While *Formal Kneel* has a ceremonial and rigid element, '*Relaxed Kneel*' is for comfort and sustained kneeling. It is just as the name implies, used when kneeling is required, but comfort necessary. I use it everywhere in countless situations. Many slaves are prohibited from using chairs, stools and sofas in the presence of their masters so it behooves us to give them a realistic position that is comfortable. In all its permutations and variants, this is it. She will spend a lot of time here.

When she hears the command to *relax*, she kneels but has permission to sit back on her haunches, or roll onto her butt to find comfort. As long as her legs are tucked beneath her or folded to the side I will not bite her. Most slaves can roll around varying their position to maintain comfort and avoid cramps. This is not an exact position by purpose. It is a position of comfort on the floor. If she ends up sitting on her ass leaning against my knees with legs stretched out while munching popcorn watching a movie that works for me. She is essentially where I want her, on the floor so the rest I leave to her own reality check. However if the movie is a chick flick then she can forget relaxed kneeling. Then she lies between my legs; her head on my chest munching her popcorn as I stretch out on the couch mauling her tits. I will be as quiet as a titmouse so she can hear her movie.

Slaves will play footloose and fancy-free with relaxed kneeling at times and occasionally a reminder of the position is good. With friends for an evening I am pretty liberal in allowing her position. But if the visitors are lifestyle folk we are just getting to know, or a little more formality than flopping around on the floor like a beached whale is called for, a *your legs*' command reminds her decorum is required and to get those legs under or beside her. Easy-peezy. No maintenance, fun, livable, yes this works.

NADU

If you are unaware of the *Gorean Nadu* position then no big deal. It is not essential. But it is pretty to see and you might want to teach it to her anyway. It is fun having her demonstrate it to guests and the squeal when her labia rings catch in the kneeling furs is cruel, but typical Gorean humor.

FORMAL STANDING

There are times when you require the slave to stand formally focused only on you. Do not use this at the checkout counter, nor the Christmas party when she is talking to her boss, unless of course she works for me.

The purpose like most positions, is to provide structure, focus and humility with enforced behavior. Slaves readily identify with this position reading about it often in erotic stories of slavery. They already associate it with their own slavery. Understandably then, when not taught this they feel deprived. So use it, make her *'feel her submission'* and deprive her of an orgasm instead.

The position could not be simpler. The slave stands tall, again, no slouching because I said so, with her feet together. Her wrists are crossed on her tummy with fingers extended and straight. It is much like the hand position of the *Formal Kneel* except now the palms are inward towards her body and in front. Many masters allow clasped hands rather than crossed wrists and extended fingers. There is no right or wrong so do as you wish, but the handclasp is reminiscent of how vanilla woman hold their hands and that is the last image I want for her. This is a formal slave stand so anything vanilla is out.

Head is bowed and eyes are again on the floor in front of her. She is a slave and has no right to look around. She is also again, prohibited from talking, with minor exceptions.

Keeping her feet together is to affect an image totally femininity. Graceful standing with feet together creates that feminine dignified look. With legs spread wide the image is lost. She looks like a tramp. There is nothing wrong with her looking like a tramp, and to slut her up just order her legs apart. But this is a *Formal Stand* to convey feminine peace, not a formal piece of female.

BEGGING POSITION

There are many flavors in the BDSM culture and again, you can make any part as simple or complicated as you want. This applies when addressing a slave's need to beg. Oh do not deny it slavegirls, you love begging… or better learn to.

Successful masters keep to the KISS principle and take the simple route. Operating on the premise that the less time administering the relationship, the more time there is to enjoy your slave is a popular theme. While called the *"Begging Position"*, it can also be for *"Forgiveness"* or *"Mercy"* if you are into that. The more you can do with one position the less you have to remember, thus, the less chance to err and raise inconsistencies.

Because for some slaves, begging sounds so much like whining, take time to explain this is not the *"Whining Position"*. The *"Whining Position"* is the

"Toothbrush". Whining gets her firmly planted on my arm so far up her ass I can pick her teeth clean from the inside. Such is my love of whiners. No, this is for legitimate begging, seeking forgiveness and mercy. She can learn it the hard way, or throw out her toothbrush. It matters not to me.

Begging has a supplication tone to it, so naturally the position is on the knees. Kneeling in front, she puts her arms around your legs and looks up, often with tears as you will discover, and pleads forgiveness, mercy or any reason she might have to beg. It will not take long for her to realize it is very effective to beg.

PLEASURE

The *"Pleasure Position"* is the first position I ever taught over three decades ago and oddly, neither its name nor position has ever changed. The decision is now made - it is a keeper.

"Pleasure" is used for exactly what one might expect by its name. When you want complete access to her pussy, she hears the word *"pleasure"* or *"pleasure, girl"* or some such phrase, and she does not even think of hesitating. Up goes the skirt, or down come the jeans, and neither can happen fast enough. Onto her back, legs pulled up as far and wide as she can, and arms over head extended flat. She is exposed, open and ready for use in either hole. The purpose is having her fully displayed and accessible for my sexual pleasure and occasionally, if she is a good girl, her pleasure too. I fucking love this!

BEND 'N' BRACE

This is a favorite. Those knowing me have heard it many times. It is a *"quickie"* punishment position for disobedience, usually some saucy infraction that has me laughing. *BendNBrace* is done clothed by bending over and bracing against her legs as far down as possible without bending her knees. She can expect a fanny smack or ten, and more often than not, a quick grope between her legs just as a reminder of who owns there too.

That reminds me of a wee skill masters are cleverly wise to learn. Apparently, I got good at it somewhere along the line. When you are kissing your slave in the kitchen, or anywhere for that matter… oh heck, you do not have to be kissing, just when she is standing nearby, poke her crotch with a finger, a half grab little pokey thing. The trick is to nail her right on the clit every time. Practice until you master it. You got it when, she bends over suddenly, gasps and says *"Oh, right on the spot!"* I just laugh.

INSPECTION

No, this is not a health inspection given to restaurants by some civic-minded bureaucrat justifying an inflated salary. Well, now, come to think of it, it may be similar. There is meat on display, it can be branded *Certified Grade AAA Rump Roast,* and causes some inflation. Throw in a company car and I will take it.

Why we inspect slaves is explained in *Behavior Rituals.* For now, we just want to know how to do it. When a slave hears *"Inspection"* she must know your expectations. Some masters do not require a slave naked for inspection and that makes me chuckle. Why not? If not just on modesty removal grounds alone, we would still do it. It is fun and sometimes even for the slave. Man does not survive on cultured behavior alone. We often need to return to our roots, to unreservedly grope and leer at the beauty of feminine body. Said often, is that men are voyeurs. Ok, I can live with that, but I want the benefits too.

To inspect your slave she stands slightly to your left or right. I use left for everything because I am left-handed. She strips, folding clothes neatly to the side. Then, standing with legs spread as wide as possible, she places her hands behind her bowed head. A nice touch is having her arch the back slightly. Bringing attention to her snapper is never a bad thing. Do not allow any rights of privacy by slouching. Her modesty belongs in your back pocket. Know also, half the slaves reading this are wet, the other half hear *"Suck it up princess."* Life is good!

HUMILITY

Slaves need to reflect on their position in their *master-slave* relationship from time to time. If not diligent in maintaining focus, their commitment can stray, or deteriorate, often manifested in assuming powers previously offered. Then a lesson in *attitude* is necessary. This is not about humiliation though. It is about humility, two distinctly different words. It is important enough to dedicate a position to and wise masters use it frequently. It is not a negative thing at all. It is a physical act she identifies with reinforcing that she is a slave by choice. The purpose is to make her feel humble, not humiliated. Very much used so she knows there are no choices for her ego, or self-importance, as opposed to stripping self-respect and esteem.

Kneeling, she bends forward until her face is on the ground, or on her arms, whichever is comfortable. She remains in this position until released from it. Combine a bit of silent pacing around her and she feels the full effect of her decision to submit.

Using and leaving her in this position is very effective. This is not sexual or intended as a lesson in modesty. Keep her clothed with knees together. Remaining clothed is more effective to focus her. Experiment and find what works for you and your slave.

POINT'N'BEND

Has it been mentioned the lifestyle is fun? *Bend* is a fun command and position best combined as part of *PointNBend*. It is exclusively for sexual purposes. It is a raw, primal command ordering her bent over whatever you point at. She will be fucked, or fondled, possible immodestly groped as well, so unless she wants her jeans cut off, which you are more than happy to do, she drops them without hesitation or protest. Once bent over she spreads her legs, arches her back and extends her arms over her head when there is room. Her cute, tight little pussy will start moistening about now, knowing she will not wait long for some bumthwaps and penetration. Lest this becomes too routine, switch it up.

After a few Point'N'Bend commands and a pain in the ass, she will remember to keep a supply of lubricant in her purse at all times. More than her pussy is used and lack of lubricant does not stop many masters.

This is also a terrific position for application of the *LTCureall*. Does your slave have a headache, a stubbed toe, or sore nipples? You have the answer. She will forget all those maladies and any other pain she feels, when the pain in her ass from rough anal sex is liberally applied. Just call me *Doc*!

OTK

"Over the knee, let's go pet." She knows exactly what is coming. She is going to be spanked and if lucky, have her G-Spot massaged too, sometimes at the same time. Being left-handed she lies across my lap facing to the right, freeing my left hand to inflict the damage. She knows this is for bare bottoms.

If your slave resents you watching a little Sunday afternoon football on TV, this is a perfect position to introduce her to the game. A good spanking while your team has the ball is great fun and when they score, a little spike in her end zone is appropriate celebration. No flag on the play. She will soon be a big fan of the game. Test her knowledge on Monday morning and if she does not remember who was playing, well then, there is always *Monday Night Football*.

BREEDING

Within most masters resides a part of him that is savage and raw, with primordial animal needs. Fortunately, slaves have a corresponding need to be taken. It is hot being their *alpha man's bitch*. A woman on elbows and knees, with her back arched and knees spread, exposed and ready, a bitch-in-heat, creates intense slave feelings, perhaps more than any other. She is your cum slut bitch, grabbed by the hair, growled at, fucked raw, used, and surrendered to the natural order.

Exploring her sexuality and sensuality is part of the freedom of this lifestyle. While slaves need quiet time with intimacy, affection and tender loving care, they also need to be his bitch, lustily mounted, bred, made his receptacle, fucked raw and put away wet. Growl, smack her ass and take her. Breeding her savagely is fucking hot, for both of you.

BOOTS

A simple, neat clean, position and command to your boots is a place she will or should enjoy being. It is a supplication position, but more than that to her. It is home, her haven, a place representing dedication and unconditional surrender. It is safe.

A pointing or uttering the word *"boots"* brings her kneeling with face on your boots. Whether her arms are around your legs is your choice. The position is one of emotional comfort, similar to *"her place"*, representing the dynamics of your relationship. It is respectful and appropriate, particularly when developing intimacy.

To the casual and vanilla world, it may appear a position of humiliation but it is not in the hands of a wise master. Security and fostered feelings of submission in her soul is the intent and it serves that purpose well. She may have initial resistance to the position, that it is too representative of god-like adoration, but that is not the purpose. Teach her it has a different meaning between you. She will come around.

HER PLACE

A master's home is his Castle, a sanctuary for them both. It must be so. It is where peace reigns supreme. Within that Castle there is *"Her Place"*, a spot reserved for no other, a spot where she is treasured and special in her master's heart. That spot is at his feet.

"Come to your place" is a command of great comfort to a slave. She is summoned to her master's side for no other reason than he wants her close. She is that important to him.

The actual position can vary depending on the situation, but her place is in a *Relaxed Kneel* just slightly to her master's left. If he is sitting, she can rest her head in his lap, or keep an arm on his leg, but she should be touching him whenever feasible. It is indeed her special place and slaves will appreciate their master cares enough to provide one.

Where *"Boots"* is a position recognizing her devotion and loyalty to master, this position is more relaxed, a place to share space and chat.

MIND FUCK #29 "HOOKER"

"How do I look Sir?"

"You need more makeup, pet."

"But Master, this will look great with the dress. It's perfect."

"Pet, you are a whore, a hooker, I want you to look like Corrine- Corrine-the-Makeup-Queen!. Slather the shit on. You are not supposed to look like a beautiful callgirl, you are supposed to look like an over made up tart. Got it?"

"Yes Sir" she grumbled.

"Now pile on the eyeliner and that stuff that makes your cheeks red and get on with it!" They were headed to a bar tonight and this was going to be fun.

"Ok, you know your role pet? Do you have any questions?"

She looked like a million bucks, well, in a fake over slutted-up trashy sort of way. The dress was terrific, a sleek gold skintight low cut tramp dress. Her tits half hung out and the hem barely covered her ass. She had a matching purse and stilettos that screamed CFMPP's.

"Master, what is the PP for again?"

"Come Fuck Me Party Pumps pet. Sheesh."

"Right, got it Sir", they laughed together.

"Do we have to do this Sir? I'm going to be so embarrassed."

"Do we have to pet? No, we do not have to. But we are going to," he said, biting her nose. *"Suck it up princess, it will be fun."*

An hour later they parked beside the bar. It was an upscale place and the clientele were out of town businessmen on the prowl. The setting was perfect.

"Ok, you go in first pet, and sit at the bar. I will be ten minutes behind you, and remember, you do not know me!

It was crowded when he walked in. He spied her over near the far end of the bar. There was no stool nearby, so he sat at the other end. Already the plan was in trouble and he saw her glance at him nervously.

"I'll have a Scotch bartender please" and sat back to watch.

It took thirty minutes for a stool to open up beside her, so he signaled the bartender to get the lady in gold a drink and headed over.

The charade was on and they chatted. The bar was busy but not overly noisy, so their voices would carry. When it came time to order another drink, he started. The bartender and nearby patrons could hear it all. After some innocuous bar chit chat and flirty come-ons he hit her up. He started by acting surprised.

"That is a lot of money honey. What exactly do I get for a thousand dollars?

"Whatever you want sugar" she replied seductively.

That had the bartender's attention. He was discreetly listening now as were the other patrons close by.

"Honey, for that kind of money, you need to be more specific, or at least tell me it is lined in gold." She was blushing behind her caked on makeup. Talking dirty was not one of her strengths, something she did not enjoy, especially if others could hear. But that was the point of this. She was learning obedience and that modesty was not hers to control.

"It is better than gold sugar, I want it full of your cum" she cooed. There was no holding back now. If she had to do this, it would be memorable. Besides, it was fun and she was getting into it. The drinks were working. Maybe a pro callgirl is not so bad she thought.

The graphic filth from her shocked him. It was turning him on. He shook his head remembering he did not have to buy her.

The bartender listened intently as did the nearby patrons, all of whom hung on every word. The plan was working, much to the slave's mirth and embarrassment.

"Well honey, that sounds wonderful, but a thousand dollars is a little steep for me." He picked up his drink, "Best of luck honey." Her master stood and headed to a side table. He watched with amusement. Action began immediately. The vultures swept in. Now it was her task to lure them in and then fend them off. The game was to keep driving up the price.

Her night would not end until she found a man to pay the money. She had to play high-class hooker and verbally seduce until someone agreed to go take her to his hotel room. The price was high enough to challenge her seductive charms. Every "extra", drove the price up even more.

He smiled from the table watching one after another make their move, hear the seduction and then wilt at the price. But liquor was on her side.

He had scouted the bar and she knew the drill. She just had to get one careless drunk horny enough to take up her offer. On the stroke of midnight the fish landed.

At ten minutes past the witching hour they were driving home, laughing hilariously. She was drunk as a skunk and flying high. The stories got better with each passing mile.

"Start at the end pet, did you have any trouble getting out?"

"Not at all Sir. Once he agreed we were going to go back to his hotel, I did what you said and told him I needed to visit the ladies room and then slipped out the back door. I forgot about the alarm, but you had the car ready, so it worked. I felt like a bank robber." They laughed.

"So what did you think? Enjoy yourself? Learn anything?"

She was giggling now. "Oh I found out I liked talking dirty to them after awhile. I got better at it as the night went on and was a great cock tease. But some of those guys are nasty."

"What do you mean pet?"

"Well, most of them wanted me to pee on them and dominate them."

He laughed. "Oh I can imagine the fun you had with that."

"Yes Sir, I was an awesome little dominatrix. You would have been proud of me. I used your tricks on them."

Now he was really laughing and reached over grabbing her hair.

"Well pet, what I heard coming from your filthy little mouth was turning me on. I was almost ready to pay. I am glad you came out of your shell, but I am pulling over. I will not pee on you, but you are going to swallow. Now get my pants open!"

176 / LT Morrison

10

BEHAVIOR RITUALS & PROTOCOLS

There are as many *protocols* and *rituals* masters create to structure their slave's life as he wishes. Some are very sophisticated. They represent elaborate *ritual* of symbolic significance. Often they are themed to reflect a particular style or fetish. *Gorean Rituals, Geisha Tea Service,* and *Harem Wenches* fall into that realm. They are fun and serve a variety of purposes.

The *Behavior Rituals* espoused below are designed for one primary purpose. Fantasy and role-play were not considered in their development. *Rules, Protocols* and *Rituals* build structure and the goal is to develop these to ensure livable and sustainable structure for years of happiness.

As you have come to see, rules are not always *rituals*. A slave required to obtain master's permission for her daily activities is a rule but not a *ritual*. *Rituals* are assertive procedures a slave sometimes initiates of her own volition or upon a command, adhering to specific preset behavioral expectations. She learns these *Rituals* from the teachings of her master.

Rituals serve many purposes with structure building a primary one. But none is more important than the benefit of daily vanilla transformation. *Rituals* are ideal tools to reinforce her slave mindset on a daily basis. It is yet another tool, often invisible, in the practice of the *master-slave* lifestyle daily. Do we not often hear that from folks in the lifestyle? How can we live this each and every day in a vanilla world? *Rituals* are a significant part of that answer.

Obviously, a master and slave cannot be together every moment of every day, nor would most want that. Familiarity breeds contempt. When apart, they are relentlessly bombarded with vanilla issues and influences as the part of normal daily living. That is expected and welcome, after all, both live and interact a balanced life in the vanilla world. Living together as master and slave is their personal dynamic and focus, but it is not their entire world. Masters thinking slavery is one-dimensional, eliminating balance from a slave's life are delusional, if not psychotic.

The first issue confronting *master-slave* couples and in particular the slave is making the transformation each and every day from her healthy and required vanilla mindset needed to function and succeed outside the home, to focus on who they are and who she is when reunited each day. It is a challenge faced by every couple, so do not ignore or fear it. Instead, learn to manage it. Each slave must almost instantly switch from vanilla behavior to slave behaviors the moment she walks in the door. Notice how that is worded. Her *"behaviors"* have to alter, not belief in what she is. That never wavers. She is aware of her slavery constantly and bases her daily decisions on that reality. While out in society, she processes thoughts and interactions with co-workers, friends, teachers and the butcher using vanilla thought processes. Good for her, as it should be, after all, she is not submitting to them.

Experienced slaves reading this know of the challenge of changing vanilla thinking to refocus on her master and his wishes after a long day. It must happen when she walks in the front door and that is very difficult. Until the transformation process becomes habit, it is a significant problem and each master has to address it. One, or a series of *Rituals* helps develop that habit.

No master worth a pinch of salt allows his slave to interact with him in vanilla terms. That statement is controversial and too often misunderstood, but true. The statement does not say a master does not want to hear about her vanilla day, or their relationship is unbalanced to exclude vanilla from her life. We all have vanilla friends and interests and they do not threaten our mastery, nor preclude her from service. Master's in fact encourage those interests in their slave. They are critically important to live fulfilling healthy lives. A life of consensual slavery and one full of exciting vanilla interests are

178 / LT Morrison

neither mutually exclusive, nor adversarial goals. They can and should co-exist peacefully. I have never quite understood some masters being threatened because their slave has a life.

The statement simply reflects the slave must be mindful of how she interacts with her master in his presence. He is not her vanilla buddy and he has *protocols* to guide her interaction with him. If she is cranky and passionate about something in her day, he does not want, nor will ever accept her venting, screaming, yelling, or relating her day's activities disrespectful of her position. He wants her passion and is very interested in hearing what happened, but he did not collar a vanilla wife, nor will he be thrust into the role of vanilla husband. Pussy-whipped belongs on her genitals, not a description of his standing in the relationship.

So this transformation is difficult and necessary every day. How do we do it?

There is no one magical panacea. It is a process of using *Ritual* and *Protocol* techniques repeatedly to develop habits. *Behavior Rituals* when consistently applied create habits in her behavior. Some of these are easy, some difficult. In time they not only become easier, she comes to rely on them and anticipate the positive effect they have on her day and peace of mind.

The *Behavior Rituals* described here are in no particular order, except the first three. They are important in creating livable structure and each addresses directly the transformation from vanilla to slave behavior she faces daily.

Aside from the wonderful transitional benefits *Rituals* provide to sustaining *master-slave* structure, there is an even more important reason, perhaps the most important of all. She radiates when doing them. If you have never seen a slave perform a personalized greeting of your design, then you have missed a wonder of the world. Regardless what *Ritual* she is doing, the look in her eye cannot hide the incredible feelings of loyal submission in her heart. *Rituals* look good, feel good and taste good! Her beauty is magnified and highlighted. *Behavior Rituals* are sheer beauty. One cannot help but smile when she obeys flawlessly.

GREETING MASTER

This *protocol* serves several purposes. Fun is one, respect another, and focus yet one more. It is a terrific first step for the slave in making the transformation to slave behavior each day. Depending how well you design your *protocol*, she will immediately focus at least to some degree on her master, the important priority in her life, and of course her position as his slave.

Two *greeting rituals* cover most circumstances, be they part of the master-slave private, or more public vanilla life. Teaching her the appropriate greeting is simple. A *Private Greeting Ritual* when used alone, or among those understanding their personal dynamics is very intimate and should be unlike any vanilla counterpart. A *Public Greeting Ritual* is more vanilla appearing but the necessity to obey the rule is no less stringent. The two important *"givens"* regardless of which greeting is used are first she must initiate the greeting and the second is always done.

To greet, the slave does not wait for her master to come to her, either when he is returning home, or she is. Nor does it matter if it is even in the house. Anytime they are apart for a pre-determined period, the greeting *ritual* is in effect. It is an ad hoc *Ritual* requiring no command. You do not live a mundane suburban vanilla take-it-for-granted relationship. Dad drops the briefcase, comes to wifey, who is slaving over a hot stove as the three point two screaming brats fight over the blaring cartoons on TV, then pecks her cheek with an *"Hi dear, I'm home"* is not going to happen.

What will happen is a slave comes to her master when he arrives home and greets him, sometimes in front of the kids, who see two people showing affection and love to each other every day. That is not a bad lesson for them in my book. The kids do not need to know the rest of the relationship of course, unless they are over twenty-one, in a different gene pool, and think age-play is fun. Either way, it is not a bad deal.

The slave must initiate the greeting. Consensual slavery is not about things just done to her. She signed on to be pro-active too.

Have her perform the greeting every time regardless of circumstances. You need to pick a time window that triggers the *Greeting Ritual* as a minimum standard for your slave to greet and she of course can do it more often, just not less. I use three hours. Regardless if you are away from the house or she is, if you are apart more than three hours she must initiate a greeting.

This *Ritual,* as a simple bit of structure, has an amazing effect on the relationship. It focuses you both to prioritize your relationship each day. It creates affection and intimacy, two of the *Four Pillars* of all relationships. It is simple and effective. As time moves forward in the relationship and you grow together, the *Ritual* becomes habit for your slave and she relies on it; takes comfort in it; and uses it as tangible evidence structure exists. She knows her master is not taking her for granted and he cares. If he did not he would not do it.

As master it is your responsibility to keep the greeting interesting. She is going to greet you everyday come hell or high water. She can use some creativity but as a *Ritual* her options are limited. Yours are not. The greeting is an opportunity for your creative juices to flow. Make them memorable. Some greetings will be routine, but throw in some hair pulls, unexpected slam fucks and deep kisses that catch her off guard. She is after all, the girl you love. Use the three questions on her regularly, *"Who are you"; " What do slaves do"* and *"Whose slave are you?"* Your own *Ritual* has presented an opportunity on a silver platter to use her, so do it. Be creative. She has obeyed you, now re-enforce and stimulate the slave mindset that the moment evoked.

The greeting can take but a moment or an hour, it is up to you. Use the time to begin transforming her vanilla thought processing. Slave thinking does not occur instantly after a hard day, so encourage it.

PUBLIC GREETING

No command is necessary. She simply assesses the circumstances she finds you in and when the *Private Greeting* might offend others she comes to you, stands slightly to your left (or right), smiles and kisses your cheek. Some vanilla words of greeting can accompany the greeting if you choose. My slave took initiative each time to discreetly whisper in my ear *"Hello Master".* She was a little scamp that way. But, she did it quickly so not appearing rude to others. It was a lovely addition. She understood taking initiative to please was part of her duty and the simple words created an intimacy we enjoyed together. It was our private *"in your face"* to the vanilla world and we laughed.

PRIVATE GREETING

Over the years, this *Private Greeting* thing has evolved, grown, shrunk, expanded again and changed many times. Partly because I got bored with whatever was then used, sometimes because of physical ailments the slave suffered, but mostly to reflect our maturing in the lifestyle over the years. At one time, she knelt and kissed my boots remaining prone until released. That changed when she knelt in a puddle of melting snow in the front hallway the first spring when I arrived home in slushy mud covered snow boots. Another time for a while, I required her naked with her ass lubricated in the *Breeding Position*. That was great fun. It only lasted until her period cycle started. Messy. I did not mind changing the greeting from time to time. It was fun and added some zest to life.

Eventually as it is today, the importance of livability, simplicity, functionality and a *Ritual* that achieved focusing her mind on slavery and feminine grace won the day.

A *Private Greeting* today is facing me, always slightly to my left. As noted before, standing directly in front of a master is subliminally, if not overtly confrontational, a condition never permitted. Dressed as she was, she assumes the *Formal Stand* position. As my leather collar is to be worn in the house, she usually has that on as well.. She does not speak, or move, or raise her eyes until directed. She will wait there all night if necessary and at times that is an effective way of focusing her. It also helps her avoid taking the greeting and you for granted. Time and silence are wonderful tools for a master to use.

Picture along now. She has presented herself in a *Formal Stand* and patiently awaits her master's attention. She stands in strength with grace and humility, the very essence of femininity. She is respectful with eyes lowered, disciplined by remaining motionless, and mindful of the position you hold in her life. Beautiful! Fucking beautiful!

Yet this simple feminine *Private Greeting Ritual* accommodates the reality we live in. Who has time these days for her to drop everything to don slave robes, grease up the hiney and recite some liturgy of selfless idolatry every time you walk in the door? This is easy, yet effective. If she greets you in this simple *Private Greeting*, but you want her naked and ass fucked, then just haul out your knife and cut off her clothes. If she is a goodgirl, she still will not move until ordered.

Be creative, you are the master. Touch all her emotions and enjoy your slave. She is standing there for you, so cup her face, look in her eyes and ask her who she is. A lovely, *"Your slave Master"* is good for both your souls. *"You look beautiful pet"* in reply never hurt a slave's attitude. By adding a hair pull and kiss, you have her undivided attention. *"You are my treasure, slavegirl"* and she might think of raping you.

An old adage in coaching circles says, *"Praise the positive first"*. Show her we are not always cantankerous, horny beasts with whips. Only on days starting with "F". Like Fucking Monday, and Fucking Tuesday and.... .

FOCUS

By far and away the most important *Ritual* you can develop to focus a slave's mind and speed the transition from vanilla mindset to her slavery is teaching her the *Focus Ritual*. The *Ritual* is simple. She is required at least once a day (and anytime needed), immediately after greeting you, to retire into the bedroom. If there are kids in the home, they are taught when the bedroom door is closed Mommy is not to be disturbed. As Mommy knows Daddy is home, she has peace of mind that the kids are supervised.

The slave then kneels on *"her"* pillow, one you specifically acquired for this purpose. She must spend at least five minutes, but for as long as it takes kneeling and re-focusing on the most important thing in her life, her relationship with you (kids notwithstanding). If it is not you, release her, you have the wrong slave.

The purpose of this *protocol* is specific. She has this time every day, sometimes more than once a day, to calm herself, dispose of the vanilla issues pressing on her, and focus on what is important in her life, her master. She is aware he is going to want to know of her day and will demand to hear it without the vanilla baggage learned through a lifetime of teachings prior to entering service. She spends her time on the pillow organizing how she will present her day to her master in such a way to please him and honestly communicate all there is. This is the slave's opportunity every day, to do what she can in accepting responsibilities for her own behavior, to stay on track with her commitments as his slave. His needs come first and that she is there to serve and obey is important to her. Remember, she wants this. . The *Focus Ritual* is the trigger that shoots the vanilla world in the ass.

The effect of the *protocol* is profound. Like many aspects of her new life, at first it will seem awkward and an imposition on her time and because in the beginning she is so focused on her master, it will seem unnecessary. Tough! As master you are looking beyond the beginning to a time when she will need the benefit of peace the *Ritual* provides. The day is coming when the bloom falls off the rose and the lusty romance period ends. When the daily vanilla pressures take hold and are pushing to influence the relationship more and more, the benefits of the *Focus Ritual* will grow. It helps enormously in re-position her mind each day, a major piece of the transformation process. It too, provides a daily opportunity to *"feel her submission"*. That is always a good thing.

Teach the *Ritual.* Explain to her the long-term benefits and that she may not begin to realize them for months. Do not accept debate she may offer to avoid the discipline. It may seem silly, unproductive and artificial at first but you are the master and know better. Stay with her the first few times ensuring she understands the purpose and until she is able to achieve your goal. Enforcing this *Ritual* is an essential tool of your mastery. Is that clear enough?

REQUESTING DISCUSSION

Of all the rules and requirements a master has for his slave, none is more important than those facilitating communications between them. Developing channels of communications is the enabling tool for masters to maintain integrity in keeping with their responsibility of emotional and physical safety. Communicating with your slave is fun and interesting and a core need in everyone. It would be inconsistent of you and near impossible for your slave if you want her pro-active; useful not just used; and then fail to provide a method for her to talk to you openly and respectfully without intimidation.

Regrettably and contrary to popular fiction, reality is not flogging, fucking, training and whipping up devilish punishment scenes every moment of every day. Sorry to break that news to you. Reality is that you interact with your slave by speech more than any other way. That is true of any relationship and thus requires the most thought of how a master will structure that communication.

"That was a delicious breakfast pet, but I have to run. It is going to be a long hectic day and I need an early jump."

"Thank you Master, enjoy your day."

He grabbed his briefcase and ready to head to the door, he stopped and turned to her, pausing for a moment then spoke.

"Ah, and one more thing pet, tonight I am going to use you and fist your ass."

Her mouth dropped open.

Now this girl had never experienced a good old fashioned down home, salt of the earth ass fisting up to that moment. She knew it could be demanded, but she was deathly afraid. So what is going to happen?

Masters who have taught the importance of how a slave communicates will get one type of response, and masters unwilling to explore this aspect and control of her behavior, quite another. The slave has two responses she can give and two styles with she can deliver them.

The first is acknowledgment of the command and the second is expressing she really does not want his arm up her ass. The acknowledgment response usually runs something like this:

Trained-slave:	*She gasped and looked at him, took a deep breath and murmured "Yes Master."*
Untrained-slave-mouth:	*"Oh goody, it is about time too Masterly-one."*

Then there is the *'cold-day-in-hell'* response. It is more like this:

Untrained-slave-mouth:	*"Over my dead body Big Boy!"*
Trained-slave:	*She gasped... "Ummmm, Master, may we talk about this please?"*

Which style of response do you prefer? To some masters either style is acceptable, or a difference not noticed, or even cared about. To others how she talks to him is a very important part of his structure. Channels of communication start with the *Twenty-Four Hour Rule* but are dressed up with an attending *Protocol*.

The *Twenty-Four Hour Rule* provides a slave the opportunity to have a discussion on anything she wants by simply asking for it. Well, that is misleading. The wise master insists she actually ask by abiding this *Protocol*. She kneels formal slightly to the left, and because she initiated and was not summoned to the position, the speech restriction is lifted and she simply asks politely for a discussion and names the topic. No more words are required. Asking is not having, so she best not use sly trickery disguising the request as in fact the beginning of the discussion. Once she has requested, she does not talk, just waits to be spoken to.

There is a difference between having a conversation and a discussion and this *Protocol* is not intended for the former. It is reserved for more serious issues than what whip length to buy next. Wait... oh never mind!

This is yet another effective *Protocol* to assist in her daily transformation and structure she can feel.

PRESENTING ITEMS

After speech, the next common interaction for many masters is when your slave brings something to you. Fetching, retrieving, presenting, they are all the same thing. Developing a *protocol* for this is tricky because so often it is done in a vanilla setting. Some elaborate *Rituals* in flowing robes, dangling buttplugs and pussy soaked coffee cups do not work at Starbucks. Rather than developing, teaching and remembering two *protocols*, one vanilla and one master-slave, resorting to the *"No Master Maintenance KISS Principle"* makes sense. Using a combination of techniques accommodates both settings. In a private setting the slave uses them all. Wonderful, structure achieved and everyone is happy.

The individual pieces making up the Ritual are subtle and collectively look odd in public, but individually are virtually invisible and rarely raise an eyebrow. Even then, if someone questions or is offended a quick *"this is the custom in my country, so go bugger yourself silly on an armadillo"* is quite an appropriate retort. Social conformity need only go so far.

It is especially respectful dominance when your slave uses the full *Ritual* when presenting items to other known dominants in the same manner she would you. The practice is usually appreciated.

The full presenting *Ritual* involves six individual components. The first was added after the *Ritual* was developed, but should have been included from the start. It is positive structure and respect.

The slave verbally acknowledges what was ordered of her. A simple 'Yes Sir' is enough unless she develops a bad habit of bringing the wrong thing. Then have her repeat the full command before proceeding, while a pain in the ass for both master and slave it quickly develops her listening skills before resorting back to 'Yes Sir'.

Acknowledging the command was added because of a slave who was deaf in one ear. Many times despite growing annoyance from her master, she messed up simply because she did not hear him. While the partial deafness caused angst at first, it sustained the relationship for years. By sleeping on her good ear, she had no idea the snoring lump beside her was raising the roof. Any assumption of this being an autobiographical reference, will be denied. This tape self-destructs in ten seconds.

Good posture is used when presenting items. Posture reflects much of what is happening in a slaves mind so demanding it re-enforces a good attitude. Combined with posture, body language, elegance of motion, grace, submission and, respect convey happiness. Practice this and if necessary explore sending her to a Finishing School course to acquire the skill.

Items are presented with two hands, palms up when possible. Lastly, the slave never thrusts the item at her master. The norm is to present and hold it until accepted. You can and will come up with countless exceptions to *'present and hold'* but that is the ad hoc *Ritual* unless there is a legitimate reason to vary. The fun part of mastery is you decide what is legitimate.

ENTERING A ROOM

Entering and leaving a room is a lifestyle specific protocol used only when her master is present, or when he has authorized other dominants making them aware of the *protocol*. They of course must be willing to enforce it. It is not used when vanilla folk are present. That includes children in the house, the in-laws, vanilla guests and obviously out in public. That she has to remember this *protocol* requires work, concentration and is undoubtedly inconvenient at times. Too damned bad, suck it up princess, or *BendNBrace*. Masters never promise everything will be easy, convenient, or to their liking. She did not vote when developing the *protocol* but many thrive and enjoy it.

This wonderful *protocol* directly addresses those people expressing concern of how to live *master-slave* day-to-day. It can be practiced each day even with kids in the household, when they are out playing, at school, or in bed. The only condition needed is that master is present and vanillas are not. Those conditions come up regularly, every day.

The *Entering the Room Protocol* is easier than leaving the room. She simply pauses at the threshold before entering then continues in. No fuss, no muss, no maintenance. All that is required of the master is to watch and that she obeys. If you miss a few times when she forgets, oh well, it happens, but develop the habit of watching as she develops the habit of pausing. Transgressions call for a quick *BendNBrace* and throw in a pussy grope just for the hell of it. It is fun, real, and you will love the act as much as the structure.

LEAVING A ROOM

The conditions to enable this *protocol* are identical for *'Entering the Room'.* It is a lifestyle specific *protocol.* The only difference between them is when given permission to leave, if that is part of your structure, she faces you, takes one step away then turns and departs. The reason she does not require permission to enter but does to leave is simple practicality. You may not see her arrival and likely will not if you are busy. So she just pauses and enters. But a slave should not be empowered to leave your presence solely at her discretion. Hence, nod, bite her ,or give her a tickling. She will know she is dismissed.

This may seem onerous on you but it is a simple learned habit that becomes effortless. And it is beautiful. Once taught it she performs with grace, subservience, and dignity, that becoming a constant reminder she is your trained slave..

Some masters add to the *protocol* having their slave ask permission to leave their presence and some go so far to insist this be done in all circumstances, vanilla or otherwise. All circumstances seems onerous and high maintenance, but it is doable. Their rationale is sound. They realize vanilla wives come and go as they please and they do not have one of those creatures. They own a slave, so develop subtle, virtually invisible looks, nods, winks and gestures to ask for, acknowledge and grant permissions.

Seeking permission is the ad hoc rule and again can be amended for specific events, or situations. During supper for example, it is normal as supper is prepared and served for her to be moving back and forth to the dining room and you may be chatting with her in the kitchen as she does. That may happen a dozen times during the course of a meal. Simply suspend the *Entering and Leaving a Room protocol* for the meal, all meals, or perhaps, just between the kitchen and dining room. The purpose is not to be onerous or stupid about this, so make the *protocol* work for you.

Throw in a little creativity sometimes to kick it up a notch. Next time you are watching a movie and she asks to go pee, smile and say, *"Yes girl. Go and fetch the big metal bowl and you can pee right here in the middle of the room."* As she shyly squats, just grab her by the hair, *'Well, go girl'*. Do not b surprised if she did not have to go as badly as thought.

BEDTIME

Too many people complain you cannot live *master-slave* in reality because it is not practical, or is offensive when the general populace sees it. Stop the belly aching and whining please. Think a little. Anything is possible if you want it. Those making excuses most likely would not live *master-slave* if it were handed to them on a silver platter anyway. If *master-slave* is only about living in Chateau Roissy, or as Princesses captured and enslaved in mythical castles by strict but benevolent Queens and Sultans, sure it is unlivable. If that is the only thinking or energy you put into it, so be it. Have fun on the magic carpet ride. This book says otherwise, and it is certainly my reality and many others.

But naysayers have a point. *Master-slavery* must co-exist with the vanilla world and can when masters accept the reality of both lifestyles and are prepared to exercise enough intelligence to take the opportunities presented each day. Choosing to impose their structure and thus influence their own and slave's life can be enriching on a daily basis.

There is no better opportunity than at bedtime each night. It is every day, it is private and with the exception of when kids are young and constantly climbing into bed with you, it is uninterrupted. It behooves masters to use this golden opportunity to support their structure. To those advocating it is too impractical living *master-slave* every day, here is your chance. Here is but one of many chances each day.

There are as many *Bedtime Protocols* as there are masters to teach them. The one described here essentially keeps to the *"No Master Maintenance KISS Principle"* again but with added flourishes because a little work dedicated to each other is good work. It is a chance to show your slave at the end of each day that you care. Those opportunities do not necessarily come along each day, so this is a chance to express how appreciated she is and re-enforce intimacy. She loves knowing structure exists. Performing this *Protocol* each night is an act of intimacy and consistency.

Now let us examine the *Protocol* and start immediately with a disclaimer. A very fine gentleman I have mentored and his slave have a problem each night that we have never constructively solved despite their asking. He falls asleep on the couch watching TV every night before she goes to bed. This excludes any chance of reaping the benefits of a bedtime *ritual*. They do not know how to solve this problem and short of the master's self-discipline to alter his behavior, neither do I.

That exception notwithstanding whether she goes to bed first, or he does or ideally together, the *Protocol* works. First establish who's bed is whose, where they are and accommodate any physical issues that exist. Some slaves respond to and identify the floor as their rightful place. Others must have a waterbed, or endure constant back pain. Whatever the reason, where a slave sleeps must be decided before any *Protocol* can be established. While the straw in the corner, a slave shackled to a stone wall and a tin pot to pee in is a lovely vision, it is not very practical, but once or twice a year.

Before finalizing your *Protocol* consider too, if she sleeps in your bed, where is that on the bed. Will she be bound, if so, how will it be safely done? A subtle but effective piece of bed *Protocol* I enjoy is that her head position cannot be closer to the headboard than mine. In effect, she is below me on the bed and this serves to place her head near my chest or cuddled into my shoulder and arm.   Again, this subtly re-enforces her standing in the relationship. When resting on your chest it also is easy to give her a push southward when the Titanic needs rising. Ignore her distress signals, or you are sunk.

Binding a slave at night is a controversial subject often debated in the BDSM community. The primary argument against the practice is safety with secondary concerns related to children in the home. There are many voices shouting the practice is dangerous and if a fire occurs she is trapped or heaven forbid her master kicks the bucket in bed beside her and she has to sleep with a corpse (and how is that different than a vanilla man?). Bind her as part of your nightly *ritual*. Ignore the *Busybody Police*.

While the safety argument has surface merit, it fails the logic test by making invalid assumptions when you examine the slave mind and apply the principles we know she needs and craves. By examining too, the two styles of bondage, *'forced'* and *'mental'*, you begin to have a more realistic understanding that bedtime bondage is not only safe, but necessary. It is also *asymmetrical* for you bondage aficionados out there.

The safety argument presumes she will be bound in a way effectively incapacitating her ability to free herself. That forced style of bondage ignores her slave needs as discussed earlier in the *SODS Principle*. There it was discussed a primary slave need is to obey. A slave wants to obey and she needs to obey. She does not have to be forced to obey. As such *mental bondage* at night is far more effective in meeting her needs than restrictive forced bondage. It creates a healthy mindset long-term and a *protocol* required every night is more conducive to peace and tranquility.

If you are to bind her at night, just do not bind her neck. It is not worth it. If she suffocates, you are likely going to jail. Use *mental bondage*. Bind her in a way she can release herself in an emergency but with strict orders she is not to under any other circumstances. When she rolls over and feels the tug of a strap on an ankle or wrist, immediately she feels who she is, literally. As uncomfortable as that is at first, it grows to be her safety net, her place, allowing her to feel her position.

As part of the preparation for bed have her put on at least one leather wrist or ankle cuff. Lying on her back, the most ideal in my experience is the outside ankle cuff. That is where the bondage will occur. To attach her, use a simple leather strap(s) attached to the bed leg that comes up and with scissor clips, fasten around the D-ring on whatever limb cuff you are securing. There, all done. Her leg is bound to the bed restricting movement. That took about four seconds.

She knows she cannot release herself and her sleeping positions are restricted. Not nastily so, because she needs her sleep to function too, but the subtle message is there, she is a bound slave. There is enough restriction on her leg or arm, that if it becomes uncomfortable in the middle of the night, she can move, but calls on mental discipline not to self-release. It is a win/win situation for everyone. She can move about with some restriction, yet is bound and able to release herself in an emergency. Perfect. If she does an unauthorized release (and that has happened), then she will think twice about a recurrence when she sees the wrath of *Disappointment Hell* that reigns down on her life come morning.

I cannot tell you how many times slaves, both others and mine have extolled the virtues of being bound at night. They love it.

Bind her at night. Call on her need to obey and use mental bondage techniques. Give her structure and give her the security she needs. Then in the morning tell the *Busybody Safety Police* to take a Valium.

Another nice practice to incorporate into a *Bedtime Protocol* is requirement she must wear your leather collar to bed. Now she has your leather cuffs on her limbs and collar on her neck. She is going to look beautiful. It will be uncomfortable at first, but within a week or two she will feel naked without them. Your only adjustment is getting used to feeling cold D-rings on you from time to time but it is a small imposition for the benefits received.

"No Master Maintenance", the sustenance of mastery. I have long thought the ritualizing of putting your collar on the slave each night, or anytime other time than the moment of taking possession of her is unnecessary and foolish. The collar symbolizes who she is and when not wearing it the look from me is astonishment and *"Get it on now girl"*. She is not to be in the house without it, visitors notwithstanding. It is her duty and assumedly her desire, to be wearing it. It is not there as a make work project for the master putting it on her every day. That practice smells of the *"hoity-toity-submission-is-a-gift"* nonsense. Master put it on when he collared her. It was intended to last a lifetime and he gave her conditions for its removal temporarily to accommodate the vanilla world. Her ability to take it off at times is not a permanent right. She cannot arbitrarily decide when she will wear it to suit

her convenience. When the situation is appropriate, she should want it back on and best do so. Make it clear to your slave the collar was put around her neck and you own her. It was put there permanently and if she removes it temporarily it is to go back around her neck immediately at the next opportunity. Make her very aware she is a collared slave, figuratively and literally.

That requirement notwithstanding, it is very romantic to surprise her by having her neck presented after a shower and put the collar back on with special words. A smile and how you remember that day it was first fastened and that she is more beautiful today, is magic for a relationship. You have to love this lifestyle, a little something for everyone.

So now with the preliminary decisions made, what goes into a *Bedtime Protocol*? First, she must request permission to go to bed. She cannot just wander off to flop into the sack hogging all the pillows and blankets. As time inevitably takes its toll and the benefit of having a *Protocol* is more important than the specifics of it, the position from which she asks permission has evolved.

From kneeling with her face on my feet, to *Formal Kneel* to now *Formal Stand* what you do is particular to you, but I have evolved to simplicity, livability, with a realistic approach recognizing some night we are exhausted and others quite frisky. The purpose is always my pleasure in seeing her feminine grace and submission and providing an opportunity to appreciate her enslavement.

The *Ritual* I find most practical and meaningful, is having her approach and *Stand Formally* slightly to my left, (see a pattern here), and simply ask permission to go to bed. By custom she uses the word *"Master"*, but the specific words are not important. Once given permission she is free to come into my arms for her hug and kiss.

Asking permission is near the end of the *ritual*, or the beginning depending on your definition. There are tasks at bedtime she must perform before asking to go to bed that change from time to time, thus I look upon asking permission as the start of the *protocol*. Tasks of turning down the bed, cleaning and setting my reading glasses beside the book I am currently reading on the end table, having a glass of ice water ready and turning on the end table light must be done first. Completing her bathroom needs, donning any nightie she is allowed and of course putting on her cuffs and collar if not already on, all must be done before asking permission.

More often than not, the routine is for her to ask to get ready for bed before actually permission to do so. That is because we are usually together in another room and she might need to ask to leave that room and customarily gives the reason. Then she completes her tasks before returning to ask permission.

Asking permission is the final intimate sequence of the day so she must be ready to climb into bed to be used, or bound for sleep. If I am staying up later, or if I am in another room when ready for bed, I make it a point to leave what I am doing and go to the bedroom for her to ask there. I do this deliberately as it is 'our' moment everyday away from the vanilla world to be alone. It is time set aside that she can count on for intimacy and affection, or sometimes just a good smack on the ass. There is a time and place for everything so mix it up.

Once she has permission and her kiss, she lays over the edge of the bed and bares her ass, if it is not already. She extends her arms over her head, spreads her legs and arches her back. It is her final act of the day, to present the very core of her femininity to me. I then use her as I see fit, from a sound fucking, to fisting, to whipping, to a slap on the ass and a good night, they all are used at different times. When finished she is put to bed and one leg or arm cuff is attached to the bed bondage strap.

Simple, elegant and totally in keeping with my responsibilities and love of her, it is a poignant *ritual.* For the slave, she goes to bed knowing she served well and is appreciated. With a little luck, she drifts off more in love with her master, than when she woke up.

There are wrinkles life throws at you that can cause the need to adjust the *Ritual.* The obvious first one is if you go to bed first. Follow the identical *protocol* except she fastens the leg strap when she comes to bed. But she must go through the *ritual* to that point, even though she may stay up later. Also, my slave and I are addicted night readers. We often went to bed very early and read for hours. Again she was required to go through the *protocol* but the leg restraint was left off until she was finished reading. If I nodded off first she was responsible for fastening it.

If the slave needs to pee during the night she is well advised not to wake her master for such a trivial issue. She unfastens herself, does her business and refastens herself on return to bed. The benefits of bedtime bondage are not in forced restriction. They derive from the little tugs on her movement as she is drifting off, a wonderful reminder of her slavery.

WAKEUP

A wakeup *protocol* is actually more difficult to develop and sustain than at bedtime. The demands on each person vary so much from day to day, routine can be difficult and accommodations must be made. If she routinely arises before her master, does she just lie there until he awakens and unfastens her? That is silly, a waste of time and accomplishes nothing. If he is up first does he force her up too? Sure, sometimes but some people be they slaves or not, require more sleep than others. So keep it simple and prioritize what is most important then focus on a *ritual* or *protocol* that accomplishes what that is. COFFEE!

Does anything else matter first thing in the morning besides coffee? Not in this household. She has two choices. She can unfasten herself, get up before her master without fail and make sure the coffee is perked, or she can risk the wrath of hell if the coffee timer she set the night before fails.

The simpler it is in the morning the better. I like my slave up with me and if that is particularly early, she can go back after I am gone or nap later in the day. The *protocol* is easy. Present me with my coffee and *formally stand* for her kiss and hug. That is all I can handle first thing in the morning. That I throw some curves at her sometimes and use the three questions on her, jump her bones, or push her to her knees, just goes with the job and someone has to do the dirty work. But, for the slaves reading this please note... fresh perked, milk, no sugar, please.

USE

Of course, she will be useful. That is fostered in her as an indispensable part of her service. It is typically a term used for non-sexual tasks. But there are times when you need to *'use'* your slave. It is fun. Commonly, this is time for sexual and or sado-masochistic use. Make this distinction for her. Slaves love being useful and being used. As her master, have the maturity to positively define the difference between used and useful. Like the core *Ritual* this is, the command and procedure could not be more beautiful or simple. There is no flowery nonsense. She is being summoned for use.

"Come here girl, I want to use you."

In any variation of that statement, when she hears it, she it she drops whatever she was doing without hesitation, excuse or protest and presents herself immediately in the *Formal Kneel* position. She then waits.

The command and *Ritual* is peaceful and strikes at the core needs of her slavery. There can be no more profound command for a slave. Hearing it often instantly produces the mindset for a fast-track journey to happy-happy land and a wet thong. Slaves love it and so will you.

The tricky master of course, will not always announce his intentions to use her, nor should he. They unexpectedly just yank her by the hair growling she is going to be used, not giving her a chance to kneel, then without ceremony whip her. Slaves will love that too. They get hot and bothered in the presence of their Alpha male doing his thing.

SPEECH RESTRICTION

Use a scarf, stuff panties in her mouth, duct tape her closed, hold her face against a friends vagina, or use one of the variety of gags available be it a ball gag, ring gag or dental spreader, there are many ways to gag a slave. The Scots seem to have it right though. Enjoying a libation in an Edinburgh pub many years ago, a kilted Scotsman who obviously spent hours getting around many a pint of bitters was asked by my innocent, though equally beer saturated slave what a Scotsman really kept under his kilt. In a lilting brogue quite in need of translation to my provincial ears and much to the embarrassment of the wee lass, he hauled up his kilt and bellowed

"It's me gag lass. A gag to use on the wee lass when she be getting overly loquacious."

My wee-ass-lass-slave looked down and giggled.

"Well Sir, she is getting quite a mouthful then."

The next day, after a quick trip to the bookstore, it was back to the hotel and the wee-lass slavegirl knelt, remaining gagged according to Scottish tradition, while I researched clan tartans in hopes to adopt this wonderful custom as my own. Alas, none were found. But, with only tenuous ancestral Scottish bloodlines, their custom was adopted and their gagging tradition continues just the same. All of those though, are forced speech restrictions and certainly useful and used by many masters.

Forced gagging has its place, to be sure. There is a time and place for everything in this wonderful lifestyle and it is good discipline and good mastery to forbid rather than force, your slave from speaking at times. *Forbidding* speech is an excellent technique to re-enforce position. *Forbidden* speech has several degrees of use. They range from complete silence, to restricted speech, allowing only certain phrases, or words be used. *Speech Restriction* is often used in conjunction with other *protocols*, but most commonly when she is leashed, in a *Formal Kneel*, or *Stand* position; and when a master uses rigidly structured levels of formality, often called *High/Medium/Low Protocol* levels.

Speech Restriction cannot be a permanent part of your structure obviously, but it certainly has its place and should be used. It is excellent discipline for her and again another virtually invisible way of practicing the lifestyle, anywhere, everyday. Try it while you are grocery shopping. At least you will not end up with tofu in the basket. More fun though, is taking her for a haircut. More than a few hairdressers get a twinkle in their eye when they realize answers are coming from you, not her.

For those of simpler mind, *Speech Restriction* is a total ban on talking unless asked a direct question. She responds only to you and never initiates any verbal communication, unless of course you are about to be smacked by a bus walking across the road. If required to respond while in *Speech Restriction*, structure your questions, or commands in a way that directs response to one of three answers. *"Yes Master"* (there is no '*Sir*' allowed), *"May I ask a question please Master"*, or a derivative of *"Not as yet Master"* the '*No*' word being prohibited. Her voice must be low and respectful. Beyond those responses, there is nothing you want to hear from her.

Stick to simple commands summoning her to *Speech Restriction*. They again are no maintenance, useful and effective.

"You are on speech restriction girl", is enough.

When commanded to a position or *protocol* that has *Speech Restriction* included, a second specific command is not required. If it is, she needs a lesson in using her head. Avoid the little used practice of cutting her tongue out. It is unnecessary when clothespins on her tongue work just as well.

LEASHED

An unbroken pony bucks, rears, resists and throws hissy fits. A leashed slave does not. This *Protocol* is not about teaching her ponygirl play, though that is fun too.

The leash is a control device and a symbol of her standing in the relationship, so exacting behavior is taught. The simple act of leashing her enacts a *protocol* of behavior that controls eye contact, speech, position, restricts movement, structures the way she moves and likely evokes both intense slave feelings and pride of demonstrating her discipline to please master. Others that see flawless leash behavior often have a positive impression about that couple.

On the other hand, it is not common, but at times some viewing a leashed slave remark that it appears a cold, mean, juvenile, contrived and very much in the realm of role-play and fantasy *protocol*. So be it, one will never please everyone.

Many years ago, on seeing a leashed slave for the first time, I expressed to members of Wayne's group that leashing a slave gave me the impression that the master could not control his slave. It bothered me, the practice seeming a paradox to what I was learning was mastery. They indulged my youth and had me look again this time at the slave's face. The peaceful subservience and loyalty were evident. That came not from the leash, but from knowing her master cared enough to use her training. The leash became but a symbol of that care. He was as proud of her, as she of him. Leashed was very much a small public expression of their unique relationship. More experienced masters recognized this and respected the care he had for the leashed girl.

Leash Protocol is simple and no commands are necessary. He attaches the leash and that does the trick. She knows she is on *protocol*. She immediately comes to a *Formal Stand* and resumes that when movement ends. When unmoving, she stands to the side of the hand holding the leash, a half step or so to the side and behind. When walking, or being walked, depending on your viewpoint, she walks gracefully, softly, femininely and sublimely. She walks slightly behind and side and at a pace to ensure the leash never goes taut. Her eyes are lowered but not enough she cannot see the leash controller and her immediate path. She is on full *Speech Restriction* and will not speak even when addressed by others.

Any variation her master wants he orders, but in the absence of them her behavior never varies. The seamless feminine grace of a well-trained leashed slave is a wonder.

GREETING DOMINANTS – THE CURTSEY

"Your slave is lovely, so beautifully mannered and respectful."

"Thank you. She is a joy and pleasure. I am very proud of her."

In the lifestyle among peers, there are times your slave needs to acknowledge a greeting from other dominants of either gender. How she is taught to do this, if she is even taught, is your choice and style. Whether you care or not, it makes a statement to others about you and more importantly is noticed by and affects your slave. She is of course looking for structure and what a perfect opportunity to provide something unique. Developing a *protocol* or *ritual* you enjoy and she can rely on to acknowledge greeting has positive benefits on many levels.

In the vanilla world regardless of gender, a handshake is the universal greeting between two people. It is a shame but understandable in this age of gender nullification. Many masters refuse to accede to this trend however, and act to distinguish gender differences. Handshakes between a slave and other known dominant are widely banned by many masters as a small kick in the ass to the pansexual and vanilla custom. They prefer a lifestyle specific *protocol* reflective of her respect to kneel in service and the choice by the dominant to be involved in the lifestyle. It is a token symbol of the *"camaraderie of difference"* between niche lifestyle peers. A mannerly curtsey serves the purpose to a tee.

It is not uncommon to see formally trained male slaves, be they heterosexual, or in gay service, bow routinely when introduced. What is good for the goose works for the gander. Did I say that cliché right? Perhaps I meant a deep curtsey by a cute bare-bottomed slave is an invitation for a goose and gander. But I digress again.

Done well a curtsey is graceful and uniquely feminine. It is traditional, elegant, formal and respectful. Perhaps for this reason, in a more casual world it has fallen into disuse. Then again, for the uppity master, the rarity of the practice just increases its appeal. Dominants are like that, stubborn mules sometimes, or is it a renaissance style?

There is a fashion rule that guides selection of what to wear to social gatherings. If in doubt about what to wear, overdress, never under dress. The polite abide by this rule of thumb. A couple in jeans and sneakers stick out like sore thumbs at a semi-formal cocktail party, but a couple in suit and dress, do not at a backyard BBQ. So it is with your slave when acknowledging greeting from dominant peers. Teaching a *protocol* perceived as too formal for the occasion can be dumbed down when the occasion calls for it. Whether she respects the dominant she is curtseying to is unimportant. She is curtseying to the dominant position, not the person. In doing so she displays respect for the lifestyle and avoids social gaffs and turmoil. Her act is peaceful and calming for everyone.

There are a number of curtsey styles from the exaggerated flourish to the token dip. The earmark of a graceful curtsey is in neither extreme though. The depth of the knee bend and the exaggeration of the skirt tug are both curtsey variables you can play around with to get the style you want. Two other elements though distinguish a graceful courteous curtsey and reflect well on everyone, the lifestyle included. Her eyes must move away from the person to the floor as her head bows during the curtsey and secondly the speed at which the curtsey is performed is critical to acknowledge appropriate respect. Practice speed. Too fast is disrespectful and amateurish. She looks embarrassed to do this and too slow is silly, too theatrical and a mockery. Elegant understated grace is the goal.

Practice by having her curtsey different ways until you are satisfied and then drill it into her. If she has trouble, resort proven slave-training methods. Slide ever-bigger buttplugs up her fanny until she gets it right. *"Motivation through Dilation"*, it works every time!

SHAVING

"Where's that fucking cat" he roared.

"Is there a problem Master", turning to him with a concerned look.

"There are scratch marks on my leather chair and that freaking animal is going to get a lesson. Bring me the isopropynol and a candle slave girl. I'm going to practice fireplay on that little beast!"

She gasped. *"Master you wouldn't! She is so little and soooooooo cute."*

"Cute huh! Well we'll see how cute it is when it has no fur left!"

"OMG Master, you wouldn't. That's awful. She'd be ugly."

He started to laugh.

"Girl, cats were put on this earth for but one reason. So dominant studmuffins can practice fireplay techniques. And if you don't believe me pet, just ask how many of us love bald pussy!"

She swatted her master's arm.

"You are so bad."

It is true, freely admitted, many of us like the bald beaver tail. Certainly with but one small exception my slave has been kept bare. Just once for a few months, she was she told to grow out the great goatee. It was around the birth of our daughter and it was not long before she was home from the hospital and I had to change the little poopy-pants diaper. Well like many Daddies I freaked, but not for the rotten mess and smell she must surely have inherited from her mother's side, but for a different reason. She was hairless like Momma and it totally squicked me for about six months. I could not handle my slave looking like my princess baby girl, so made her grow it out.

Was it irrational? Sure. Silly? Of course. Was I made the butt of my Dom pals jokes? Relentlessly. But it did not change anything. I was squicked.

Now who says masters cannot grow? One afternoon, months later, when the baby was down for her nap I got over myself. Grabbing the momma-slave by the hair I thrust a hand down her pants and tugged.

"Say bye-bye to the furry-burry-creature pet. I'm over it! No more hair, get the gear."

"Oh thank you, thank you Master, I hate this feel."

I laughed.

"Well pet, it's coming off and I know how you like sentimental things like keeping the baby's first tooth to bronzing their baby shoes, but this goes down the drain or I'll put it in the scrapbook labeled "Mommy after baby."

She danced away to prepare. She knew she was going to get fucked.

The shaving *ritual* is fun. Save the last Sunday afternoon of each month for her *ritual* shaving. Make sure it starts with proper apparel.

None!

Naked in cuffs and collar, then have her retrieve the gear. If she is a talker, put her on speech restriction, but once through this *ritual* a few times she generally tends to stay quiet. Know that as she prepares, she has begun the journey to happy-happy land. Undoubtedly, she is already getting wet.

Bind her to the bed, a towel beneath her bottom. Blindfold her sometimes too if you want, especially if you are not good at this and prone to mishaps. Do not let her see the bloodbath yet. The tray has a bowl of warm water, shaving cream, a hand towel and any lotion or cream she uses to reduce the likelihood of ingrown hairs. And, of course the razor! If you are feeling particularly sadistic have her bring a dull one, otherwise assume she brought the sharpest one ever made. She is not stupid.

Now your preparation and forethought comes in. Remove the hanging plant from over the bed. You know the one. The one friends laugh and tease you about, thinking your eclectic decorating style is nuts. This despite your slave passionately telling them she just loves plants and flowers hanging over the middle of the bed. You are whacked and this just confirms it for everyone.

Hook the spreader bar to the craftily disguised eyebolt in the ceiling and attach her ankle cuffs pulling her legs back and well apart. Then you will hear the first small moan from your well-displayed, immodest little furball. Now to work. A quick *'SlashNDash'* or the *'KinderGentler'* approach, it is your choice.

SlashNDash is fun though. Some growly-snarls in her ear; cunt spanks aimed perfectly, a finger or two up her ass, oh, and do not forget to shave her at some point. Use the advanced shaving technique. Unless you love the *Tomato-Dicer-Slicer-gone-amok* look, you might want to use care in executing those wild razor slashes. Her resemblance to bruschetta at the end is only cool some times. But what the heck, a few nicks and open wounds never harmed a slave. Rubbing blood on your lips and kissing her afterwards is always fun too. Very intimate!

On the other hand, the *"kinder-gentler-I'm-such-a-nice-Master"* style works too. Lovingly pat her pussy and giving her little booboo kisses is nice. I am particularly fond of the *"PinchNPull"* technique. Pinch her *girl-fin*, (aka clit) and pull it aside to get at those stubborn spots. If there are not any, pretend there are and be glad you blindfolded her. Slaves will not mind. In fact, you might find your hand covered in *girl-goo*. They moan and shake their heads a lot too. Occasionally you will hear a whimper. I am not sure if that is a smile or grimace at times, but since I am the Boss, I have decided it is a smile. Take your time and throw in a few optional orgasms for her if you want, but do not spoil her too much, after all you are doing the shaving for her. Ten or so sounds about right.

This is also a good time to make sure the speculums still fit. She is already there, so you may as well grab them from the freezer and go ahead. Have a look at her cervix and upper colon mumbling something about the pictures being on the Internet by dinnertime.

So now she is done. Use the old card trick to make sure you did not miss any sneaky spots. Scrape the edge of your credit card against the grain of her hair. Yelps will direct you to missed spots faster than a high-speed flogger tail. There is also something seriously ironic too, knowing how much men spend on pussy, to have your credit card right there.

Shaved, checked and double-checked, reward yourself for a job well done. Fuck her silly. Either hole, it does not much matter. Her orgasms are optional. Have her expel your semen and use it to cream her mound. It works better on the nubblies than commercial brands.

There, smooth as a baby's bum and now the baby's nap should be over too.

BODY INSPECTION

"Ritualized inspections", yummy.... oops, I mean here is another way if desired, to re-introduce the *master-slave* lifestyle into daily routine. Inspecting

her naked body is another tool, and a good way to release the vanilla activities and bring headspace back to slavery. It is also a good time to point out changes in her body, sometimes good and sometimes, well, not-so-good. Use the *protocol* for positive re-enforcement, but do not be so timid to avoid pointing out disappointments. At times, incorporate an element of humiliation into the *Inspection*. But be careful here. Women are extremely sensitive to their body image and it might not take much to push too far.

As she stands naked, a pinch of the tummy and *"are you gaining weight girl?"* can be a slave's undoing. On the other hand, fingers in her cunt and a growl in her ear *"squeeze"*... then *"good girl"*, can also be a wonderfully intimate moment. Use *"Body Inspection"* for positive re-enforcement as much as possible, knowing this can be an emotional minefield for any woman. When necessary though, do what you must and be honest.

The *protocol* is simple. Have her strip all clothing folding it neatly and placing them to the side. She presents herself slightly to the left. Standing with back arched, breasts thrust forward, legs well spread, hands clasped behind her head, head bowed and with eyes lowered, she thrusts her hips forward. She then waits, only responding to further instruction. Have her turn ninety degrees and inspect all aspects of her body. Bend her over and while clutching her legs, examine her anus. This can be humbling to a slave. It can also be erotic, maybe more so for you than the slave. A body inspection is intimate in the extreme and a delicious way to enjoy her.

SCENE PROTOCOL

There are times you may take your slave to specific BDSM events, parties or fetish nights. These are opportunities to be among peers, often like-minded souls participating in some niche variation of the *Three Powers*. They can be wonderful opportunities to be who you are in a controlled public environment. One of the themes throughout this book is to respect the lifestyle, not just your choice to be involved but others choice as well. The scene *protocol* outlined here is but one that works. It respects the lifestyle, lets her feel submission and gives you another opportunity to enjoy your slave.

BDSM events are not opportunities to flit about like some social butterfly, hugging and kissing anything in leather, thereby making a spectacle of herself like a giggling schoolgirl. Nor is it her chance to either lord it over single slaves that she has a master, or flaunt her knowledge and understanding of consensual slavery. Doing so assures she does not.

Scene Protocols are behavior expectations at a BDSM event and vary with purpose. Reasons change during the course of an evening. Until she acquires some experience at events, the simplest *protocol* is to leash her. That is not a bad way to start any fetish evening. It serves to focus her mind knowing she cannot speak, look around or move from your side. Plus she has to pay attention to your movement keeping the leash from going taut ensuring she has no other focus. The drawbacks and why many masters move away from leash control in the course of an evening is to give her a chance to enjoy the surroundings. You may want her seeing the S&M happening and often friends she wants to socialize with are there. Leaving her on the leash all night is a tad unfair simply because you do not attend these events every night and she loses the chance to fully enjoy the experience.

Too often collared slaves are seen running about all willy-nilly with nary a restriction on their behavior and that is fine if that is what their *master* wants. Unfortunately though, they often lack experience or knowledge of *protocol* and end up trampling other's *protocols*. That it reflects poorly on the slave and her master is a given, but it too often spoils the evening for others and certainly lacks respect for the choices made by others if not her own choice. It tends to dumb down the lifestyle. But, to each their own. It is not the end of the world when some big bosomed woman supposedly in slave mode gets grumpy at a lack of response after greeting a leashed slave.

With the extremes thus defined, leashed or free to roam, a *Protocol* somewhere in the middle works well and accomplishes what the master wants. It allows both to enjoy the evening to the fullest. That the slave has restrictions on her behavior at an event is normal, and do not for a minute think you are imposing on her. A slave is just like any person; she has some ego and takes pride showing off her training to please you, particularly so among those who appreciate it. She has pride in her master and she enjoys showing off even if subliminally that he has taken the time, effort and cares enough to train her. She enjoys the compliments you receive about her and enhancing your reputation as a quality master. She beams. This is her chance to use her training that reflects on her, but importantly on you. The last thing she wants to do is behave poorly or embarrass you. She wants a Protocol to know what to do and it is up to you to provide it.

Develop what works best for you of course. Experience has taught that on arrival, leave her leashed long enough to acclimate to the event and venue. Once comfortable and settled remove the leash. If she does not know automatically tell her she is in *Scene Protocol*, but it should not be necessary. She knows the *Protocol* beforehand. The *Protocol* is fun and intensely rigid yet allows her to fully enjoy the evening within structure.

So what is it? She must ask permission for everything. A drink, to hit the ladies room, to cross the room, to greet friends, everything. She cannot leave your side without permission and when she does must return promptly. She is free to look about, talk to people, greet slaves and dominant friends and introduce you if you do not know someone she does. She is wearing your collar so theoretically should not be bothered by dominants trolling for meat, but if she is either you hear the troll and deal with him, or she politely refers him to you. Let her lovely personality shine. She knows the line and will not embarrass you.

She stands to your left or right, or where you direct, perhaps kneeling at your feet. Adjust to the event. Her speech to you is formal, using *'Master'* frequently. Her manners are flawless and of course, she knows how to acknowledge greetings from other dominants and does so. It is not her position to initiate contact with another dominant and would not, but can bring then to your attention so you may.

"A good Master makes her a good slave."

You are in her head, do yourself proud. Train her and let her show what you have taught. It is as important to her as you. Make her a good slave.

THREE DAY MIRROR PROTOCOL

Once in a while it benefits all of us to take time to pause and reflect about ourselves. Stepping away from the moment, the daily grind and routine to see who we are and have become what we want to be. Have we grown, changed, are fulfilled and happy? We all need to do this, but few ever do. Most have never thought to do it, others lack the honesty to be objective and some fear what they will see. Self-examination is never easy, but you are a master. You have the courage, acquired the technique and not only do it yourself but make your slave do it too. You always act to move deeper into her head, constantly probing and pushing her to be the best and happiest she can.

There is a *Protocol* you can institute with her to facilitate this process. It is fun and builds incredible intimacy. She may find it tough, self-examination always is, but the benefits are wonderful.

"Pet your birthday is on Saturday. How old will you be again?"

She looked up from her book. It was Tuesday evening and they were quietly reading together on the couch.

"Master, you know it is impolite to ask a lady's age."

He laughed, *"You are quite right now drop the lady crap and spill toots."*

Thirty-eight again Master" she smirked.

"Pfffffffftttt, again is right. Well regardless I will do one hundred swats just for your sauciness."

Her eyes bugged out and before she could say a word he laughed.

"And that is each check pet. And every master at the party will be having a go. By my count that puts your cute ass in the two thousand swat category. Think you might fly pet?"

She gulped but he knew she felt a stirring between her legs.

"Put your book down and take your place please pet. There is something I want to do with you."

She obeyed without hesitation kneeling at his feet. She looked up curious at what was coming.

"Pet, the rest of your week after dinner is now booked. Whatever you have on your schedule, clear it please."

"Yes Master, consider it done."

"Goodgirl. Starting tonight, you are going to learn a new ritual that you are going to perform twice a year. It takes four days to complete, but only an hour or so each day. You will do it on the four days before each of our birthdays, so about six months apart. Make a note on the calendar to remind me to block the evening of the fourth day so I do not schedule anything please."

"Yes Master."

Now she was very curious and excited. Her master made life interesting to say the least.

"Pet, this is the Three Day Mirror Protocol. Ever heard of it?"

"I have not Master."

"The reason I bought the full length mirror for the back of the bedroom door, believe it or not was not to admire my rippling pecs and washboard tummy. I'd need a fucking fun house mirror for that. I put it up because you are going to use it starting tonight and for tomorrow and Thursday night as well. You are going to do three things, one per night."

He went on and explained about self-examination and the reasons for the examination he wanted.

"Tonight you will pull up a chair, sit down and look into the mirror. For fifteen minutes look at nothing but your face. Examine it, look at it and see who you are. What woman do you see staring back at you? Examine yourself and see what you see. Then after fifteen minutes write down what you saw, what you thought, who was looking back at you. Write everything down. Be honest, we both want to know. Do you understand pet?"

She nodded, "Yes Master."

"Then tomorrow night stand in front of the mirror, fully clothed and look at yourself. Not just your face this time, but your whole body. How you stand, your posture, what you see is good, the not so good, whatever you see remember it and after fifteen minutes again write down everything you saw and thought about. Who are you, who is looking back at you. Do you understand pet?"

Again she nodded now realizing this was going to be difficult. She did not like some things about herself and he was forcing her to address them.

"Then on Thursday pet, I want you to stand and do it again naked. Examine your image, what you see and who you are stripped of all barriers and walls to hide behind. Front and back pet, I want to know all of you and write it down again. Do you understand?"

"Yes Master," but her voice was quiet now.

She knew he was asking her to do something very difficult that she hated doing. They had two kids and she was not eighteen anymore, and while he thought she was beautiful she knew her flaws. She felt like crying. She had never hidden anything from him, but he had never asked for anything quite like this. It was a new level of intimacy when she thought it could go no deeper.

"On Friday night pet we will discuss what you have written. Do not disappoint me.

Oh my gawd she thought. This might be the most difficult thing she would ever do, but she would not disappoint him.

POINTING THE HAND

SLAVE when together in private; and socializing in public; will ensure a hand or foot is pointed at Master in the minimum, but preferably a hand on Master at all times when she is idle.

This is another discreet (almost invisible) rule ideal for private and vanilla occasions. People express wanting new and clever *protocols* and ways of sustaining the master-slave structure while coping with our intrusive vanilla society and culture, especially on a daily basis. Well here is another for you.

The discipline and attention teaching this rule and the difficulty for the slave to focus consistently on this task, often results in many *master-slave* couples dropping or amending it too quickly. But then not all rules are for all folks. The real long-term benefit is to create, intensify and deepen the intimacy between master and slave through an ongoing physical touch.

Now some master's and men in general do not like being touched. They are not the touchy feely kind of guys. But this rule can work well for those gentlemen as well, and why pointing is sometimes preferred to touching. The effects are similar.

It is interesting to note that this rule is a *"proactive"* or *"assertive"* rule for the slave. It requires her to do something ad hoc, or without being told. It is neither an attitude, nor passive rule for her. This rule requires her to initiate, a condition of slavery many center-of-attention-slaves do not enjoy. More experienced readers will have run across slaves that embrace slavery as *"something being done to them,"* and of course many times many things are *'done'* to them. Some dominant men abide by that singular dimension of slavery. By observation over the years though, that slaves who are passive and not required to be assertive in pleasing, become self-absorbed. This rule goes to prevent that condition from developing.

Application of the rule is very simple. If the slave is eating, or busy the rule is not in effect. Certainly though when she is idle and in her master's presence, she is required to be touching her master, maybe with just a hand on his thigh, or leaning against his legs as they watch TV and relax. But in the minimum she must have a hand, or foot pointed at her master. The point is to create an ongoing and continuous bond and focus on her master. The purpose is not to create a puppy drone that cannot leave her master's side (though come to think of it, that can be fun some nights too) but to emphasize she is a slave and her master her priority, as she is his. The rule is particularly effective at lifestyle events and functions amidst other like-minded souls.

A unique feature of the rule unlike many is this rule can become oppressive. A wise master knows when to turn it off. A slave needs time to daydream and think, relax and depressurize from the day. She does not need *"timeouts"*, but rather just some time when her master knows she is there and is happy to let her center herself.

PUNISHMENT

There is no *protocol* for punishment. Disobedience is not an anticipated behavior and a *protocol* in expectation of the unwanted is inappropriate. That there is no *protocol* conveys a message in and of itself.

MIND FUCK #30 "INTIMACY"

He liked the bar. It was dimly lit and fun. The crowd was younger, mostly beer drinkers out for a good time. Jeans and boots, plaid shirts on the guys and the women were hot, mostly in tank tops and cowboy hats. The band was churning out the tunes and folks filled the dance floor.

Yesterday was the hard drive, eating up miles of dusty road. Last night at a roadside motel they checked in exhausted. After some beers and a steak in the local saloon, they headed back to the room and crashed.

This morning they rose late, a more leisurely day planned. Talking over eggs and coffee in the diner, they were refreshed with not a care in the world.

It was after all a well deserved vacation, a special one too. They made no plans. Just pack up and go and see where the road took them and today found them in a small town in Texas, thousands of miles from home as free as the birds.

Sauntering back to the room they began packing the gear when he stopped, admiring his slave, the woman he loved. Tight jeans rounded her pert bottom stirring his libido as it had, relentlessly for years. Suddenly there seemed no reason to rush their departure.

Grabbing her hair from behind he growled, "Pants down now slut." Pushed over the dresser, she squealed at the slap on her ass and moaned as he thrust in. They liked it sudden, fast and rough.

The knock came as she cried out and came.

"Everything all right in there?" the old man yelled through the door.

"Just sex, she's cum now and pulling her pants up is all. We'll be out of here in five minutes," he yelled back.

He laughed as she turned, struggling to pull her jeans up, beet red... "Oh my gawd Master, did you have to say that?" He kissed her beet red face.

"Hush girl, now go pay the man the room money and I'll get us loaded up."

Her eyes went saucer and cheeks beet red at the prospect of going to the office and seeing the man from the door. But she knew there was no choice, and besides, she would never be here again. That thought helped overcome her flushed embarrassment and she headed to the door.

"Hey, slavegirl! What the fuck? Are you going to march off like some princess who just used her boytoy for pleasure?"

She scurried back and wrapped her arms around him with a big smile. "No Master, thank you for the fucking" and she kissed him hard. They smiled as he slapped her ass, "that's better, goodgirl, now git... oh, and pet... you are beautiful."

"Thank you Sir." She happily sashayed out the door, wiggling her ass as only well-fucked women can do.

The lazy afternoon drive was gorgeous. They followed back roads along the edge of a meandering river. Stopping alongside the slow moving water in the shade of nature, they picnicked. It was a perfect day. Tonight was a chance to let their hair down and make good on a promise to take her dancing.

It was a small outdoor cantina as the sun set to the west. They touched, kissed and held her hands through dinner. The margaritas and food were spectacular and the wandering Mexican minstrel serenaded the lovebirds perhaps sensing the special bond of master and slave.

"Well, let's do a little two-step pet, time to hit the dance floor and shake that booty for me!" They headed inside to the bar.

The music was lively and the place was hopping. "You look spectacular pet. I could fuck you right here". She smiled, more than a little worried he might, but the wine was working and she just cooed. "Oh fuck me then mister." She had on her short jean skirt, bare legs and cowboy boots. He really could just fuck her here. She certainly had no panties on. Maybe in the bathroom later, he thought.

Well she could flat out dance. He struggled just to avoid knocking her over. When she danced she took over the floor, she was that good. Folks moved back, giving her room, smiling and cheering her on. She was sex in a skirt. Always though, her eyes never left her master as she tore into the music, her energy a combination of artistry and tantalizing slut. She was trying to turn him on, the grin on her face told everyone so. She pressed into him as she danced, all eyes glued on this incredible sex machine. Straddling his leg, her arms wrapped around his neck and she ground herself onto his thigh, in perfect harmony with the music. Her skirt was riding up and he felt her bare cunt on his jeans. Surely half her ass was hanging out the back. If she knew, she was beyond caring, her eyes glazing in rhythmic lust. She ground, humped and rode his leg to the music. The circle around them now, voyeuristically cheered them on. It was apparent she was going to cum soon.

And she did! Like an explosion! Squeezing her tiny frame into him, she rode his leg, her skirt merely a belt now. She came and gushed, screaming lust searing her face. Animal passion took over and the crowd cheered wildly. He carried her off the dance floor to enormous cheers and waiting drinks at the bar.

Flush with lust and embarrassment she sat quietly on his lap sipping her drink.

"You are my slave forever pet". "That is all I want Master", then rested her head on his chest.

11

TRILOGY AFTERCARE

A GREAT MASTER

We are nearing the end of this *Trilogy* on the *Art of Mastery*. It has been a journey, not just for the readers, but for me as well. Reminiscing about the great stories and events of the past brought many smiles over coffee with old friends. For that, I thank you. Those memories might have been lost but not for this project.

Reading three volumes on the *Art of Mastery* has been a journey for you as well. Revealed are the mysteries of mastery, not that there was any great magic. Regardless, those secrets and knowledge are yours now.

The question arises what will you do with this knowledge, and what is the next step? The answer differs by master.

Three groups of masters I believe have read these books. The first are those experienced, slave owners already, who are dedicated to the craft and lifestyle. They are the wily old veterans who probably did not need anything from these works. They had it figured out long ago. They read anyway, because they are masters. I salute and thank them.

Also, there are the masters who own a slave, but who are wise enough to understand there were aspects of their structure, perhaps their motivations, or understanding of the slave mindset, and just wanted to improve their mastery of the one they already love. Slaves to those men are lucky. Regardless of past failings, or mistakes, those men remain dedicated to learning, perfecting and aspiring to master themselves and their slave well. I particularly thank and salute them.

For these first two master groups, they own a slave already and are well along the path of peace and tranquility this lifestyle affords. They might finesse or pick up a trick or two to massage their relationship, but they essentially are happy with their progress into and along the *master-slave* continuum.

Yet, it is the third type of man reading these books that especially interests me. He is the neophyte, the rookie, the man with no experience who wants to own, but does not yet. For those men, if they have grasped and identified with the messages contained in these books, there is a logical next step and an easy one. The answers to two simple questions reveal that path.

Are you a master?

What does a slave want?

A slave recently said to me, *"You are clearly a confident, experienced master, one that any slave would love to serve. When you come upon a new slave, you already know what to do, what you want and what you expect. And that is what I think every slave wants. A master who knows what he is doing."*

What does the new, aspiring master learn from that statement? Being neither new, nor aspiring to much more than walloping a cute fanny, I put her over my knee and in perfect cadence told her *"Flattery will get you spanked,"* over and over, until my hand was sore.

There is a message there for those new, just starting out and aspiring to mastery. It is profound and you will love it.

You do not need experience to be a master. You just have to know how to do it and then do it. That is the message my slave friend conveyed.

This *Trilogy* provides every tool you need to be a great master. Learn them, memorize and prepare yourself by taking the necessary pre-ownership steps, and voila, you are a master. Sure, I know, you have to be able to explain it, and do it, but all the tools are before you to do that. Read and re-read this *Trilogy* until you have it down pat.

Now, I know that sounds arrogant and know there are other paths to mastery. I know this too, that the path, tools, and knowledge laid before you works. Is not that all you need to know to start, that you are not wasting your time learning from internet audacity? Anonymous internet sources that cannot even be verified, identified, or the veracity of their statements validated serves no constructive purpose. I am not trying to sell you anything. Whether you decide this is the path for you is as important as a Nun's pinched nipple to me. It affects me not.

My slave friend's offhand comment was poignant though. She said, *"When you come upon a new slave, you already know what to do, what you want and what you expect."*

So do you, if you have prepared yourself, regardless if you have experience.

Listen to what my slave friend said in those last sentences. She answered the second question, *"What does a slave want?"*

She wants a master who knows what he is doing!

In Closing

It is with humility and hope; through these words, you have acquired a deeper appreciation for the *Art of Mastery*, the living of a loving relationship of *master-slavery* in all its beauty and perils. It is a lifestyle of passion and compassion. I appreciate that you invested the time to read these books, to study and learn. You obviously have great interest to have come this far. Now, my job is done. It is up to you to go forward with new skills and appreciations, to build the structure and relationship you want.

To many newcomers it must seem that the scope of mastery is enormous. The purpose of this *Trilogy* was never to overwhelm aspiring masters; rather it was to educate, clarify and provide the necessary tools. The lifestyle is simple, and so is mastery. While there may be as much, or as little as you wish, it is always your choice, and always your fundamental truths and values. You are the responsible alpha man and she will have it no other way. Accept that responsibility, for with it comes dedication and love that I believe is unequalled in other relationship dynamics.

The concepts, theories and practice of *master-slavery* are real, not intangible abstract debating points. Rather, for those prepared to apply thought and effort they are quintessentially simple and easily understood. That most will not find peace in the narrow confines of mastery detailed here, is irrelevant. You are not most. You are special. You are a man dedicated to personal happiness through mature, responsible control of your slave, environment and of course yourself. What is nobler than that? In your happiness, others embrace, rejoice and celebrate their own wondrous joys. By looking after yourself first, you create the platform to give. By extending the benefits of your responsibilities, you offer the same happiness to a woman of slave needs. There is nothing confusing about it. It is the American dream. It is freeing and freedom itself. Work hard and you can be anything you want. By aspiring to your dreams, you enable the dreams of others.

Mastery requires learning, but that is no different from any aspect of life worth achieving. It is there for your asking, believing and knowing it is yours. Imagine yourself the master of your dreams, your universe and your identity.

As the alpha male, you do not need anyone, yet you share. You are self-sufficient, quietly confident, mature and grounded. You are fun. You have a vision of life for yourself, your slave, and the world. Those values are your soul. Your slave partner is out there to share that life. You will thrive and grow together, in your own way, because it is right for you. It is for her too. She will see into your soul and the compassion at its very core. She sees you are strong and vulnerable; open and empathetic. You are a leader. You are romantic, loving, and demand the same. You are her knight, representing integrity, with humor. That is your way.

Sadistic and caring, hard yet loving, harsh and passionate, these are you. These are words rarely spoken together in the vanilla world, yet ring true for you.

Use these books as reference as you travel along your journey. Learning and absorbing the *Three Powers*, the *Three Tenets of Mastery*, the *Theory of the Two Decisions*, the *Four Pillars of a Relationship*, the *SODS Principle*, and the *Training Triumvirate* such that it is habit and consistent; and you are there. It truly is not rocket science.

You have come to this with passion and a hunger for knowledge; open to education, asking questions, observant, absorbing explanations, and seeking answers. Your leadership is valid. But, you will face the one question all masters must. The question remains now, as it did at the outset of these books.

Is a lifestyle of consensual master-slavery sustainable?

Still, the answer never changes.

A consensual master-slave relationship intended to endure, within the total power exchange, same roof, 24/7 niche, is reality in the presence of responsible mastery.

Asked to describe a real life master-slave relationship, in a sentence or two, long ago, I remembered this small adage:

A master-slave relationship exists when she thoughtfully offers control of all, or part of her life, in return for his accepting the incumbent responsibilities for that control, mindful of both their needs and desires. What makes it real, is when neither owns a keyboard.

Thirty-five years ago, I undertook an unspoken obligation and trust. This *Trilogy* of books relieves that obligation. To Wayne Innes and his group who were generous enough to take a young kid into their world many decades ago, thank you. They patiently taught a lifelong set of values that brought so very much happiness. In doing so, they hoped their experiences and knowledge would go forward to a new generation of masters. The *Devil in the Details Trilogy* continues that tradition.

The torch of responsible mastery is now yours to enjoy. Reap the rewards, you deserve them. Mastery is in your hands. Mold your structure, create your happiness and know,

"A great master will make her a great slave."

I have passed on the knowledge and experiences, the values and responsibilities, to the best of my abilities. Having met my obligations to Wayne, and the entire leather community, it is time to sit back, watch, teach, oh and, well, I am not that old, put a slave or two, over my knee, every now and then.

There is one last thing I ask of you the reader. This final book in the *Trilogy* is specific, and makes developing your own structure a relatively easy task. You have most if not all the tools now to build as you wish. You will pick what works for you and that unique structure is yours. Do it, enjoy it, and then do us both a favor, and re-read the first two *Volumes*. I venture to say, armed with the knowledge you now have, you will get far more from it than the first time through.

My parting advice to all in the *master-slave* realm is that first and foremost you are the alpha. With that power comes responsibilities, not the least of which is remembering, you are in a relationship. You are not alone. She wants your leadership and to be part of your life.

And lest we forget...

The lifestyle is fun!

Finally, I leave you with a simple parable, drawn from the North American Native culture that parallels choices we make as masters, and seems a fitting conclusion.

TWO WOLVES

"Son, there is a battle that goes on inside us all. It is a battle between two wolves."

"One is Evil. It is anger, jealousy, sorrow, regret, greed, arrogance, self-pity, guilt, resentment, inferiority, lies, false pride, and ego.

"The other wolf is Good. It is joy, peace, love, hope, serenity, humility, kindness, benevolence, empathy, generosity, truth, compassion and faith."

His son thought about it, then asked.

"Which wolf wins, Dad?"

He smiled and looked at this young man, so much like him.

"Son, it is always the one you feed."

Thank you and good luck.

LT Morrison

Perge!

ABOUT THE AUTHOR

LT Morrison is a penname. It is used it to protect his children. That is the only reason. While they are adults, he understands many in our society do not accept the BDSM lifestyle and look upon practitioners as odd, sick, perverted, or dangerous. He does not want that stigma, however false, associated with his children. They have their own lives with the freedom to choose, unencumbered by their parent's choice.

LT developed a series of lectures on the master-slave lifestyle, and gives freely to community groups. He can be found at book signings, BDSM events, and considers all opportunities to talk with groups on the lifestyle. Contact him by email, at LT@LTMorrison.com.

LT is widowed, and spends time between homes in Canada and the United States.

APPENDIX A

MASTER-SLAVE CONTRACT

) In the matter of the personal relationship

) contract and the allocation of rights thereto;

) and regarding the ownership of property and

) rules that govern the relationship between the

) parties dated xxxxxxxx xx, xxxx

CONSENSUAL MASTER & SLAVE CONTRACT

1. Preamble

THE essence, spirit and intent of this contract are based on the simple notion of a structured personal relationship between the parties identified hereinafter, wherein the responsibilities of both parties are clearly defined. Hereinafter the party known as the Master will exercise responsible control for the day to day living of both parties. The other party hereinafter referred to as the slave being fully informed of the responsibilities and expectations placed upon her, consensual without coercion or undue influence agrees to obey the Master in all asked of her within the Laws of Canada. Master will not command the slave to act, plan or conspire to act outside the law.

THIS private contract is provided as a binding agreement, which defines in specific terms, the relationship and interaction between the participants, hereinafter termed the Master and the slave. The contract defines the personal relationship structure of the parties. This agreement is binding only between the two parties listed and is binding only by the integrity of the parties. This contract in no way supersedes the Laws of Canada. This agreement is entered into voluntarily, both parties being fully informed with both parties agreeing to the conditions and stipulations set out herein.

2. Parties

Hereinafter, the term "Master" refers to:

Xxxx X. Xxxx,

And furthermore, the term "slave" refers to:

Xxxxxxx X. Xxxxxxxxx

3. Master's Responsibility

MASTER accepts the responsibility of slave's body; to do with as he sees fit, under the provisions determined in this contract. Master undertakes responsibility to define slave's behavior and attitudes and teach, then enforce these elements to please him. Master agrees to care for the well-being of slave and to arrange for her physical and emotional safety. Master accepts responsibility to fulfill slave's needs to the best of his abilities, for as long as he owns her. Master also accepts the responsibility to treat slave properly; to train, punish and use slave for pleasure and useful service. Master recognizes slave's desire for this relationship structure and works to build a life of peace and tranquility together, through intimacy, affection, honest communication, trust, love and romance, embodied in structure. Master accepts the responsibilities incumbent in this contract and undertakes to make the decisions entrusted to him, for the betterment of both.

4. Slave's Responsibility

SLAVE agrees to submit completely to Master in all ways. There are no boundaries of place, time, or situation in which slave may willfully refuse to obey the directive of Master without risking corrective measurements and punishment by Master, except in the activities relating to boundaries covered in this contract under Section 9 - Boundaries. Slave also agrees that, once entered into this Contract, her body belongs to the Master, to be used as seen fit, within the guidelines defined herein. She agrees to be useful, utilizing her skills, talent, knowledge and experience in service, taking direction and using initiative within the structure of rituals, protocols and rules taught by Master. Slave agrees to please the Master to the best of her ability, with her primary focus now Master's pleasure, needs and wants. Slave is expected to seek the Master's comfort, pleasure and well being, above all other considerations slave may have. Slave will carry out these expectations conveying her pleasure to undertake her responsibilities. Slave will be loyal to her integrity and Master.

5. Alteration of Contract

THIS contract may not be altered, except when both Master and slave agree. If the contract is to be altered, the new contract shall be prepared, executed and the old contract destroyed.

6. Termination of Contract

MASTER may terminate this agreement as and when he sees fit. Master will not release slave without adequately providing for slave's welfare, as best able and sees fit.

SLAVE has the right to terminate this contract, only after exhausting all avenues available to her to overcome differences between Master and herself and after discussion, or discussions with Master as to her reasoning. Master will determine whether all reasonable efforts have been exhausted. Master will accept slave's request for release, only after a seven-day waiting period and upon return of Master's collar.

SLAVE understands Master will not ever collar and own slave again once she has been un-collared and released from this contract.

Master accepts that should this contract ever be voided and slave released from service, it is his solemn oath to part ways having enriched slave's life, both parties having grown, enjoyed and savored their time together.

7. Agreements between Master and slave

WE agree that our relationship will always come first in our lives. We will not put work, or other outside interests before the relationship.

WE agree to be fully truthful to each other at all times regardless of situation. Untruths, omissions and lies are forbidden in the relationship. Full honesty is committed to, in all things including feelings, thoughts and actions. There is no need for dishonesty and it is prohibited.

WE agree that emotional monogamy is required in this relationship. There will be no additional partners brought permanently into the relationship.

WE agree the slave may not seek any other Master, or lover, or relate to others in any sexual, or submissive way without Master's permission.

WE agree Master may engage sexually with others, but will consider slave's emotional response to such action and involve slave emotionally, or physically.

WE agree Master may give slave to other Masters, Mistresses, or others on a temporary basis, provided the terms of this contract are upheld. In such a circumstance, Master will inform the new parties(s) of the provisions stated herein and any breach by them is a breach by Master.

ALL sado-masochistic equipment required by Master is paid for by Master and remains his property.

WE agree that household tasks will be distributed between Master and slave at Master's direction.

WE agree that no commands will be given causing extreme damage to slave's life.

WE agree that Master will never strike slave in anger.

8. Rules

THERE are to be discussion times regarding the relationship, or any other issue, concern, need, or interest anytime Master, or slave feels it is necessary, except when Master is using the slave, or while being given an instruction. A request for discussion will assure one, within twenty-four hours at Master's convenience.

SLAVE is required to fully obey Master's directions. When given instruction, slave will neither negotiate with Master, nor hesitate to complete the instruction. Slave's only choice is to ask for clarification, if necessary and obey Master. Discussion will be allowed later if needed. Hesitation will be met with corrective measures and punishment. Slave will obey the literal and spirit of the direction.

SLAVE will conduct herself with integrity and self-respect while exhibiting complete loyalty, honor and respect for Master.

SLAVE must display an ability to be totally submissive to Master and furthermore display a positive attitude about her relationship choice and having entered this agreement. Discernable pleasure to be in service to Master is slave's predominant outward image and emotion.

SLAVE must express her feelings, wants, state of health, likes and dislikes, at all times. Slave is free to express those needs consistent her position as slave, expressing not demanding.

SLAVE'S speech to Master will always reflect a submissive, respectful tone and choice of words. Slave will never scream, yell, or argue with Master. Master provides opportunity and protocol to ensure slave is able to voice all her thoughts and feelings. Use of submissive speech in tone and choice of words is not to restrict expression of thoughts and feelings, but rather to reflect on the unique structure and tenets of this relationship. Speech patterns are enforced to kindle harmony, peace and tranquility.

A period of reflection and focus is required when slave returns home after absence from Master for more than four hours. "Focus" is done on her knees in a spot designated by Master and lasts for a period not less than five minutes. Slave will focus during the reflection period to release her daily tensions and concerns outside the relationship dynamic and focus on Master and the happiness she feels in service and the consensual choice made to enter this Contract.

SLAVE will express her femininity in appearance, behavior and attitude.

SLAVE will conduct herself with dignity and grace in public.

SLAVE will respect others known to practice the Master-slave lifestyle, mindful she only submits to Master.

ANY errors, or breaches of this contract by Master, do not abrogate slave's obligations provided for herein. Slave may request a discussion, but should not expect an apology from Master for any perceived, or real errors, or omissions. Acceptance of this contract is sufficient for the slave to understand Master's intent is to provide a safe, healthy structure and life for the slave and that errors are reflective of the human condition, not motivated by malfeasance, or desire to harm the slave. Slave accepts any errors on an ad hoc basis.

SLAVE will accept corrective measures in her heart. Slave must learn to understand that when Master deems slave to be in error and corrective measures and punishment occurs, she accepts that Master has the right and control to make these decisions, whether she agrees an error occurred.

SLAVE has at her disposable the Laugh Rule. When slave is due punishment and can make Master laugh in context of her disobedience, she may request this rule be invoked. The Laugh Rule, when granted, relieves slave of punishment and the Forgive & Forget mechanism of the punishment regimen is immediately invoked, ending the punishment and dismissing the disobedience to ancient history. Asking for the Rule does not automatically grant it, application of the Rule is solely Master's discretion.

MASTER'S leather collar is to be worn by slave at all times when in the home, unless guests who might be offended by it, or not understand, are present. Master will provide a more discreet marking of ownership available to slave for use inside and outside the home where discretion is required. Slave is never to spend a moment un-collared except when bathing, or directed.

SLAVE is the only person in the world ever permitted to wear Master's collar. The collar is never to be shared, or loaned by slave.

SLAVE'S clothing will be selected and, or approved by Master.

MASTER will approve all modification of slave's body including haircuts.

SLAVE will be clean of hair on legs and underarms at all times. The genital area including the vaginal and anal areas will be hairless. Slave will ask Master's permission when shaving is required.

SLAVE is not permitted use of chairs, sofas, ottomans, stools, or other furniture to sit on when in Master's presence, unless specific permission is granted by Master.

SLAVE will not use the words "No" or "Ok" to Master.

THE sanctity of the bathroom is inviolate. When Master is in a washroom and the door closed slave will not enter unless commanded to.

SLAVE will be taught additional rules exclusive of this Contract and recorded in a Ledger entitled House Rules. Slave is expected to honor those rules as she would these. House Rules can be altered as Master sees fit to reflect change and growth. The Ledger is always available to slave for review. No expectations are imposed on slave, until a rule is taught and recorded.

SLAVE will be taught Rituals and Protocols, which can be altered as Master sees fit and recorded in a Ledger entitled Rituals & Protocols. The Ledger is always available to slave for review. No expectations are imposed on slave, until a Ritual, or Protocol is taught and recorded.

9. Boundaries

THE following list of boundaries both Master and slave agree upon. Boundaries can only be altered and amended upon agreement by both Master and slave.

NO acts involving feces.

NO acts involving children, or animals.

NO acts leaving deliberate permanent injury to slave.

NO acts resulting in un-due risk of contracting venereal disease.

NO snakes, pictures of snakes, replications of snakes, or any other representation of snakes are permitted in Master's home, car, office, or any other area he may be present if the area can be controlled or influenced by slave.

10. Slave Signature

I have read and fully understand this contract in its entirety. I agree to give myself completely to my Master, and further, accept his claim of ownership over my physical body. I understand that I will be commanded, trained and punished as a slave and promise to be true and to fulfill the pleasures and desires of my Master to the best of my abilities. I understand that I cannot withdraw from this contract, except as stated in this contract.

Signature: _____

Date: _____

11. Master Signature

I have read and fully understand this contract in its entirety. I agree to accept this slave as my property; body and possessions, to care for her to the best of my ability. I shall provide for her security and well-being and command, train, and punish her as a slave. I understand the responsibility implicit in this arrangement and agree that no deliberate harm shall come to the slave, as long as she is mine. I further understand that I can withdraw from this contract at any time abiding by the terms of Termination.

Signature: _____

Date: _____

APPENDIX B

HOUSE RULES(SAMPLE PAGE)

HOUSE RULE	
DATE TAUGHT:	**JANUARY 16, 2005**

DO NOT EVEN THINK OF STRINGING PANTYHOSE OR NYLONS OVER THE SHOWER CURTAIN ROD TO DRY!

APPENDIX C

SAMPLE - ME LIST

M E   L I S T

Likes	Taught	Dislikes	Taught
Penn State Football		Notre Dame anything	
Michigan Football	√	Slave swearing	√
A clean house	√	Sushi	
A perfect lawn	√	Gardening	
Manners		Complaining the toilet seat is up.	√
Showers	√	My car not running	
A clean car		Being late	√
Coke-Cola		Beets	

APPENDIX D

MASTERY TOOLS

TANGIBLE

1. Me List
2. Master/Slave Contract
3. House Rules Binder
4. House Rules Insert Sheet
5. Rituals & Protocols Binder
6. Rituals & Protocols Insert Sheet
7. BDSM Checklist
8. The slave's "How can I be useful to her Master" list
9. A "No" Stick

INTANGIBLE UNDERSTANDINGS

1. A Vision
2. Three Tenets of Mastery
3. Theory of the Two Decisions
4. Three Powers
5. Four Pillars of a Relationship
6. SODS Principle
7. One Year Training Discipline
8. The Training Triumvirate
9. Conflict Resolution – The Twenty-Four Hour Rule
10. The Laugh Rule
11. Role of Punishment

Made in the USA
Middletown, DE
16 May 2020

95022301R00128